# *Past Praise for the Author's Work*

"David Swanson is a truth-teller and witness-bearer whose voice and action warrant our attention." —Cornel West, author.

"David Swanson predicates his belief that nonviolence can change the world on careful research and historical analysis." —Kathy Kelly, activist and author.

"The world needs more true advocates of democracy like David Swanson!" —Thom Hartmann, radio/TV host and author.

"Our times cry out for a smart, witty and courageous Populist who hasn't forgotten how to play offense. Luckily we have David Swanson." —Mike Ferner, activist and author.

"David Swanson, who has been a one-man wonder leading the charge for accountability, writes a compelling narrative that inspires not just outrage, but ACTION." —Medea Benjamin, activist and author.

"David Swanson despises war and lying, and unmasks them both with rare intelligence. I learn something new on every page." —Jeff Cohen, activist and author.

"Swanson's book is far more uplifting and inspiring than virtually any other book in its genre, as it devotes itself to laying out a detailed plan for how American ci        is through the activism which he has devoted himself—ca        our political values." —Glenn Gre

D1287854

"David Swanson is the most consistently great writer of this generation." —Jean Athey, activist.

"David Swanson is an antidote to the toxins of complacency and evasion. He insists on rousing the sleepwalkers, confronting the deadly prevaricators and shining a bright light on possibilities for a truly better world." —Norman Solomon, activist and author.

"I am always impressed and inspired by David's prolific energy and I admire his unwavering opposition to *all war,* not just the ones started or continued by Republicans." —Cindy Sheehan, activist and author.

"David Swanson writes like he talks; that is to say, in clear, sharp language that gets to the root of the issue, but in a very personal way...as if you are having a one-on-one conversation with him." —Leah Bolger, activist.

The author, hard at work.

# Killing Is Not a Way of Life

by David Swanson

Charlottesville, VA
First edition—2014

*Also by David Swanson*

WAR NO MORE: THE CASE FOR ABOLITION (2013)

TUBE WORLD (2012)

THE MILITARY INDUSTRIAL COMPLEX AT 50 (2011)

WHEN THE WORLD OUTLAWED WAR (2011)

WAR IS A LIE (2010)

DAYBREAK: UNDOING THE IMPERIAL PRESIDENCY
AND FORMING A MORE PERFECT UNION (2009)

THE 35 ARTICLES OF IMPEACHMENT (Introduction, 2008)

davidswanson.org

• • •

Swanson, David, 1969 Dec. 1-

Killing Is Not a Way of Life

Book design by David Swanson
Cover art by Wesley Swanson

Printed in the USA

First Edition / December 2014

ISBN: 978-0-9830830-6-1

# CONTENTS

**War Culture**

## What Is Imaginable

# Introduction

This is a reorganized—or, rather, organized for the first time—record of nearly a year's worth of immediate reactions to the world. These bits of writing originated between January and November of 2014. My thanks go to the great radio host Lila Garrett for suggesting that I publish such a collection (though all blame is my own for what I've chosen to include).

This year has been busy, globally and personally. My wife Anna and I welcomed our second little boy into the world. Oliver joined his big brother Wesley with great enthusiasm. I dedicate this book to Anna, Wesley, Oliver, and our dog Tilly.

During the course of a year, I write many activist emails, lengthy reports, and strategy arguments. I produce many radio shows. Plus, of course, tons of social media posts and emails, etc. None of that is included. Also I'm usually working on full-length books, but not this year. My writing energy this year has been broken into pieces, the pieces that make up this collection.

I always write a great many essays, book and movie reviews, and other blog posts. What follows is drawn from these relatively short -- sometimes very short -- creations. Some have been written as "news" for news outlets, others as "opinion" columns, but most purely for my own purposes and from a point of view that has no use for the news/opinion distinction.

I've organized articles by topic and, for the most part, kept them in chronological order within each section. I begin with a section aimed at suggesting what I think we need to be talking about more than we are. I close with a section pointing toward directions in which we might move forward. In between, the topics include the earth, justice, a selection of wars currently underway, and finally a section on war culture.

I would love it if the reader finished this book with some thoughts firmly in place on why and how we should move from a culture of violence to one of nonviolence. As I was putting this book together I happened upon an article[1] (not by me) titled "UN Ambassador Warns Against Intervention Fatigue." It began: "Samantha Power, the U.S. Ambassador to the United Nations, warned the American public against a kind of intervention fatigue, emphasizing that U.S. leadership is needed now more than ever amid global threats from Ebola to the Islamic State. 'I think there is too much of, "Oh, look, this is what intervention has wrought" … one has to be careful about overdrawing lessons,' Power said." The article seemed to suggest that if you look too closely at what bombing Libya did to Libya you won't be supportive enough about bombing Syria. I guess I agree. I just favor looking, eyes wide open.

I welcome your thoughts at davidswanson.org.

—David Swanson, November 2014

---

1    http://www.defenseone.com/threats/2014/11/un-ambassador-warns-against-intervention-fatigue/99485/

# What Is Hidden

## Letter From Happy Town

It's hard to know whether to be pleased each time the place I live, Charlottesville, Va., is named[2] the happiest city in the United States. I grew up largely in Northern Virginia (suburbs of Washington, D.C.) and Charlottesville is a long ways away in Central Virginia. I remember hearing that Fairfax County schools, which I attended at the time, were ranked best in the country. Wow, I thought, other people's schools must be truly awful!

So, I haven't discovered that I'm happier; I've just been informed that everyone else is less happy. Not being much of a schadenfreudist, I can't really find that anything but depressing. I knew that the United States fell behind a lot of nations in international attempts to measure happiness, but the idea that the rest of the United States falls behind my bit of it seems pretty gloomy.

I wasn't interviewed for the latest survey, don't know who was, and have no idea how meaningful it is. Of course I find the analysis interesting that says people in other cities are wealthier but less happy, and concludes that people are willing to be paid to be less happy. Again, I'm sorry not to be pleased, but doesn't that suggest we're a nation of morons? (Well, except for we enlightened few who've moved to Charlottesville.)

---

2    http://www.dailyprogress.com/news/joy-town-u-s-a-charlottesville-named-america-s-happiest/article_394b5170-127b-11e4-94db-0017a43b2370.html

Of course, I don't know most people in Charlottesville or have any idea how happy they are or why. Charlottesville, like most places, suffers from income inequality, poverty, pollution, too many cars, ugly sprawl, racial segregation, ignorance, consumerism, and lack of imagination. It's no paradise, and my experience of it is not the same as anyone else's. But let me offer a few ideas on how it manages to win these happiness rankings.

Charlottesville is significantly smaller than the other top-ranked cities. That it is a city is a legal matter; many people would call it a small town. It's even smaller when the University of Virginia is on break. Charlottesville is close enough that people can go to the Washington, D.C., area when and if they need to or want to, by car or train or bus. But the traffic jams and crowds are there, not here. And, importantly, we know it. We know that we have many things better than they have it up north: we can get anywhere in 10 minutes or less; we can walk or bicycle; we can expect to bump into people we know; random people say hello; and there are no lines to wait in when we get where we're going. And, significantly, when we get organized our local government often listens to us—in stark contrast to many people's experience in larger places.

Charlottesville is heavily populated by people who chose to be here, as I did. People must be happier when they are somewhere they've chosen to be. I suspect that many, like I, appreciate the balance between a small town and a city. Charlottesville is culturally and intellectually rich for its size. It has a pedestrian downtown square—or, rather, street—so there is a there there. It has hills and farms and vineyards, a river, mountains, parks. It's an athletic town, and exercise makes happiness. And, importantly perhaps, at least some of us are aware that rural areas not far from Charlottesville can sometimes be politically and culturally akin to stepping back decades or centuries in time, and not in a good way. One hopes we manage to be appreciative without being blindly arrogant.

Charlottesville has a university and two big hospitals and lots of other businesses, but I could never find a decent job here back in the days of real-world jobs. Only after I'd figured out how to work online could I move back to Charlottesville. I could do my job from anywhere and choose to do it from here, in part to be near family, in part to be somewhere that speaks my mother tongue, but in large part because I like the place.

And yet I'm haunted by some of the darker reasons that it's possible to be so happy in Cville. Like most places in the United States, a good chunk of Charlottesville's economy comes from the military and its contractors and subcontractors. Only because the military does what it does very far away and out of sight, and only because we tell ourselves lies to justify those evil deeds, can we enjoy our cafes and bike lanes and farmers markets. There are U.S. weapons companies in Charlottesville and U.S. weapons leveling houses in Gaza—not such a happy thought.

Like most places in the United States, Charlottesville unsustainably pollutes the earth's air and water. That we're in the piedmont, unlike those low-lying folks in Norfolk who are going to have to get very used to wetness, gives us a false sense of security.

Weather extremes have begun reaching us here too, and there's more to come.

Like most places in the United States, Charlottesville locks too many of its most troubled, and untroubled, people up behind bars and out-of-sight. Like most places, Charlottesville consumes products from around the world created in severely inhumane conditions.

I'm not sure I could spend my time writing about violence and injustice if I weren't living in a place that suggests that's not all that's possible, but we all must work on making our happy places possible without hidden dependencies on violence and injustice.

## Society as a Failed Experiment

There's little dispute among social scientists that most of our major public programs are counter-productive on their own terms. There is also little analysis of this phenomenon as a pattern in need of an explanation and a solution.

Prisons are supposedly intended to reduce crime, but instead increase it. Young people who when they commit crimes are arrested and punished become much more likely to commit crimes as adults than are those young people who when they commit crimes are just left alone.

Fixing public schools by requiring endless test-preparation

and testing is ruining public schools. Kids are emerging with less education than before the fix. Parents are sending their kids to private schools or charter schools or homeschooling them or even pulling them out of school for a few months during the worst of the test-preparation binging.

Free trade policies are supposed to enrich us. Trickle-down tax cuts for the wealthy and corporations are supposed to enrich us. We keep trying them and they keep impoverishing us.

War preparations are supposed to enrich us, but impoverish us instead. War is supposed to protect us, but generates enemies. Or war is supposed to benefit some far away place, but leaves it in ruins. Is more war the answer?

When a road gets crowded, we enlarge it or build another road. The traffic responds by enlarging to fill the new roads. So we cut funds for trains in order to build yet more roads.

We're several times more likely to be killed by a police officer than by a terrorist. So, we give police officers weapons of war to make us safe.

We're making the earth's climate unlivable by consuming fossil fuels. So we ramp up the consumption of fossil fuels.

Guns are supposed to protect us, but the more we spread the guns around the more we get killed intentionally and accidentally with guns.

What causes us to pursue counterproductive programs and policies? And why does it seem that the bigger the program is the more we pursue its counterproductive agenda? Well, let's look at the above list again and ask who benefits.

We've made prisons into a for-profit industry and an economic rescue program for depressed rural areas. Enormous profits are being made from children who abandon public schools; from the point of view of those profiteers there's every reason to fix schools in a manner that actually makes them horrible. Corporate trade pacts and tax exemptions for billionaires don't impoverish everyone, just us non-billionaires. Some people get rich from road construction. Weapons companies don't mind when one war leads to three more (especially if they're arming all sides), or when police pick up used weaponry that can then be replaced. Oil and coal profiteers aren't focused on the inhabitability of the earth. Gun manufacturers aren't worried about how many people die so much as how many guns are sold.

What keeps us from seeing this as a pattern is the myth that we live in a democracy in which decisions are made by majority opinion. In reality, majority opinion is badly distorted by anti-democratic news media and largely ignored by anti-democratic officials.

Major public pressure will be needed to change this situation, to strip corporations of power, ban bribery, provide free media and public financing of elections, and create a democratic communications system.

We should begin by dropping the pretense that we're rationally testing policies and adjusting them as we go. No, the whole thing is broken. Experiments keep failing upward with no end in sight. Enough is enough. Let's change direction.

## *Free College or Another New War?*

Noting that U.S. college costs have gone up 500% since 1985, the *Washington Post* recommends[3] seven countries where U.S. students can go to college for free without bothering to learn the language of the natives or anything so primitive.

These are nations with less wealth than the United States has, but which make college free or nearly free, both for citizens and for dangerous illegals visiting their Homelands.

How do they do it?

Three of them have a higher top tax rate[4] than the United States has, but four of them don't.

What does the United States spend its money on that these other countries do not? What is the largest public program in the United States? What makes up over 50% of federal discretionary spending in the United States?

---

3          http://www.washingtonpost.com/blogs/worldviews/wp/2014/10/29/7-countries-where-americans-can-study-at-universities-in-english-for-free-or-almost-free/
4 http://en.wikipedia.org/wiki/List_of_countries_by_tax_rates

If you said "war," it's possible you were educated in a fine foreign country.

A comprehensive calculation of U.S. military spending puts it at over $1 trillion a year. The International Institute for Strategic Studies puts it at[5] $645.7 billion in 2012. Using that smaller number, let's compare the seven nations where Americans can find their human right to an education respected:

France $48.1 billion or 7.4% of U.S.
Germany $40.4 billion or 6.3% of U.S.
Brazil $35.3 billion or 5.5% of U.S.
Norway $6.9 billion or 1.1% of U.S.
Sweden $5.8 billion or 0.9% of U.S.
Finland $3.6 billion or 0.6% of U.S.
Slovenia $0.6 billion or 0.1% of U.S.

Oh, but those are smaller countries. Well, let's compare[6] military spending per capita:

United States $2,057
Norway $1,455 or 71% of U.S.
France $733 or 35% of U.S.
Finland $683 or 33% of U.S.
Sweden $636 or 31% of U.S.
Germany $496 or 24% of U.S.
Slovenia $284 or 14% of U.S.
Brazil $177 or 9% of U.S.

5 http://worldbeyondwar.org/wp-content/uploads/statplanet/StatPlanet.html
6 http://worldbeyondwar.org/wp-content/uploads/statplanet/StatPlanet.html

It's worth noting that in wealth per capita, Norway is wealthier than the United States. It still spends significantly less per capita on war preparations. The others all spend between 9% and 35%.

Now, you may be a believer in militarism, and you may be shouting right about now: "The United States provides these other nations' warmaking needs for them. When Germany or France has to destroy Iraq or Afghanistan or Libya, who does the heavy lifting?"

Or you may be an opponent of militarism, and you may be thinking about its many additional costs. Not only does the United States pay the most in dollars, but it generates the most hatred, kills the most people, does the most damage to the natural environment, and loses the most freedoms in the process.

Either way, the point is that these other countries have chosen education, while the United States has chosen a project that perhaps a well-educated populace would support, but we don't have any way to test that theory, and it doesn't look like we're going to any time soon.

We have a choice before us: free college or more war?[7]

---

http://worldbeyondwar.org/individual

# Mayor From Okinawa to Bring Surprising Message to Washington

Imagine if China were stationing large numbers of troops in the United States. Imagine that most of them were based in a small rural county in Mississippi. Imagine—this shouldn't be hard—that their presence was problematic, that nations they threatened in Latin America resented the United States' hospitality, and that the communities around the bases resented the noise and pollution and drinking and raping of local girls.

Now imagine a proposal by the Chinese government, with support from the federal government in Washington, to build another big new base in that same corner of Mississippi. Imagine the governor of Mississippi supported the base, but just before his reelection pretended to oppose it, and after being reelected went back to supporting it. Imagine that the mayor of the town where the base would be built made opposition to it the entire focus of his reelection campaign and won, with exit polls showing that voters overwhelmingly agreed with him. And imagine that the mayor meant it.

Where would your sympathies lie? Would you want anyone in China to hear what that mayor had to say?

Sometimes in the United States we forget that there are heavily armed employees of our government permanently stationed in most nations on earth. Sometimes when we remember, we imagine that the other nations must appreciate it.[8] We turn away from the public uproar in the Philippines as the U.S. military tries to return troops to those islands from which they were driven by public pressure. We avoid knowing what anti-U.S. terrorists say motivates them, as if by merely knowing what they say we would be approving of their violence. We manage not to know of the heroic nonviolent struggle underway on Jeju Island, South Korea, as residents try to stop the construction of a new base for the U.S. Navy. We live on oblivious to the massive nonviolent resistance of the people of Vicenza, Italy, who for years voted and demonstrated and lobbied and protested a huge new U.S. Army base that has gone right ahead regardless.

Mayor Susumu Inamine of Nago City, Okinawa, (population 61,000) is headed to the United States, where he may have to do a bit of afflicting the comfortable as he tries to comfort the afflicted back home. Okinawa Prefecture has hosted major U.S. military bases for 68 years. Over 73% of the U.S. troop presence in Japan is concentrated in Okinawa, which makes up a mere 0.6% of the Japanese land area. As a result of public protest, one base is being closed—the Marine Corps Air Station Futenma. The U.S. government wants a new Marine base in Nago City. The people of Nago City do not.

Inamine was first elected as mayor of Nago City in January 2010 promising to block the new base. He was reelected this past January 19th still promising to block the base. The Japanese government had worked hard to defeat him, but exit polls showed 68% of

8        http://www.huffingtonpost.com/2014/01/02/greatest-threat-world-peace-country_n_4531824.html

voters opposing the base, and 27% in favor of it. In February U.S. Ambassador Caroline Kennedy visited Okinawa, where she met with the Governor but declined to meet with the mayor.

That's all right. The Mayor can meet with the State Department, the White House, the Pentagon, and the Congress. He'll be in Washington, D.C. in mid-May, where he hopes to appeal directly to the U.S. government and the U.S. public. He'll speak at an open, public event at Busboys and Poets restaurant at 14th and V Streets at 6:00 p.m. on May 20th.

A great summary of the situation in Okinawa can be found in this statement: "International Scholars, Peace Advocates and Artists Condemn Agreement To Build New U.S. Marine Base in Okinawa."[9] An excerpt:

"Not unlike the 20th century U.S. Civil Rights struggle, Okinawans have non-violently pressed for the end to their military colonization. They tried to stop live-fire military drills that threatened their lives by entering the exercise zone in protest; they formed human chains around military bases to express their opposition; and about a hundred thousand people, one tenth of the population have turned out periodically for massive demonstrations. Octogenarians initiated the campaign to prevent the construction of the Henoko base with a sit-in that has been continuing for years. The prefectural assembly passed resolutions to oppose the Henoko base plan. In January 2013, leaders of all the 41 municipalities of Okinawa signed the petition to the

9     http://peacephilosophy.blogspot.ca/2014/01/international-scholars-peace-advocates.html

government to remove the newly deployed MV-22 Osprey from Futenma base and to give up the plan to build a replacement base in Okinawa."

Here's background on the Governor of Okinawa.[10]

Here's an organization[11] working to support the will of the public of Okinawa on this issue. And here's a video worth watching: http://www.youtube.com/watch?v=rzAw-jOQwME#t=0

## *Do We Care About People If They Live in Bahrain?*

I had a heck of a time making sense of the U.S. Navy's new motto "A Global Force for Good" until I realized that it meant "We are a global force, and wherever we go we're never leaving."

For three years now people in the little island nation of Bahrain have been nonviolently protesting and demanding democratic reforms.

For three years now the king of Bahrain and his royal thugs have been shooting, kidnapping, torturing, imprisoning, and terrorizing nonviolent opponents. An opponent includes anyone speaking up for human rights or even "insulting" the king or his flag, which carries a sentence of 7 years in prison and a hefty fine.

---

10      http://www.japanfocus.org/events/view/208
11      http://closethebase.org

For three years now, Saudi Arabia has been aiding the King of Bahrain in his crackdown on the people of Bahrain. A U.S. police chief named John Timoney, with a reputation for brutality earned in Miami and Philadelphia, was hired to help the Bahraini government intimidate and brutalize its population.

For three years now, the U.S. government has been tolerating the abuses committed by Bahrain and Saudi Arabia, continuing to sell weapons to Bahrain and Saudi Arabia, and continuing to dock the U.S. Navy's Fifth Fleet in Bahrain. In fact, the U.S. military has recently announced big and pricey plans to expand its bases in Bahrain and add more ships.

For three years now, the U.S. government has continued to dump some $150 billion (with a 'B') each year into the U.S. Navy, a large portion of which goes for the maintenance of the Fifth Fleet in Bahrain. Withdrawing and disbanding that fleet would save that gargantuan expense. Retraining and re-employing in peaceful activities all personnel would cost a fraction of $150 billion. Providing aid to nonviolent pro-democracy activists in Bahrain would cost a tiny fraction of a fraction. Establishing a policy in the case of this one country of supporting human rights over brutal dictatorship would be, as they say, *priceless*. It would create a very useful model for a transformation of U.S. policy in numerous other nations as well.

Accurate and timely information about the horrors underway for the past three years in Bahrain are available online[12], via Western human rights groups, and via small back-page stories in U.S.

12 http://warisacrime.org/category/categories/bahrain

newspapers. There's little dispute over the general facts. Yet, there's little outrage. There appears to have been no polling done of the U.S. public on the topic of Bahrain whatsoever, so it's impossible to know what people think. But my impression is that most people have never heard of the place.

The U.S. government is not shouting about the need to bomb Bahrain to protect its people. Senators are not insisting on sanctions, sanctions, and more sanctions. There seems to be no crisis, no need for "intervention," only the need to end an intervention we aren't told about.

Which raises a tough question for people who give a damn. We're able to reject a war on Iran or Syria when the question is raised on our televisions. But we can't seem to stop drone strikes nobody tells us about. How do we create a question nobody is asking, about a topic nobody has heard of, and then answer it humanely and wisely? And how do we overcome the inevitable pretense that the Fifth Fleet serves some useful purpose, and that this purpose justifies a little teargas, a bit of torture, and some murders here and there?

The Fifth Fleet claims to be responsible for these nations[13]: Afghanistan, Bahrain, Egypt, Iran, Iraq, Jordan, Kazakhstan, Kyrgyzstan, Lebanon, Oman, Pakistan, Qatar, Saudi Arabia, Syria, Tajikistan, Turkmenistan, United Arab Emirates, Uzbekistan, and Yemen. None of these nations have ships in U.S. waters claiming to be responsible for it. None of these nations' peoples have indicated majority support for having the Fifth Fleet be responsible for

13 http://www.cusnc.navy.mil/command/aor2.html

them. Afghanistan has suffered under U.S. occupation for over a decade, with chaos and tyranny to follow. Egypt's thugs are rising anew with steady U.S. support, money, and weaponry. Iran has threatened and attacked no other nation for centuries, has never had a nuclear weapons program, spends less than 1% what the U.S. does on its military, and moves away from democracy with every U.S. threat. Why not leave Iran alone? Iraq, Jordan, Qatar, Saudi Arabia, Yemen, and others of these nations, including Bahrain, suffer under the rule of U.S.-backed governments. One might reasonably add Israel and the lands it occupies to the list, even if the Navy cannot bring itself to mention them. Yemen and Pakistan suffer under the constant buzzing and missile launching of U.S. drones, which are creating far more enemies than they kill. In fact, not a single nation falling under the past 19 years of benevolent "responsibility" of the Fifth Fleet has clearly benefitted in any way.

At a third annual conference recently held in Lebanon, Bahraini activists laid out a plan of action. It includes building international connections with people who care and are willing to help. It includes supporting the International Day to End Impunity on November 23rd. It includes pushing Bahrain to join the ICC, although that may be of little value until the U.S. can be persuaded to do the same and until the United Nations can be democratized. The plan includes calls for an end to weapons sales and the initiation of sanctions against the Bahraini government (not its people).

Those would certainly be good steps. The first question in my mind remains: do the people in the nation that screams most loudly about "freedom" and does the most to support its repression wherever deemed useful, care?

# A 15-Year Murder Spree

*"The notion of a 'humanitarian war' would have rang in the ears of the drafters of the UN Charter as nothing short of Hitlerian, because it was precisely the justification used by Hitler himself for the invasion of Poland just six years earlier." —Michael Mandel*

Fifteen years ago, NATO was bombing Yugoslavia. This may be difficult for people to grasp who believe the Noah movie is historical fiction, but: What your government told you about the bombing of Kosovo was false. And it matters.

While Rwanda[14] is the war that many misinformed people wish they could have had (or rather, wish others could have had for them), Yugoslavia is the war they're glad happened—at least whenever World War II really fails as a model for the new war they're after—in Syria[15] for instance, or in Ukraine[16]—the latter being, like Yugoslavia, another borderland[17] between east and west that is being taken to pieces.

The peace movement is gathering[18] in Sarajevo this summer. The moment seems fitting to recall how NATO's breakout war of aggression, its first post-Cold-War war to assert its power, threaten Russia, impose a corporate economy, and demonstrate that a major war can keep all the casualties on one side (apart from

14 http://davidswanson.org/node/4358
15  http://therealnews.com/t2/index.php?option=com_content&task=view&id=31&Itemid=74&jumival=11539
16 http://davidswanson.org/node/4360
17 http://www.counterpunch.org/2014/03/21/ukraine-and-yugoslavia/
18 http://www.peaceeventsarajevo2014.eu

self-inflicted helicopter crashes)—how this was put over on us as an act of philanthropy.

The killing hasn't stopped. NATO keeps expanding its membership and its mission, notably into places like Afghanistan and Libya. It matters how this got started, because it's going to be up to us to stop it.

Some of us had not yet been born or were too young or too busy or too Democratic partisan or too caught up still in the notion that mainstream opinion isn't radically insane. We didn't pay attention or we fell for the lies. Or we didn't fall for the lies, but we haven't yet figured out a way to get most people to look at them.

Here's my recommendation. There are two books that everyone should read. They are about the lies we were told about Yugoslavia in the 1990s but are also two of the best books about war, period, regardless of the subtopic. They are: How America Gets Away With Murder: Illegal Wars, Collateral Damage, and Crimes Against Humanity[19] by Michael Mandel, and Fools' Crusade: Yugoslavia, NATO and Western Delusions[20] by Diana Johnstone.

Johnstone's book provides the historical background, the context, and analysis of the role of the United States, of Germany, of the mass media, and of various players in Yugoslavia. Mandel's book provides the immediate events and a lawyer's analysis of the crimes committed. While many ordinary people in the United States and Europe supported or tolerated the war out of good intentions—

19 http://us.macmillan.com/howamericagetsawaywithmurder/MichaelMandel
20 http://www.amazon.com/Fools-Crusade-Yugoslavia-Western-Delusions/dp/158367084X

that is, because they believed the propaganda—the motivations and actions of the U.S. government and NATO turn out to have been as cynical and immoral as usual.

The United States worked for the breakup of Yugoslavia, intentionally prevented negotiated agreements among the parties, and engaged in a massive bombing campaign that killed large numbers of people, injured many more, destroyed civilian infrastructure and hospitals and media outlets, and created a refugee crisis that did not exist until after the bombing had begun. This was accomplished through lies, fabrications, and exaggerations about atrocities, and then justified anachronistically as a response to violence that it generated.

After the bombing, the U.S. allowed the Bosnian Muslims to agree to a peace plan very similar to the plan that the U.S. had been blocking prior to the bombing spree. Here's U.N. Secretary General Boutros Boutros-Ghali:

> *"In its first weeks in office, the Clinton administration has administered a death blow to the Vance-Owen plan that would have given the Serbs 43 percent of the territory of a unified state. In 1995 at Dayton, the administration took pride in an agreement that, after nearly three more years of horror and slaughter, gave the Serbs 49 percent in a state partitioned into two entities."*

These many years later it should matter to us that we were told about fake atrocities that researchers were unable to ever find, any more than anyone could ever find the weapons in Iraq, or the evidence of plans to slaughter civilians in Benghazi, or the evidence of Syrian chemical weapons use. We're being told that Russian troops are massing on the border of Ukraine with genocidal intentions. But when people look for those troops they can't find them[21]. We should be prepared to consider what that might mean[22].

NATO had to bomb Kosovo 15 years ago to prevent a genocide? Really? Why sabotage negotiations? Why pull out all observers? Why give five days' warning? Why then bomb away from the area of the supposed genocide? Wouldn't a real rescue operation have sent in ground forces without any warning, while continuing diplomatic efforts? Wouldn't a humanitarian effort have avoided killing so many men, women, and children with bombs, while threatening to starve whole populations through sanctions?

Mandel looks very carefully at the legality of this war, considering every defense ever offered for it, and concludes that it violated the U.N. Charter and consisted of murder on a large scale. Mandel, or perhaps his publisher, chose to begin his book with an analysis of the illegality of the wars on Iraq and Afghanistan, and to leave Yugoslavia out of the book's title. But it is Yugoslavia, not Iraq or Afghanistan, that war proponents will continue pointing to for years to come as a model for future wars—unless we stop them. This was a war that broke new ground, but did it with far more effective PR than the Bush administration ever bothered with. This war violated the UN Charter, but also—though Mandel doesn't mention it—Article I of the U.S. Constitution requiring Congressional approval.

21      http://my.firedoglake.com/fairleft/2014/04/01/new-big-ukraine-lie-russia-amassing-troops-at-the-border
22 http://warisalie.org

Every war also violates the Kellogg-Briand Pact[23]. Mandel, all too typically, erases the Pact from consideration even while noting its existence and significance. "The first count against the Nazis at Nuremberg," he writes, "was the 'crime against peace . . . violation of international treaties'—international treaties just like the Charter of the United Nations." That can't be right. The U.N. Charter did not yet exist. Other treaties were not just like it. Much later in the book, Mandel cites the Kellogg-Briand Pact as the basis for the prosecutions, but he treats the Pact as if it existed then and exists no longer. He also treats it as if it banned aggressive war, rather than all war. I hate to quibble, as Mandel's book is so excellent, including his criticism of Amnesty International and Human Rights Watch for refusing to recognize the U.N. Charter. But what they're doing to make the U.N. Charter a treaty of the past, Mandel himself (and virtually everyone else) does to the Kellogg-Briand Pact, awareness of which would devastate all arguments for "humanitarian wars."

Of course, proving that every war thus far marketed as humanitarian has actually harmed humanity doesn't eliminate the theoretical possibility of a humanitarian war. What erases that is the damage that keeping the institution of war around does to human society and the natural environment. Even if, in theory, 1 war in 1,000 could be a good one (which I don't believe for a minute), preparing for wars is going to bring those other 999 along with it. That is why the time has come to abolish the institution[24].

23 http://davidswanson.org/outlawry
24 http://worldbeyondwar.org

# Lies About Rwanda Mean More Wars If Not Corrected

Urge the ending of war these days and you'll very quickly hear two words: "Hitler" and "Rwanda." While World War II killed some 70 million people, it's the killing of some 6 to 10 million (depending on who's included) that carries the name Holocaust. Never mind that the United States and its allies refused to help those people before the war or to halt the war to save them or to prioritize helping them when the war ended—or even to refrain from letting the Pentagon hire some of their killers. Never mind that saving the Jews didn't become a purpose for WWII until long after the war was over. Propose eliminating war from the world and your ears will ring with the name that Hillary Clinton calls Vladimir Putin and that John Kerry calls Bashar al Assad.

Get past Hitler, and shouts of "We must prevent another Rwanda!" will stop you in your tracks, unless your education has overcome a nearly universal myth that runs as follows. In 1994, a bunch of irrational Africans in Rwanda developed a plan to eliminate a tribal minority and carried out their plan to the extent of slaughtering over a million people from that tribe—for purely irrational motivations of tribal hatred. The U.S. government had been busy doing good deeds elsewhere and not paying enough attention until it was too late. The United Nations knew what was happening but refused to act, due to its being a large bureaucracy inhabited by weak-willed non-Americans. But, thanks to U.S. efforts, the criminals were prosecuted, refugees were allowed to return, and democracy and European enlightenment were brought belatedly to the dark valleys of Rwanda.

Something like this myth is in the minds of those who shout for attacks on Libya or Syria or Ukraine under the banner of "Not another Rwanda!" The thinking would be hopelessly sloppy even if based on facts. The idea that SOMETHING was needed in Rwanda morphs into the idea that heavy bombing was needed in Rwanda which slides effortlessly into the idea that heavy bombing is needed in Libya. The result is the destruction of Libya[25]. But the argument is not for those who pay attention to what was happening in and around Rwanda before or since 1994. It's a momentary argument meant to apply only to a moment. Never mind why Gadaffi was transformed from a Western ally into a Western enemy, and never mind what the war left behind. Pay no attention to how World War I was ended and how many wise observers predicted World War II at that time. The point is that a Rwanda was going to happen in Libya (unless you look at the facts too closely) and it did not happen. Case closed. Next victim.

Edward Herman highly recommends[26] a book by Robin Philpot called *Rwanda and the New Scramble for Africa: From Tragedy to Useful Imperial Fiction,* and so do I. Philpot opens with U.N. Secretary General Boutros Boutros-Ghali's comment that "the genocide in Rwanda was one hundred percent the responsibility of the Americans!" How could that be? Americans are not to blame for how things are in backward parts of the world prior to their "interventions." Surely Mr. double Boutros has got his chronology

25   http://www.theguardian.com/commentisfree/2014/mar/24/libya-disaster-shames-western-interventionists
26   http://www.globalresearch.ca/rwanda-and-the-new-scramble-for-africa-an-eye-opener-and-essential-reading/5365737

wrong. Too much time spent in those U.N. offices with foreign bureaucrats no doubt. And yet, the facts—not disputed claims but universally agreed upon facts that are simply deemphasized by many—say otherwise.

The United States backed an invasion of Rwanda on October 1, 1990, by a Ugandan army led by U.S.-trained killers, and supported their attack on Rwanda for three-and-a-half years. The Rwandan government, in response, did not follow the model of the U.S. internment of Japanese during World War II, or of U.S. treatment of Muslims for the past 12 years. Nor did it fabricate the idea of traitors in its midst, as the invading army in fact had 36 active cells of collaborators in Rwanda. But the Rwandan government did arrest 8,000 people and hold them for a few days to six-months. Africa Watch (later Human Rights Watch/Africa) declared this a serious violation of human rights, but had nothing to say about the invasion and war. Alison Des Forges of Africa Watch explained that good human rights groups "do not examine the issue of who makes war. We see war as an evil and we try to prevent the existence of war from being an excuse for massive human rights violations."

The war killed many people, whether or not those killings qualified as human rights violations. People fled the invaders, creating a huge refugee crisis, ruined agriculture, wrecked economy, and shattered society. The United States and the West armed the warmakers and applied additional pressure through the World Bank, IMF, and USAID. And among the results of the war was increased hostility between Hutus and Tutsis. Eventually the government would topple. First would come the mass slaughter known as the Rwandan Genocide. And before that would come the murder of two presidents. At that point, in April 1994, Rwanda was in chaos almost on the level of post-liberation Iraq or Libya.

One way to have prevented the slaughter would have been to not support the war. Another way to have prevented the slaughter would have been to not support the assassination of the presidents of Rwanda and Burundi on April 6, 1994. The evidence points strongly to the U.S.-backed and U.S.-trained war-maker Paul Kagame—now president of Rwanda—as the guilty party. While there is no dispute that the presidents' plane was shot down, human rights groups and international bodies have simply referred in passing to a "plane crash" and refused to investigate.

A third way to have prevented the slaughter, which began immediately upon news of the presidents' assassinations, might have been to send in U.N. peacekeepers (not the same thing as Hellfire missiles, be it noted), but that was not what Washington wanted, and the U.S. government worked against it. What the Clinton administration was after was putting Kagame in power. Thus the resistance to calling the slaughter a "genocide" (and sending in the U.N.) until blaming that crime on the Hutu-dominated government became seen as useful. The evidence assembled by Philpot suggests that the "genocide" was not so much planned as erupted following the shooting down of the plane, was politically motivated rather than simply ethnic, and was not nearly as one-sided as generally assumed.

Moreover, the killing of civilians in Rwanda has continued

ever since, although the killing has been much more heavy in neighboring Congo, where Kagame's government took the war—with U.S. aid and weapons and troops—and bombed refugee camps killing some million people. The excuse for going into the Congo has been the hunt for Rwandan war criminals. The real motivation has been Western control and profits[27]. War in the Congo has continued to this day, leaving some 6 million dead—the worst killing since the 70 million of WWII. And yet nobody ever says "We must prevent another Congo!"

## *Token Anti-War Guest on Television*
September 23, 2014, on MSNBC

Ed Schultz: Welcome back to the Ed Show. Thanks for watching tonight. With the United States carrying out air strikes on Syria to combat ISIS we are at war once again. But many war weary Americans are speaking out against the President's plan. As the President spoke on the South Lawn of the White House about the latest military action, the National Campaign for Nonviolent Resistance staged a die-in outside the White House in protest. The crowd took issue with the president's escalated action.

Joy First: I think what we're doing is escalating the war over there again in that area of the world, and a lot of innocent people are going to be killed.

David Swanson: There is no rationale and there is absolutely no legal basis for what he is proposing, and we need more people in

27  http://davidswanson.org/node/4299

the streets protesting it.

Ed Schultz: Their voice of dissent is being echoed by some members of Congress. Senator Time Kaine of Virginia says that the President should have sought out Congressional approval before carrying out strikes in Syria.

Tim Kaine: The Constitution is pretty clear. The president always has the ability to defend the United States against any kind of an imminent attack. But as soon as a president decides, as the President described it to Chuck Todd a few weeks ago to "go on offense" against ISIL, if it's not just a defensive mission but an offensive one, that's when Congress is needed, that's what the Constitution says.

Ed Schultz: During the run-up to the war in Iraq in 2003 I believe the mainstream media neglected to listen to the antiwar voices and cover them. We should not let this happen again. You'll get both sides of the story on this show as we cover what's unfolding in the Middle East. I'm joined tonight by David Swanson. He's the director of WorldBeyondWar.org who spoke at today's protest. David, good to have you with us tonight. I want to say that I have read your material with quite interest and I would go so far as to say that you're probably on of the most antiwar anti-military-action activists in this country, and I want to tell our audience that, and I don't think you'd take exception to that. Go ahead.

David Swanson: I completely agree. I agree 100 percent, and I'm not war weary, I'm war aware. I've come to recognize that war makes us less safe, it doesn't do us any good, so it's not so much weariness as awareness of what it is.

Ed Schultz: Has the President overstepped his Constitutional authority in your opinion?

David Swanson: Oh, there's no question. I agree with Congressman Garamendi and my own senator, Kaine. This is a blatant violation of Article I Section 8 of the Constitution. But even if Congress comes back and votes for it, it's a blatant violation of the U.N. Charter. This is illegal, to go into another country and bomb it. But more importantly it's counterproductive, it's almost knowingly counterproductive. There is no military solution, they keep saying that. And, by the way, candidate Barack Obama strongly agreed with everything I've just said; it's President Obama who's changed his mind. And we have to bring him back to that desire to end the mindset that gets us into war, because there are numerous useful nonmilitary actions here that don't involve doing what ISIS openly explicitly wants the U.S. military to do. And it's almost guaranteed to be counterproductive. Look at the disaster in Libya. Look at the past quarter-century and the past several years and the past six weeks in Iraq. It makes things worse to go in and bomb a bad situation.

Ed Shultz: What do you view the UN how the UN plays out here, I found it interesting that the UN informed the Syrian ambassador that these air strikes were taking place, and the UN has not formally said for this coalition to back off. What do you make of that?

David Swanson: I think the UN ought to, I think it is absolutely obliged to, but one of its permanent Security Council members with permanent veto status is involved in this. The UN needs to be reformed, it needs to be democratized, it needs to be strengthened, but the fact is that this is an operation going around the UN. And the fact that you can get five kings and dictators to say they're on your side shows that you have a great deal of influence over them. Why not get them on your side for an arms embargo? Seventy-nine percent of the weapons shipped into the Middle East, according to the United States Congress, are from the United States, not counting the U.S. military's weapons. An arms embargo would be three-quarters of the way, just with the United States initiating it. If it can get these Sunni governments to bomb Sunnis, it can get them to join an arms embargo, join discussions that include Iran and Russia and Syria and Iraq, which the U.S. government is willing to talk to about war but not about peace. And send in actual aid, a Marshall-plan scale of restitution to that region, which would be far cheaper than these $2 million missiles.

Ed Schultz: Dissenting voices, such as yourself, what are your expectations as all of this military action unfolds?

David Swanson: I think the public support for it is exaggerated and is likely to be short-lived. I think it's driven by irrational fear based on slick beheading videos and reports on beheading videos. I think people are going to realize that bombing the opposite side of the side they were told they had to bomb a year ago and arming the other side at the same time is madness, that this is benefitting ISIS, it's benefitting the weapons companies. It's not benefitting the people of Iraq or Syria or the world. And it's tearing down the rule of law, which we would like to uphold for this nation and every other nation going forward. And they are unwilling to say how many years and what cost in any measurement of the cost. People are not going to stand for this very long, and the Congress members have given themselves a little bit too lengthy of a vacation, I think. They're going to start hearing pressure from people who want this ended.

Ed Shultz: All right. David Swanson, good to have you with us tonight. I appreciate your voice and your opinion. And if you're watching tonight, you can follow us on Twitter at EdShow.

# Earth

## What Do World's Two Biggest Dangers Have in Common?

Anyone who cares about our natural environment should be marking with great sadness the centenary of World War I. Beyond the incredible destruction in European battlefields, the intense harvesting of forests, and the new focus on the fossil fuels of the Middle East, the Great War was the Chemists' War. Poison gas became a weapon—one that would be used against many forms of life.

Insecticides were developed alongside nerve gases and from byproducts of explosives. World War II—the sequel made almost inevitable by the manner of ending the first one—produced, among other things, nuclear bombs, DDT, and a common language for discussing both—not to mention airplanes for delivering both.

War propagandists made killing easier by depicting foreign people as bugs. Insecticide marketers made buying their poisons patriotic by using war language to describe the "annihilation" of "invading" insects (never mind who was actually here first). DDT was made available for public purchase five days before the U.S. dropped the bomb on Hiroshima. On the first anniversary of the bomb, a full-page photograph of a mushroom cloud appeared in an advertisement for DDT.

War and environmental destruction don't just overlap in how they're thought and talked about. They don't just promote each other through mutually reinforcing notions of machismo and domination. The connection is much deeper and more direct. War and preparations for war, including weapons testing, are themselves among the greatest destroyers of our environment. The U.S. military is a leading consumer of fossil fuels. From March 2003 to December 2007 the war on Iraq alone released[28] more CO2 than 60% of all nations.

Rarely do we appreciate the extent to which wars are fought for control over resources the consumption of which will destroy us. Even more rarely do we appreciate the extent to which that consumption is driven by wars. The Confederate Army marched up toward Gettysburg in search of food to fuel itself. (Sherman burned the South, as he killed the Buffalo, to cause starvation— while the North exploited its land to fuel the war.) The British Navy sought control of oil first as a fuel for the ships of the British Navy, not for some other purpose. The Nazis went east, among several other reasons, for forests with which to fuel their war. The deforestation of the tropics that took off during World War II only accelerated during the permanent state of war that followed.

Wars in recent years have rendered large areas uninhabitable and generated tens of millions of refugees. Perhaps the most deadly weapons left behind by wars are land mines and cluster bombs. Tens of millions of them are estimated to be lying around on the earth. The Soviet and U.S. occupations of Afghanistan have destroyed or damaged thousands of villages and sources of water. The Taliban

28 http://www.naomiklein.org/articles/2009/12/fight-climate-change-not-wars

has illegally traded timber to Pakistan, resulting in significant deforestation. U.S. bombs and refugees in need of firewood have added to the damage. Afghanistan's forests are almost gone. Most of the migratory birds that used to pass through Afghanistan no longer do so. Its air and water have been poisoned with explosives and rocket propellants.

The United States fights its wars and even tests its weapons far from its shores, but remains pockmarked by environmental disaster areas and superfund sites created by its military. The environmental crisis has taken on enormous proportions, dramatically overshadowing the manufactured dangers that lie in Hillary Clinton's contention that Vladimir Putin is a new Hitler or the common pretense in Washington, D.C., that Iran is building nukes or that killing people with drones is making us safer rather than more hated. And yet, each year, the EPA spends $622 million trying to figure out how to produce power without oil, while the military spends hundreds of *billions* of dollars burning oil in wars fought to control the oil supplies. The million dollars spent to keep each soldier in a foreign occupation for a year could create 20 green energy jobs at $50,000 each. The $1 trillion spent by the United States on militarism each year, and the $1 trillion spent by the rest of the world combined, could fund a conversion to sustainable living beyond most of our wildest dreams. Even 10% of it could.

When World War I ended, not only did a huge peace movement develop, but it was allied with a wildlife conservation movement. These days, those two movements appear divided and conquered.

Once in a blue moon their paths cross, as environmental groups are persuaded to oppose a particular seizure of land or military base construction, as has happened in recent months with the movements to prevent the U.S. and South Korea from building a huge naval base on Jeju Island, and to prevent the U.S. Marine Corps from turning Pagan Island in the Northern Marianas into a bombing range. But try asking a well-funded environmental group to push for a transfer of public resources from militarism to clean energy or conservation and you might as well be trying to tackle a cloud of poison gas.

I'm pleased to be part of a movement just begun at WorldBeyondWar.org, already with people taking part in 57 nations, that seeks to replace our massive investment in war with a massive investment in actual defense of the earth. I have a suspicion that big environmental organizations would find great support for this plan were they to survey their members.

## *The Climate Is Invading the Earth!*

If an alien invader with a face were attacking the earth, the difficulties that governments have getting populations to support wars on other humans would be multiplied a thousand fold. The most common response to officials calling some petty foreign despot "a new Hitler" would shift from "yeah, right" to "who cares?" The people of the world would unite in common defense against the hostile alien.

If only it had a face. And what's a face anyway? Doctors can create faces now. You'd still love your loved ones if they lost their faces. And I hear there's a movie in which a guy falls in love with his faceless computer.

The point is that there *is* an alien invader attacking the earth. Its name is climate change. And Uncle Sam wants YOU to fight it, as does Uncle Boris and Aunt Hannah and Cousin Juan and Brother Feng. The whole family is in agreement on this one, and we *are* a family now all of a sudden.

Climate change breathes fire on our land and roasts it, killing crops, drying up water supplies, breeding dangerous diseases and infestations. Climate change circles over the oceans and blows tidal waves toward our coasts. It melts the icebergs in its evil claws and sinks our beach resorts beneath the sea.

How do we fight back? We organize quickly, as only humans can. We grab the $2 trillion that we spend on wars among ourselves each year, plus a few trillion more from some multi-billionaires who suddenly realize they don't have another planet to spend it on. We start coating the rooftops with solar panels, aimed right at the face of the monster. We put up windmills that will turn his nasty breath against himself.

And we hit him where it really hurts, we cut off his supplies with crippling sanctions: we stop buying and making and consuming and discarding such incredible piles of crap every day. Consumerism becomes rapidly understood as planetary treason, support for the Evil One. We put a stop to its worst excesses and begin reining it in systematically—working together as we never have before.

Ah, but the dark lord of the heat is subtle. He has cells of loyalists among us. They push fossil fuels on us and tell us comforting lies. No longer! We will drag them before the House UnEarthly Activities Committee. "Are you now or have you ever been a promoter of oil, gas, or coal consumption?" They'll crumble under the pressure.

Imagine how we could unite for this battle, what wits and courage and self-sacrifice we could put into it, what inspiring acts of bravery, what stunning creations of intellect!

Ah, but climate change is not a person, so forget the whole thing. Did you ever notice what a funny grin Vladimir Putin has? It's beginning to get on my nerves.

## *Peacenvironmentalism*

*Remarks at North Carolina Peace Action Event in Raleigh, N.C., August 23, 2014.*

Thank you for inviting me, and thank you to North Carolina Peace Action, and to John Heuer whom I consider a tireless selfless and inspired peacemaker himself. Can we thank John?

It's an honor for me to have a role in honoring the 2014 Student Peacemaker, iMatter Youth North Carolina. I've followed what iMatter has been doing around the country for years, I've sat in on a court case they brought in Washington, D.C., I've shared a stage with them at a public event, I've organized an online petition with them at RootsAction.org, I've written about them and watched them inspire writers like Jeremy Brecher whom I recommend reading. Here is an organization acting in the interests of all future generations of all species and being led—and led well—by human kids. Can we give them some applause?

But, perhaps revealing the short-sightedness and self-centeredness of myself as a member of a species that didn't evolve to manage a whole planet, I'm especially happy to be recognizing iMatter Youth North Carolina because my own niece Hallie Turner and my nephew Travis Turner are part of it. They deserve LOTS of applause.

And the full iMatter planning team, I'm told, is represented tonight as well by Zack Kingery, Nora White, and Ari Nicholson. They should have even more applause.

I take complete credit for Hallie and Travis's work, because although I didn't really teach them anything, I did, before they were born, tell my sister she should go to our high school reunion, at which she met the man who became my brother in law. Without that, no Hallie and no Travis.

However, it was my parents—who I suppose by the same logic

(although in this case I of course reject it) get complete credit for anything I do—it was they who took Hallie to her first rally, at the White House protesting a tar sands pipeline. I'm told that Hallie didn't know what it was all about at first or why the good people were being arrested, instead of the people committing the offenses against our loved ones and our earth being arrested. But by the end of the rally Hallie was right in the thick of it, wouldn't leave until the last person had gone off to jail for justice, and she pronounced the occasion the most important day of her life thus far, or words to that effect.

Perhaps, as it turns out, that was an important day, not just for Hallie but also for iMatter Youth North Carolina, and, who knows, just maybe—like the day Gandhi was thrown off a train, or the day Bayard Rustin talked Martin Luther King Jr. into giving up his guns, or the day a teacher assigned Thomas Clarkson to write an essay on whether slavery was acceptable—it will eventually turn out to have been an important day for more of us.

I'm a bit ashamed of two things though, despite all my pride. One is that we adults leave kids to discover moral action and serious political engagement by accident rather than teaching it to them systematically and universally, as if we don't really think they want meaningful lives, as if we imagine comfortable lives is the complete human ideal. We are asking kids to lead the way on the environment, because we—I'm speaking collectively of everyone over 30, the people Bob Dylan said not to trust until he was over 30—we are not doing it, and the kids are taking us to court, and our government is allowing its fellow leading destroyers of the environment to become voluntary co-defendants (can you imagine volunteering to be sued along with someone else who's facing a law suit? No, wait, sue me too!), and the voluntary co-defendants, including the National Association of Manufacturers, are providing teams of lawyers that probably cost more than the schools Hallie and Travis attend, and the courts are ruling that it is an individual right of non-human entities called corporations to destroy the inhabitability of the planet for everyone, despite the evident logic that says the corporations will cease to exist as well.

Should our kids do as we say or as we do? Neither! They should run in the opposite direction from anything we've touched. There are exceptions, of course. Some of us try a little. But it is an uphill effort to undo the cultural indoctrination that has us saying phrases like "throw this away" as if there really were an away, or labeling the destruction of a forest "economic growth," or worrying about so-called peak oil and how we'll live when the oil runs out, even though we've already found five times what we can safely burn and still be able to live on this beautiful rock.

But kids are different. The need to protect the earth and use clean energy even if it means a few inconveniences or even some serious personal risk, is no more unusual or strange to a kid than half the other stuff they are presented with for the first time, like algebra, or swim meets, or uncles. They haven't spent as many years being told that renewable energy doesn't work. They haven't developed the fine-tuned sense of patriotism that allows us to keep believing renewable energy cannot work even as we hear about it working in other countries. (That's German physics!)

Our young leaders have fewer years of indoctrination into what Martin Luther King Jr. called extreme materialism, militarism, and racism. Adults block the way in the courts, so kids take to the streets, they organize and agitate and educate. And so they must, but they are up against an educational system and an employment system and an entertainment system that often tells them they are powerless, that serious change is impossible, and that the most important thing you can do is vote.

Now, adults telling each other that the most important thing they can do is vote is bad enough, but saying that to kids who aren't old enough to vote is like telling them to do nothing. We need a few percent of our population doing the opposite of nothing, living and breathing dedicated activism. We need creative nonviolent resistance, re-education, redirection of our resources, boycotts, divestments, the creation of sustainable practices as models for others, and the impeding of an established order that is politely and smilingly steering us over a cliff. Rallies organized by iMatter Youth North Carolina look like moves in the right direction to me. So, let's thank them again.

The second thing I'm a little ashamed of is that it is not at all uncommon for a peace organization to arrive at an environmental activist when choosing someone to honor, whereas I have never once heard of the reverse. Hallie and Travis have an uncle who works largely on peace, but they live in a culture where the activism that receives funding and attention and mainstream acceptance, to the limited extent that any does and of course trailing far behind 5Ks against breast cancer and the sort of activism that lacks real opponents, is activism for the environment. But I think there's a problem with what I've just done and what we usually tend to do, that is, with categorizing people as peace activists or environmental activists or clean elections activists or media reform activists or anti-racism activists. As we came to realize a few years back, we all add up to 99% of the population, but those who are really active are divided, in reality as well as in people's perceptions.

Peace and environmentalism should, I think, be combined into the single word peacenvironmentalism, because neither movement is likely to succeed without the other. iMatter wants to live as if our future matters. You can't do that with militarism, with the resources it takes, with the destruction it causes, with the risk that grows greater with each passing day that nuclear weapons will be intentionally or accidentally detonated. If you could really figure out how to nuke another nation while shooting its missiles out of the sky, which of course nobody has figured out, the impact on the atmosphere and climate would severely impact your own nation as well. But that's a fantasy. In a real world scenario, a nuclear weapon is launched on purpose or by mistake, and many more are quickly launched in every direction. This has in fact nearly happened numerous times, and the fact that we pay almost no attention to it anymore makes it more rather than less likely. I imagine you know what happened 50 miles southeast of here on January 24, 1961? That's right, the U.S. military accidentally dropped two nuclear bombs and got very lucky they didn't explode. Nothing to worry about, says comedy news anchor John Oliver, that's why we have TWO Carolinas.

iMatter advocates for an economic shift from fossil fuels to renewable energy and for sustainable jobs. If only there were a couple of trillion dollars a year being wasted on something useless or destructive! And of course there is, worldwide, that unfathomable sum is being spent on preparations for war, half of it by the United States, three quarters of it by the United States and its allies—and much of that last bit on U.S. weapons. For a fraction of it, starvation and disease could be seriously dealt with, and so could climate change. War kills primarily through taking spending away from where it's needed. For a small fraction of war preparations spending, college could be free here and provided free in some other parts of the world too. Imagine how many more environmental activists we could have if college graduates didn't owe tens of thousands of dollars in exchange for the human right of an education! How do you pay that back without going to work for the destroyers of the earth?

79% of weapons in the Middle East come from the United States, not counting those belonging to the U.S. military. U.S. weapons were on both sides in Libya three years ago and are on both sides in Syria and Iraq. Weapons making is an unsustainable job if ever I saw one. It drains the economy. The same dollars spent on clean energy or infrastructure or education or even tax cuts for non-billionaires produces more jobs than military spending. Militarism fuels more violence, rather than protecting us. The weapons have to be used up, destroyed, or given to local police who will begin to see local people as enemies, so that new weapons can be made. And this process is, by some measures, the biggest destroyer of the environment we have.

The U.S. military burned through about 340,000 barrels of oil each day, as measured in 2006. If the Pentagon were a country, it would rank 38th out of 196 in oil consumption. If you removed the Pentagon from the total oil consumption by the United States, then the United States would still rank first with nobody else anywhere close. But you would have spared the atmosphere the burning of more oil than most countries consume, and would have spared the planet all the mischief the U.S. military manages to fuel with it. No other institution in the United States consumes remotely as much oil as the military.

Each year, the U.S. Environmental Protection Agency spends $622 million trying to figure out how to produce power without oil, while the military spends hundreds of billions of dollars burning oil in wars fought and on bases maintained to control the oil supplies. The million dollars spent to keep each soldier in a foreign occupation for a year could create 20 green energy jobs at $50,000 each.

Wars in recent years have rendered large areas uninhabitable and generated tens of millions of refugees. War "rivals infectious disease as a global cause of morbidity and mortality," according to Jennifer Leaning of Harvard Medical School. Leaning divides war's environmental impact into four areas: "production and testing of nuclear weapons, aerial and naval bombardment of terrain, dispersal and persistence of land mines and buried ordnance, and use or storage of military despoliants, toxins, and waste." A 1993 U.S. State Department report called land mines "the most toxic and widespread pollution facing mankind." Millions of hectares in

Europe, North Africa, and Asia are under interdiction. One-third of the land in Libya conceals land mines and unexploded World War II munitions.

The Soviet and U.S. occupations of Afghanistan have destroyed or damaged thousands of villages and sources of water. The Taliban has illegally traded timber to Pakistan, resulting in significant deforestation. U.S. bombs and refugees in need of firewood have added to the damage. Afghanistan's forests are almost gone. Most of the migratory birds that used to pass through Afghanistan no longer do so. Its air and water have been poisoned with explosives and rocket propellants.

You may not care about politics, the saying goes, but politics cares about you. That goes for war. John Wayne avoided going off to World War II by making movies to glorify other people going. And do you know what happened to him? He made a movie in Utah near a nuclear testing area. Of the 220 people who worked on the film, 91, rather than the 30 that would have been the norm, developed cancer including John Wayne, Susan Hayward, Agnes Moorehead, and director Dick Powell.

We need a different direction. In Connecticut, Peace Action and many other groups have been involved in successfully persuading the state government to set up a commission to work on converting from weapons to peaceful industries. Labor unions and management support it. Environmental and peace groups are part of it. It's very much a work in progress. It was likely stimulated by false stories that the military was being slashed. But whether we can make that a reality or not, the environmental need to shift our resources to green energy is going to grow, and there is no reason North Carolina shouldn't be the second state in the country to do this. You have moral Mondays here. Why not have moral every days of the year?

Major changes look larger before they happen than after. Environmentalism has come on very quickly. The U.S. already had nuclear submarines back when whales were still being used as a source of raw materials, lubricants, and fuels, including in nuclear submarines. Now whales are, almost suddenly, seen as marvelous intelligent creatures to be protected, and the nuclear submarines have begun to look a bit archaic, and the deadly sound pollution that the Navy imposes on the world's oceans looks a bit barbaric.

iMatter's lawsuits seek to protect the public trust for future generations. The ability to care about future generations is, in terms of the imagination required, almost identical to the ability to care about foreign people at a distance in space rather than time. If we can think of our community as including those not yet born, who of course we hope far outnumber the rest of us, we can probably think of it as including the 95% of those alive today who don't happen to be in the United States of America, and vice versa.

But even if environmentalism and peace activism were not a single movement, we'd have to join them and several others together in order to have the sort of Occupy 2.0 coalition we need to effect change. A big chance to do that is coming up around September 21st which is the International Day of Peace and the time when a rally and all sorts of events for the climate will be happening in New York City.

At WorldBeyondWar.org you'll find all sorts of resources for holding your own event for peace and the environment. You'll also find a short two-sentence statement in favor of ending all war, a statement that has been signed in the past few months by people in 81 nations and rising. You can sign it on paper here this evening. We need your help, young and old. But we should be especially glad that time and numbers are on the side of the young around the world, to whom I say along with Shelley:

*Rise like Lions after slumber*
*In unvanquishable number,*
*Shake your chains to earth like dew*
*Which in sleep had fallen on you-*
*Ye are many — they are few.*

## *Turn Left for Earth*

I appreciate that there's more[29] happening than just a march[30] for the climate[31] today on the International Day of Peace[32], and I get the idea that keeping the safe and obedient march-to-nowhere separate from protests actually at the United Nations where our corporate overlords are determining the rate of the earth's demise is intended to please all of the people some of the time, but I can't

29 http://www.beyondthemarch.org/action-calendar/
30 http://peoplesclimate.org/march/
31 http://peoplesclimate.org/peace/appeal/
32 http://www.worldbeyondwar.org/eventsforWBW/

help wishing that the march would just turn left instead of right when it reaches 42nd Street, in order to march to the United Nations rather than to nowhere.

This is not a radical idea. A nonviolent protest march expressing popular opinion should be allowed to march to the place it is protesting. The idea that insisting on that constitutes something radical or extremist bewilders me. The New York Times[33] refers to "protest or terror groups" as a category of people, but has a protest group ever engaged in terrorizing and has a terrorist ever joined a protest? Would protesting the United Nations *at the United Nations* somehow be an act of violence, perhaps purely because it would be an act of disobedience? You've got to be kidding me.

I'm in favor of mixed-use protests, not just urban developments. Don't just let the conservative marchers know about opportunities for more direct protest, but get them involved. Take a safe march to a resistance action, where its size will keep it safe and its members will be energized. Let the crowd demonstrate within sight and sound of the people it is petitioning for a redress of grievances, and let those who are ready join in disruptive protest actions.

Of course turning left in order to go where needed makes a nice metaphor for what our whole culture must do if it is to cease destroying the earth's climate. Paul Krugman figured out this week that green energy pays for itself, but he seems to imagine that therefore it will be created, as if the corrupting influence of the fossil fuel profiteers just doesn't exist. We need to turn so far left

---

33    http://www.nytimes.com/2014/09/21/us/politics/intruder-white-house.html?_r=1

that we abandon such naiveté, stop yammering about transition fuels, abandon all talk of "peak oil" as if existing oil isn't sufficient to kill us all, and forswear all pointless pursuit of the political "center."

Naomi Klein's new book does a much better job of identifying the corrupting influence of profiteers. She also points out that the sooner we act to slow down climate change the less radical our actions will need to be. The longer we wait to take meaningful action, the more drastic our actions will have to be when we finally do something. Green energy, Klein's book makes clear for anyone who was unaware, is not failing in a marketplace. It is being killed by political corruption, loan conditions, corporate trade agreements, penalties and disincentives, and the subsidies given to the fossil fuel corporations.

Klein notes that activist movements around trade and climate have, oddly, progressed while virtually ignoring each other. Klein comes closer than most environmentalists to not ignoring another big question, that of war. The military is the elephant in the room in terms of both economics and climate destruction, but is largely ignored by activists and the broader public.

In a common delusion, the government tells the truth about war, and war is worth giving up freedoms for, but scientists lie about the climate and do so in order to (somehow) attack our freedoms. In other words, the fears of bureaucrats and of limits to plutocracy are strong but perhaps not as strong as the fear of terrorists. And the fear of bureaucrats is augmented by a fear of being insignificant, because when nuclear energy or geo-engineering is proposed as a solution, those who like those ideas also see their recognition of the climate crisis increase.

When Klein mentions the military, she first proposes that the weapons companies pay their fair share toward climate protection, and then proposes (along with a bunch of other good ideas) cutting the military by 25%—while calling that proposal "the toughest sell." The U.S. military budget has doubled in the past decade. The idea that it can't be seriously cut is ridiculous. It is not a question of selling the idea to the public. Go back and look at the public's preferred solutions[34] to the supposed financial crisis in Congress a few years back. The problem is in the corruption of the U.S. government.

Elsewhere Klein says that large public sector expenditures will be needed to save the climate, but surely not as large as the military. So why talk about increasing, rather than changing, expenditures? And then again, elsewhere, Klein says what we need is "wartime levels of spending," even though base military spending is about 10 times as much as war spending. Klein also cites a study suggesting that $1.9 trillion a year, or exactly what the planet now spends on war preparations, would solve the climate and various other crises and human needs.

Congress members have skipped town in order to avoid voting on war. You can find them in their districts. November 6th will be the International Day[35] for Preventing the Exploitation of the Environment in War and Armed Conflict. The two movements

34  http://www.commondreams.org/news/2011/01/04/most-americans-say-tax-rich-balance-budget-poll
35 http://www.un.org/en/events/environmentconflictday

named in this holiday should be combined[36] and our actions should escalate. A slight left turn won't be enough to save us.

# The Conscience of a Moderate

*Angels by the River: A Memoir* by James Gustave Speth is pleasantly written but painful to read. Speth knew about the dangers of global warming before the majority of today's climate change deniers were born. He was an advisor to President Jimmy Carter and advised him and the public to address the matter before it became a crisis.

Carter and the U.S. capital of his day weren't about to take the sort of action needed. Remember, Carter was despised for a speech promoting green energy and celebrated for a speech declaring that the United States would always go to war over Middle Eastern oil. Ronald Reagan and his followers (in every sense) Bush, Clinton, Bush, and Obama wouldn't come within 10 miles of a reasonable approach to climate. But Speth has spent the decades since the Carter administration trying to maintain a career within the system, a choice that he acknowledges has required compromises. Now he's pushing for radical change and takes himself to be a radical because he was arrested at the White House opposing a tar sands pipeline.

Here's a photo of Speth at the White House wearing the campaign symbol of the man at whose house he was protesting (Speth doesn't discuss the uniqueness of this form of opposition).

36          http://act.rootsaction.org/p/dia/action3/common/public/?action_KEY=10370

Speth writes as if President Obama were trying to protect the planet from Republicans, in contrast to the real-life Obama who has sabotaged climate talks in Copenhagen and at other summits over the years. Speth gives Democrats a pass, promotes electoral work, pushes nationalism, and believes the world needs U.S. leadership to address climate change. I think the evidence is clear that the world would be fairly well along if the United States would just stay out of the way and stop leading the destruction.

This image is from a recent report[37] by the Institute for Policy Studies.

Speth's book tells a story of racist and sexist Agrarians who wanted to resist corporatism but didn't really do so; of "moderates" who blandly hinted at opposing segregation but didn't; of a Carter White House that didn't act; of a Clinton Administration that decided against even pretending to act; of a statement Speth wrote immediately after September 11, 2001, in which he took a both-and position, supporting both insane war and sane peaceful policies; and of the age of Obama in which one admits that the facts demand swift radical change while embracing lesser-evilism, not in voting but in activism and speech (that inevitable tendency being the main reason some of us oppose it in voting).

Of course I'm being unfair and Speth won't necessarily have any idea what I'm talking about. He doesn't have a chapter dedicated to nationalism, he just frames all of his proposals in terms of being a good patriot and fixing one's country—even though the problem facing us is global. And when he worked in the Carter

37 http://www.ips-dc.org/combatvsclimate/

Administration he actually did good work and got things done. We celebrate—hell, we practically worship—whistleblowers who spent decades doing *bad* work, murderous work, before speaking out. Here's a man who did good work, who nudged things in a better direction for decades, before speaking out in the way he does now. With most people contributing little or nothing to the sustainability of the planet, and with radicals living through decades of failure just the same as moderates, Speth is not someone to criticize. And his book is quite valuable. I just want to nudge him a bit further.

Speth's account of his childhood in South Carolina is charming and wise. His account of unfulfilled dreams for the South and of undesirable Southern influence on the rest of the country is powerful. Instead of losing its bigotry, the South took on the North's consumerism. Instead of losing its consumerism, the North took on the South's reactionary politics, including what Speth calls "antipathy toward the federal government"—I would add: except for that 53% of it that's dedicated to killing foreigners. Speth's account of the Nashville Agrarians' opposition to corporate consumerism is valuable. It's not that nobody knew; it's that not enough people acted. Of course, with my focus on the problem of war (which somehow, at best, squeezes into the last item on each of Speth's lists of issues) I'm brought back to wondering where we would be if slavery had been ended differently. I know that we're supposed to cheer for the Civil War even though other nations (and Washington D.C.) used compensated emancipation and skipped war. I know we're supposed to repeat to ourselves over and over "It's not Lincoln's fault, the slave owners wanted war." Well, indeed they did, but what if they hadn't? Or what if the recruits had refused to fight it for them? Or what if the North had let the South leave? It's difficult to bring up such questions while simultaneously convincing the reader that you know none of this actually happened. So, for what it's worth: I'm aware that's not how it happened; hence the need to bring it up. As it is, Vietnam has gotten over the war of the 1960s, and the U.S. South can, at long last, get over the war of the 1860s if it chooses to.

Speth was a founder of the Natural Resources Defense Council which helped win important struggles to halt a major expansion of nuclear power, to implement the Clean Water Act, and to protect wetlands. He also did great work at the World Resources Institute. Yet, he writes, there have been countless victories during an ongoing major defeat. "Our environmental organizations have grown in strength and sophistication, but the environment has continued to go downhill. The prospect of a ruined planet is now very real. We have won many victories, but we are losing the planet." Speth recounts the perils of working as a D.C. insider: "Once there, inside the system, we were compelled to a certain tameness by the need to succeed there. We opted to work within the system of political economy that we found, and we neglected to seek transformation of the system itself." And of being a global insider: "Thus far, the climate convention is not protecting climate, the biodiversity convention is not protecting biodiversity, the desertification convention is not preventing desertification, and even the older and stronger Convention on the Law of the Sea is not protecting fisheries."

Speth's conclusion is not entirely unlike Naomi Klein's. Speth writes in this book: "In short, most environmental deterioration is a result of systemic failures of the capitalism that we have today, and long-term solutions must seek transformative change in the key features of this contemporary capitalism." Klein quotes Speth in her book: "We didn't adjust with Reagan. We kept working within a system but we should have tried to change the system and root causes."

# *Justice*

## *Can We Really Blame Sociopaths?*

I've been hearing increasingly from multiple quarters that the root of our problems is psychopaths and sociopaths and other loosely defined but definitely different beings from ourselves. Rob Kall has produced a quite interesting series[38] of articles and interviews on the subject.

I want to offer some words of caution if not respectful dissent. I don't think the "because chickenhawks" dissent found, for example, in John Horgan's The End of War is sufficient. That is to say, just because a politician doesn't want to do the killing himself or herself doesn't mean the decision to order killing in war, or in prison, or through poverty and lack of healthcare, or through climate change, isn't heartless and calculating. Psychopaths could be running our world from behind desks.

But are they?

When I look at national politicians in the United States—presidents and Congress members—I can't identify any meaningful place to draw a line such that sociopaths would be on one side and healthy people on the other. They all bow, to one degree or another, to corrupt influences. They all make bad compromises. There are differences in both policy positions and personal manners, but the differences are slight and spread along a continuum. They

38 http://www.opednews.com/populum/seriespage.php?r=5

all fund the largest killing machine in history. The Progressive Caucus budget proposes slight *increases* in military spending, already at 57% of the discretionary budget. Some support wars on "humanitarian" and others on genocidal grounds, but the wars look the same from the receiving end either way.

The slightly better Congress members come from slightly better districts, have taken slightly less money, and begin with slightly more enlightened ideologies. Or at least that's true much of the time on many issues. Often, however, what makes the difference is personal experience. Senator Dianne Feinstein supports warrantless spying on everyone else, but objects when it's turned against her. Six years ago, Congressman Mike McNulty said he was voting against war funding because his brother had been killed in Vietnam. Weren't *four million* people killed there? Didn't many of them have brothers and sisters and other loved ones? Shouldn't we oppose mass murder even if nobody in our immediate family has died from mass murder? In Washington, no one is ashamed to explain their positions by their personal experiences; on the contrary, such rationales are deemed highly admirable—and not just among a certain group who stand apart as the sociopaths.

The spectrum of morality in our elected officials ranges from those who often indicate their concern and their desire to help if their own careers won't suffer in any way, to those who take tentative stands for peace or justice if their own family is impacted, to those who talk a good line and always act against it, and all the way over to those who don't even put up a pretense. But all of this is within a culture where we routinely discuss the supposed need to "humanize" humans. That is to say, we teach each other that foreigners are made more human when we see their photos and learn their names and stories and the stories of their loved ones in some trivial detail—as if we are supposed to imagine that people don't have names or quirks or loved ones until we get a specific account of those things.

When it was revealed that a bunch of TV news guest experts on war were actually getting their talking points from the Pentagon, there was no way to watch the videos and distinguish the corrupt pundits from the truly independent ones. They all talked the same. The mercenary fraudsters fit right in. It's the same with any sociopaths in Congress. They may be there, but how could one possibly spot the difference?

Kall raises the question of why people enjoy watching shows about sociopaths such as "House of Cards," and speculates that people admire sociopaths' ability to stay calm in crises, to express confidence, to project charisma, and to dominate and manipulate others. That's probably right. And such shows spread sociopathy by example. But there's also the function such shows serve of explaining (accurately or not) why our government is so bad.

There's also the joy of hoping against hope that Vice President Underwood will land in prison where so many of his real-life colleagues belong. But watch the real-life "journalists" playing themselves on fictional TV interviews in these shows. They clearly don't imagine themselves as having any value that can be lost by such charades. Watch the advertisements for which many TV shows are filler, and you'll see politicians routinely describing their opponents as behaving sociopathically.

Some experts believe sociopaths make the best CEOs of large corporations. Everybody else recognizes that the CEOs of large corporations are given incentives to behave immorally, regardless of whether it impacts them emotionally in a typical manner or not. Also encouraged to behave immorally are presidents and Congress members.

Well-designed governments encourage good behavior and bar against the potential for evil. They treat 100%—not 2% or 10% or 80%—of elected officials as *potential* psychopaths. Elections are made open and verifiable. Bribery is forbidden. Powers are checked and balanced. Abuses are exposed and punished. Secrecy is curtailed and openness required. War powers are placed in a legislature or the public, or war abolished. Standing armies are disbanded. Profiteering and other conflicts of interest are avoided. Adversarial journalism is encouraged. Our government, in contrast, treats every elected official as a saint capable of overcoming all kinds of bribery and pressure to misbehave, while our culture encourages them and the rest of us to be anything but.

Many agree that we should reform our government, but is something else needed to handle the threat of sociopaths, in public and private life alike? Kall wants sociopaths to be identified and prevented from doing damage. He wants them treated as alleged sex offenders are, despite the horrible failings of that approach and the much greater difficulty in identifying who is and who is not a sociopath. Kall goes further, suggesting sterilization. He writes that he would have happily shot and killed Nazis; and in the next breath lists billionaire Americans he considers parasites—later reassuring us that he doesn't want to kill them.

The identification process is not clear cut. Sociopathy seems to be something of a matter of degree, with some small degree reaching all of us. We allowed our government to destroy Iraq, killing some million people and making millions more refugees, and we talk about that war in terms of how many Americans were killed and how many dollars it cost, as if Iraq doesn't matter at all. Or we talk about the military investment that will generate more wars as if it were a jobs program. That behavior looks like sociopathy to others.

Congresswoman Barbara Lee is the quintessential non-sociopath on Capitol Hill, the one member who voted against launching the past dozen years of wars. But I was once in a room with her and other progressive members of Congress, relatively early in the Bush-Cheney rampage, proposing that impeachment be begun. Congresswoman Maxine Waters proposed opening an effort to impeach Vice President Cheney. Excitement gripped us. For an instant a few of us could imagine Congress pushing back against the lawlessness that has rolled on unimpeded to this day. And then Congresswoman Lee spoke up and said nobody had better do anything without getting approval from John Conyers. And that was that. Not sociopathy. But not pure principled morality either.

Studying the phenomenon of extreme cases at the other end of the spectrum from Rep. Lee is certainly desirable. What makes John McCain or Hillary Clinton tick? How could Dick Cheney contemplate ordering Americans to attack each other in the

Straight of Hormuz in order to blame it on Iran and start a war? How could George W. Bush laugh off his lies about Iraq and claim it didn't matter? How could he proudly declare he would waterboard people again if given the chance? How could Barack Obama go to Copenhagen and intentionally and maliciously block any serious agreement to confront climate change? How could he pretend to know that Gadaffi was going to slaughter Benghazians or that Assad used chemical weapons, when evidence has emerged that he couldn't possibly have known any such things?

But if there have always been sociopaths everywhere, why are some societies doing more evil than others? Has the 95% of humanity that is currently investing dramatically less in war than the United States, identified and controlled its sociopaths? Or have they, rather, created less evil paths to power and influence? If a sociopath wants power and influence, why not give him or her a system in which good behavior is rewarded? In 1928 Secretary of State Frank Kellogg, who cared not a damn for peace, worked night and day for the peace treaty known as the Kellogg-Briand Pact because he saw rewards in that direction and told his wife he might get himself a Nobel Peace Prize. Had power lain in the direction of war-making, that's the direction Kellogg would have headed. If sociopaths make great propagandists, why not train better critical thinkers to see through the lies? Mentally healthy or not, our Congress members are holding off on bombing Syria or Iran because we've rejected the idea that doing so would improve things.

There is a danger, I think, in focusing on sociopaths' existence as the problem, of developing a cure as bad as the disease. Identifying a group of people to be targeted for discrimination, eugenics, imprisonment, or death seems like the habit of a culture that is itself more of a problem than are the genes of a small minority within it likely to be. What kind of a culture would produce such an idea? A sick one, I believe.

I agree with Kall that billionaires can be identified and their billions re-claimed. Excellent proposal! But not every immoral decider is a billionaire. Nor do I find it likely that every politician who promotes some evil practice can be diagnosed as a sociopath or psychopath. Wouldn't it be easier to identify evil politicians by their evil deeds? What would be gained by identifying them instead as the sort of people likely to do something evil, and giving that category of people a scientific name? If an elected official fails to protect the environment, fails to advance peace and justice, fails to deal honestly and fairly with the people, he or she should be held accountable. If recognizing that such a person's emotions may not be functioning like ours helps us to reach them with our demands, terrific. But if it prevents us from reaching their emotions in a way that we might have, and from communicating our views more widely in the process, then it's hurting the cause of justice.

It's not as if we can't recognize the sociopaths coming. Molly Ivins warned us about Bush. He lost his election. Twice. Many of us warned about Obama. Twice. But Bush wasn't born destined to engage in extraordinary renditions. Obama wasn't born destined to drone-kill children on Tuesdays. Our entire system moves in that direction. Bush and Obama should be prosecuted along with many of their colleagues—as a step toward fixing the system. But their bodies shouldn't be studied for clues about whom to sterilize. Only a political culture already itself sterilized would think that was the solution.

# *Torture is Mainstream Now*

As Rebecca Gordon notes in her new book, *Mainstreaming Torture,* polls find greater support in the United States for torture now than when Bush was president. And it's not hard to see why that would be the case.

Fifteen years ago, it was possible to pretend the U.S. government opposed torture. Then it became widely known that the government tortured. And it was believed (with whatever accuracy) that officials had tried to keep the torturing secret. Next it became clear that nobody would be punished, that in fact top officials responsible for torture would be permitted to openly defend what they had done as good and noble.

The idea was spread around that the torture was stopping, but the cynical could imagine it must be continuing in secret, the partisan could suppose the halt was only temporary, the trusting could assume torture would be brought back as needed, and the attentive could be and have been aware that the government has gone right on torturing to this day with no end in sight.

Anyone who bases their morality on what their government does (or how Hollywood supports it) might be predicted to have moved in the direction of supporting torture.

Gordon's book, like most others, speaks of torture as being largely in the past—even while admitting that it isn't really. "Bush administration-era policies" are acknowledged to be ongoing, and yet somehow they retain the name "Bush administration-era policies," and discussion of their possible prosecution in a court of law does not consider the control that the current chief perpetrator has over law enforcement and his obvious preference not to see a predecessor prosecuted for something he's doing.

President Elect Obama made clear[39] in January 2009 that he would not allow torturers to be prosecuted and would be "looking forward" instead of (what all law enforcement outside of science fiction requires) backward. By February 2009, reports were coming in that torture at Guantanamo was worsening[40] rather than ceasing, and included: "beatings, the dislocation of limbs, spraying of pepper spray into closed cells, applying pepper spray to toilet paper and over-forcefeeding detainees who are on hunger strike." In April 2009 a Guantanamo prisoner phoned[41] a media outlet to report being tortured. As time went by the reports kept coming[42], as the military's written policy[43] would lead one to expect[44].

In May 2009, former vice president Dick Cheney forced into the news the fact that, even though Obama had "banned torture" by executive order (torture being a felony and a treaty violation before

39 http://change.gov/newsroom/entry/open_for_questions_round_2_response/
40      http://www.reuters.com/article/2009/02/25/us-guantanamo-abuse-lawyer-exclusive-idUSTRE51O3TB20090225?sp=true
41  http://thelede.blogs.nytimes.com/2009/04/15/guantanamo-detainee-phones-al-jazeera-from-prison/?_php=true&_type=blogs&_r=0
42 http://harpers.org/archive/2009/07/we-still-torture/
43  http://firedoglake.com/2010/01/04/torture-confirmed-at-guantanamo-army-field-manual-codified-abuse/
44 http://www.abc.net.au/pm/content/2010/s2908016.htm

and after the "banning") Obama maintained the power to use torture as needed. Cheney said[45] that Obama's continued claim of the power to torture vindicated his own (Cheney's) authorization of torture. David Axelrod, White House Senior Advisor, refused repeatedly[46], to dispute Cheney's assertion—also supported by Leon Panetta's confirmation hearing for CIA director, at which he said the president had the power to torture and noted that rendition would continue. In fact, it did[47]. The *New York Times* quickly reported[48] that the U.S. was now outsourcing more torture to other countries. The Obama administration announced a new policy on renditions that kept them in place, and a new policy on lawless permanent imprisonment that kept it in place but formalized it, mainstreamed it. Before long Obama-era rendition victims were alleging torture[49].

As the Obama White House continued and sought to extend the occupation of Iraq, torture continued[50] to be an Iraqi policy, as it has post-occupation. It has also remained[51] a U.S.[52] and Afghan policy[53] in Afghanistan[54], with no end[55] in sight. The U.S. military has continued to use[56] the same personnel as part of its torture

45 http://warisacrime.org/node/42892
46 http://warisacrime.org/node/42892
47            http://www.theguardian.com/world/2009/nov/01/rendition-flight-birmingham-airport-cia
48 http://www.nytimes.com/2009/05/24/world/24intel.html
49            http://www.huffingtonpost.com/2009/08/11/target-of-obama-era-rendi_n_256499.html
50            http://www.nytimes.com/2009/06/17/world/middleeast/17iraq.html?_r=1&ref=world
51 http://warisacrime.org/node/43868
52            http://www.washingtonpost.com/wp-dyn/content/article/2009/11/27/AR2009112703438.html?hpid=topnews
53 http://www.nytimes.com/2009/11/29/world/asia/29bagram.html?_r=1&hp
54 http://www.salon.com/2009/09/21/bagram_5/
55 http://news.bbc.co.uk/2/hi/south_asia/8621973.stm
56            http://firedoglake.com/2009/07/21/fdl-exclusive-sere-psychologists-still-

infrastructure. And secret CIA torture prisons[57] have continued to pop into the news even though the CIA was falsely said to have abandoned that practice. While the Obama administration has claimed unprecedented powers to block civil suits against torturers, it has also used[58], in court, testimony produced by torture, something that used to be illegal (and still is if you go by written laws).

"Look at the current situation," Obama said in 2013, "where we are force-feeding detainees who are being held on a hunger strike . . . Is this who we are?" Well, it is certainly who some of us have become, including Obama, the senior authority in charge of the soldiers doing the force-feeding, and a human chameleon able to express outrage at his own policies, a trick that is perhaps more central to the mainstreaming of vicious and sadistic practices than we always care to acknowledge.

The mainstreaming of torture in U.S. policy and entertainment has stimulated a burst of torture use around the globe, even as the U.S. State Department has never stopped claiming to oppose torture when it's engaged in by anyone other than the U.S. government. If "Bush-era policies" is taken to refer to public relations policies, then there really is something to discuss. The U.S. government tortured before, during, and after Bush and Cheney ran the show. But it was during those years that people talked about it, and it is with regard to those years that people still talk about it.

---

used-in-special-ops-interrogations-and-detention/
57    http://www.democracynow.org/2011/7/13/jeremy_scahill_reveals_cia_facility_prison
58   http://washingtonindependent.com/48370/u-s-relies-on-tortured-evidence-in-habeas-case

As Rebecca Gordon's book, *Mainstreaming Torture: Ethical Approaches in the Post-9/11 United States,* recounts well, torture has been around. Native Americans and enslaved African Americans were tortured. The CIA has always tortured. The School of the Americas has long trained torturers. The war on Vietnam was a war of mass-murder and mass-torture. Torture is standard practice in U.S. prisons, where the torture of Muslims began post-9-11, where some techniques originated and some prison guards came from via the National Guard who brought their torturing to an international set of victims for the Bush-Obama era.

One of Gordon's central points, and an important one, is that torture is not an isolated incident. Rather it is an institution, a practice, a collective endeavor that requires planning and organization. Defenders of torture often defend a widespread practice of purely vicious evil by reference to a single imaginary incident in which it would make sense to torture someone. Imagine, they say, that you knew for certain (as of course you would not) that many people were about to be killed unless a particular person revealed something. Imagine you were certain (as of course you would not be) that you had found that person. Imagine that contrary to accumulated wisdom you believed the best way to elicit the information was through torture, and that you were sure (as of course you would not be) that the information would be revealed, that it would be accurate (nobody EVER lies under torture), and that it would prevent the greater tragedy (and not just delay it or move it), with no horrible side-effects or lasting results. Then, in that impossible scenario, wouldn't you agree to torture the person?

And doesn't that fantasy justify having thousands of people prepared to engage in torture even though they'll inevitably torture in all sorts of other situations that actually exist, and even though many thousands of people will be driven to hate the nation responsible? And doesn't it justify training a whole culture to support the maintenance of an apparatus of torture, even though uses of torture outside the fantasized scenario will spread like wildfire through local police and individual vigilantes and allied governments?

Of course not. And that's why I'm glad Gordon has tackled torture as a matter of ethics, although her books seems a bit weighed down by academic jargon. I come at this as someone who got a master's degree in philosophy, focusing on ethics, back before 9-11, back when torture was used as an example of something evil in philosophy classes. Even then, people sometimes referred to "recreational torture," although I never imagined they meant that any other type of torture was good, only that it was slightly less evil. Even today, the polls that show rising—still minority—support for torture, show stronger—majority—support for murder, that is for a president going through a list of men, women, and children, picking which ones to have murdered, and having them murdered, usually with a missile from a drone—as long as nobody tortures them.

While many people would rather be tortured than killed, few people oppose the killing of others as strongly as they oppose torturing them. In part this may be because of the difficulty of torturing for the torturers. If foreigners or enemies are valued at little or nothing, and if killing them is easier than torturing them, then why not think of killing as "cleaner" just as the Obama administration does? That's one ethical question I'd like to see taken up even more than that of torture alone. Another is the question of whether we don't have a duty to put everything we have into opposing the evil of the whole—that being the Nuremberg phrase for war, an institution that brings with it murder, imprisonment, torture, rape, injury, trauma, hatred, and deceit.

If you are going to take on the ethics of torture alone, *Mainstreaming Torture* provides an excellent summary of how philosophy departments now talk about it. First they try to decide whether to be consequentialist or deontological or virtue-based. This is where the jargon takes over. A consequentialist ethics is one that decides on the propriety of actions based on what their likely consequences will be. A deontological ethics declares certain actions good or bad apart from their consequences. And an ethics of virtues looks at the type of life created by someone who behaves in various ways, and whether that person is made more virtuous in terms of any of a long list of possible virtues.

A competition between these types of ethics quickly becomes silly, while an appreciation of them as a collection of insights proves valuable. A consequentialist or utilitarian ethics is easily parodied and denounced, in particular because supporters of torture volunteer such arguments. Would you torture one person to save the lives of two people? Say yes, and you're a simple-minded consequentialist with no soul. But say no and you're demonstrably evil. The correct answer is of course that it's a bad question. You'll never face such a situation, and fantasizing about it is no guide to whether your government should fund an ongoing torture program the real aim and results of which are to generate war propaganda, scare people, and consolidate power.

A careful consideration of all consequences, short- and long-term, structural and subtle, is harder to parody and tends to encompass much of what is imagined to lie outside the purview of the utilitarian simpleton (or corporate columnist[59]). The idea of an ethics that is not based on consequences appeals to people who want to base their ethics on obedience to a god or other such delusion, but the discussions of deontological ethicists are quite helpful nonetheless. In identifying exactly how and why torture is as incredibly offensive as it is, these writers clarify the problem and move people against any support for torture.

The idea of an ethics based entirely on how actions impact the character of the actor is self-indulgent and arbitrary, and yet the discussion of virtues (and their opposite) is terrifically illuminating—in particular as to the level of cowardice being promoted by the policy of employing torture and any other evil practice in hopes of being kept safe.

I think these last two types of ethics, deontological and virtue—that is, ongoing discussion in their terms—have good consequences. And I think that consequentialism and principled integrity are virtues, while engaging in consequentialism and virtue ethics lead to better deontological talk as well as fulfillment of the better imperatives declared by the deontologists. So, the

59 http://www.newsweek.com/time-think-about-torture-149445

question should not be finding the proper ethical theory but finding the proper ethical behavior. How do you get someone who opposes torturing Americans to oppose torturing human beings? How do you get someone who wants desperately to believe that torture has in fact saved lives to look at the facts? How do you get someone who believes that anyone who is tortured deserves it to consider the evidence, and to face the possibility that the torture is used in part to make us see certain people as evil, rather than their evilness actually preceding and justifying the torture? How do you get Republicans loyal to Bush or Democrats loyal to Obama to put human rights above their loyalty?

As Gordon recounts, torture in reality has generated desired falsehoods to support wars, created lots of enemies rather than eliminating them, encouraged and directly trained more torturers, promoted cowardice rather than courage, degraded our ability to think of others as fully human, perverted our ideas of justice, and trained us all to pretend not to know something is going on while silently supporting its continued practice. None of that can help us much in any other ethical pursuit.

# Juvenile Prison: $5 Billion for Child Abuse

**Every juvenile prison must be immediately closed and all of its prisoners freed.**

Oh. Oh. Oh! That sounds too drastic and simplistic and *revolutionary.*

We talk about being reformist or revolutionary as if it were a personality choice. Yet we also talk about being scientific, about being reality-based. Unlike reactionary climate-denying racist creationists we claim, most of us, to recognize such phenomena as climate change and to act on them (leave aside for the moment whether we're really acting appropriately on that one).

The science has long been crystal clear: juvenile prisons are worse than nothing. They increase rather than reducing crime. In our failure to abolish them, we—and not the children we torture—are the seemingly hopeless recidivists.

We spend in the United States $88,000 on average per year to lock a child up, compared to $10,652 to educate a child. We have over 66,000 children locked up, 87% of them boys, and our police arrest 2 million juveniles each year.

A recent longitudinal study of 35,000 young offenders found that those who are locked up are over twice as likely to be locked up as adults compared to those who committed similar offenses and came from similar backgrounds but were given an alternative penalty or were just not arrested. In some states over 80% of those locked up as kids will be convicted of later crimes. Studies have found that, more than family difficulties or gang membership or any other factor, the best predictor of criminality is whether someone has been imprisoned in what amount to factories for crime.

Well, but then, isn't the best predictor the initial commission of a crime that led to the initial incarceration? Actually, no. Eighty to 90% of teenagers in the United States commit illegal acts that could land them behind bars. Most of those put behind bars are put there for minor, nonviolent offenses. A third of all teenagers have even committed a somewhat serious crime, but most are never arrested, much less imprisoned. Almost all grow out of it.

If the minority of young people whose lives are ruined by prison were selected randomly, we might be a bit more likely to do something about it. Anyone who is a parent and finds out what happens in juvenile prisons must be highly unlikely to tolerate their continued existence unless convinced that only other people's children will be locked up. And in fact, it is highly disproportionately kids from poor neighborhoods and with darker skin who get locked up. A non-white child is far more likely to be arrested for the same act than a white child, far more likely to be charged and detained, far more likely to be sentenced to prison, and far more likely to be given a longer sentence.

In fact, the idea that sub-human monsters, of whatever race, must be made to suffer and must be kept away from the rest of us, is the leading candidate as a major explanation of the continuation of juvenile imprisonment. If the goal were preventing crime, the prisons are worse than nothing. We've tried alternatives within the prison system, and found that reforms help but can only go so far. We've tried alternatives outside of the prison system, and found them far superior in results. We've even seen states shut down lots of juvenile prisons, primarily because of the financial cost, and seen the benefits in cost savings, in the lives of young people, and in reduced crime rates. But other states don't follow suit, and the states making the cuts need only see a rise in revenue to begin rebuilding the torture palaces.

The lessons are of course obtainable from abroad as well. The U.S. locks kids up at a higher rate than any other nation. The next closest is South Africa, which locks up children at one-fifth the rate of the U.S. While the United States slowly, reluctantly, begins to stop throwing away packaging, it remains intent on throwing away people. For many who accept disproven ways of thinking, setting those 66,000 children free would make us less safe, just as cutting the military or disbanding it would endanger us all. These are powerful myths, but the evidence overwhelmingly disproves them. If our rural communities went back to farming food instead of prisoners, we would all be better off.

Much of what is routinely done to tens of thousands of youths in the United States would be illegal if done to prisoners of war. Torture in these houses of "correction" is the norm, not the exception. Isolation is the central abuse, combined with food deprivation, assault, rape, temperature extremes, deprivation of medical care, deprivation of education, sadistic exercises in humiliation, forced nudity, stress positions, piling on, attacks by dogs, and of course indefinite detention without criminal conviction. These practices have been transferred to international prisoners after becoming routine for U.S. prisoners, including juveniles. And, while much of the abuse comes from other prisoners, most of it is committed by guards—or, excuse me, "correctional officers."

This disastrous system seems in dire need of reform, and

the idea that it can be reformed is quite tempting. Children's bodies are dug up behind an institution in Florida. A judge in Pennsylvania gets caught taking bribes to send more kids to hell. A sexual assault scandal in Texas gets big enough to make the news. Kids hog-tied and left outside in freezing weather in Arkansas create some waves. But the scandals are everywhere. A review found only eight states where there was not conclusive evidence of system-wide mistreatment. And the scandals have been there for a century and a half. The reforms have been needed and been worked on since day one. They are not what's needed. Children need love and companionship, safety and trust, respect and encouragement. They are even worse equipped to survive imprisonment than adults. Locked up kids commit suicide at a far higher rate than others, nearly rivaling that of war veterans. These facts are continually reconfirmed by new science, but they and the failure of juvenile prisons have been known practically since the invention of juvenile prisons.

Solitary confinement greatly increases suicide rates, and yet is used as a punishment for the offense of being suicidal. This is not a nifty contradiction to be examined in a master's thesis. Rather, it is part of a process that fundamentally destroys our young people, a process which we pretend improves them.

Or do we? Polls suggest that we, the public, in fact understand the madness of government child-abuse currently engaged in to the tune of $5 billion. The public prefers rehabilitation and treatment and is willing to pay *higher* taxes for those approaches, even though they actually cost less. We test this, prove it, and then don't act on it—or at least our government doesn't act on it. Oregon tried an experiment in Deschutes County, giving the county the money it would have taken to lock kids up and requiring the county to pay the bill for any kid that did end up locked up. The county spent the money on prevention, neighborhood programs, community services. In a year, the number of children sent into the fortresses of misery and horror dropped by 72%.

Everything I've just claimed, and much more, is documented in a new book by Nell Bernstein called *Burning Down the House: The End of Juvenile Prison*. This book includes numerous personal stories, countless examples, endless studies, and all the evidence anyone claiming to base policy on reality would need to become a "radical" when it comes to the malfunctioning of juvenile prisons. Bernstein looks at the worst and the best of the institutions. The best remains far from good enough. The best remains worse than nothing at all. Improving the mass abuse of children is not pragmatic; it's immoral. It's like being in favor of the war on Libya because the war on Iraq was worse; doing so requires averting one's eyes from the state Libya is in.

*Burning Down the House* should be taught in our schools. Maybe free young people would find the power to speak up on behalf of their imprisoned fellows, if they knew. Maybe parents, if sufficiently intent on discarding both sadism and racism, would act if they heard it from their children.

There is a hurdle to be overcome, however, higher than the false belief that injustice only happens to those who deserve it, or the corruption of our misrepresentative government by profiteers, or the cooption of the corporate media by the government. The hurdle is this: everything that's wrong with prisons for children is also wrong with prisons for adults. If we stop thinking about imprisoned children the way that we must think in order to allow their imprisonment, we'll be in danger of ceasing to think about imprisoned adults the way we must to allow their imprisonment. Are we willing to risk that danger? I certainly hope so.

# If Iraq Were in Central America

Just as in discussions of bombing nations for women's rights it's hard to bring up the subject of the right not to be bombed, in discussions of shipping so-called illegal children away from the border where you've been terrorizing them in reenactments of Freedom Ride buses it's hard to bring up the subject of not having your government overthrown and your nation turned into a living hell.

Imagine, however, if Iraq were in Central America. Most people in the United States don't realize how convenient it has been to have millions of Iraqis made homeless so far away from the United States, fleeing to places like Syria, and then fleeing Syria when it's Syria's turn to be destroyed.

If, during the past decades of war and sanctions and war on Iraq, Iraq had been located closer to Miami and San Antonio than New York or Seattle is, wouldn't it have been a bit harder for people to tell pollsters that Iraq was benefitting from the war? Wouldn't it have been a bit harder to continue pretending immigrants are something different from refugees? Wouldn't immigrants rights groups have been compelled to notice the military and the wars that create the justification for abuses in the United States but also the motivations for fleeing homes where the wars happen?

If Gaza were in Maryland, would the United States still provide the weapons for bombing the homes there? Would CNN still blame Gazans who remain in their homes? Or would it, rather, scream at them to get back home where they belong?

Well, Honduras is closer to Florida and Texas than much of the United States is. The U.S. government facilitated the overthrow[60] of the government of Honduras with a military coup in 2009 and has supported, funded, armed, and trained the military and the police that have turned Honduras into the most violent and dangerous place on earth, beating out Afghanistan, Pakistan, Iraq, Libya, and other top contenders in the World Cup of Hell Holes. The President of Honduras was yanked out of bed and flown to a U.S. military base and out of the country. The military that replaced him has been trained in torture and assassination at the School of the Americas in Georgia.

And now President Obama is ordering Honduran toddlers flown home from the United States where they are disturbing good democratic citizens of the land of liberty. Perhaps this is a moment, after all, in which to unite the movement for the rights of immigrants with the movement for peace and the rule of law in foreign relations.

60 http://davidswanson.org/node/4013

Imagine the strength of those two movements combined. Words like Hope and Change might actually mean something.

Until then, forgive me if I'm simply disgusted with the level of evil imposed on the world by those in power and the failure of those abused to unite against it.

## Nixon's Treason Now Acknowledged

A George Will column[61] this week, reviewing a book by Ken Hughes called *Chasing Shadows*, mentions almost in passing that presidential candidate Richard M. Nixon secretly sabotaged peace talks that appeared likely to end the war on Vietnam until he intervened. As a result, the war raged on and Nixon won election promising to end the war.

Will treats the matter as a technicality, citing the law against private diplomacy rather than the principle that one shouldn't undermine a government's attempts to halt an episode of mass-murder.

You'd almost have to already know what Will was referring to if you were going to pick up on the fact that Nixon secretly prevented peace while publicly pretending he had a peace plan. And you'd have to be independently aware that once Nixon got elected, he continued the war for years, the total carnage coming to include the deaths of 4 million Vietnamese plus hundreds of thousands

---

61        http://www.washingtonpost.com/opinions/george-f-will-nixons-long-shadow/2014/08/06/fad8c00c-1ccb-11e4-ae54-0cfe1f974f8a_story.html

of Cambodians and Laotians, with the deaths from bombs not previously exploded continuing on a major scale to this day, and, of course, the 58,000 Americans killed in the war who are listed on a wall in D.C. as if somehow more worthy than all the others.

Will is not the only one to acknowledge what Nixon did. The Smithsonian reported[62] on Nixon's treason last year, on the occasion of new tapes of Lyndon Johnson being released. But the Smithsonian didn't call it treason; it treated the matter more as hard-nosed election strategizing. Ken Hughes himself published an article[63] on the History News Network two years ago saying almost exactly what Will's column said this week. But the publication used the headline "LBJ Thought Nixon Committed Treason to Win the 1968 Election." Of course LBJ thought all kinds of things, sane and otherwise. The first two words of the headline ought to have been deleted.

The point is that it's now apparently become fashionable to acknowledge, but minimize, what Nixon did.

Will's focus is on Hughes' theory that Nixon's plan to break into or even firebomb the Brookings Institution was driven by his desire to recover evidence of his own treasonous sabotaging of peace, and that Watergate grew from Nixon's desire to coverup that horrendous crime. This differs from various theories as to what Nixon was so desperate to steal from Brookings (that he was after evidence that Kennedy murdered Diem, or evidence that LBJ

---

62    http://www.smithsonianmag.com/smart-news/nixon-prolonged-vietnam-war-for-political-gainand-johnson-knew-about-it-newly-unclassified-tapes-suggest-3595441/?no-ist
63 http://hnn.us/article/146770

halted the bombing of Vietnam just before the election to help Humphrey win, etc.) It certainly seems that Nixon had reasons for wanting files from Brookings that his staff did not share his views on the importance of. And covering up his own crimes was always a bigger motivation for Nixon than exposing someone else's. Nixon was after Daniel Ellsberg, not because Ellsberg had exposed Nixon's predecessors' high crimes and misdemeanors, but because Nixon feared what Ellsberg might have on him.

But Nixon's sabotaging of peace in 1968 has been known for many years. And that explanation of the Brookings incident has been written about for years, and written about in a context that doesn't bury the significance of the story. One need only turn to writings by Robert Parry (for example here[64], and in the book pictured on that page). Writes Parry:

"One of the Washington press corps' most misguided sayings – that 'the cover-up is worse than the crime' – derived from the failure to understand the full scope of Nixon's crimes of state." The way Parry tells the story might explain why the *Washington Post* prefers George Will's version:

*"Rostow's 'The "X" Envelope,' which was finally opened in 1994 and is now largely declassified, reveals that Johnson had come to know a great deal about Nixon's peace-talk sabotage from FBI wiretaps. In addition, tapes of presidential phone conversations, which were released in 2008, show Johnson complaining to key Republicans about the gambit and even confronting Nixon personally.*

64 http://consortiumnews.com/2012/06/12/the-dark-continuum-of-watergate/

*"In other words, the file that Nixon so desperately wanted to find was not primarily about how Johnson handled the 1968 bombing halt but rather how Nixon's campaign obstructed the peace talks by giving assurances to South Vietnamese leaders that Nixon would get them a better result.*

*"After becoming President, Nixon did extend and expand the conflict, much as South Vietnamese leaders had hoped. Ultimately, however, after more than 20,000 more Americans and possibly a million more Vietnamese had died, Nixon accepted a peace deal in 1972 similar to what Johnson was negotiating in 1968. After U.S. troops finally departed, the South Vietnamese government soon fell to the North and the Vietcong."*

Parry even puts Nixon's action in the context of a pattern of actions that includes Ronald Reagan's election following sabotage of President Carter's hostage negotiations with Iran. Parry has written as well about LBJ's failure to expose Nixon as part of a pattern of Democratic Party spinelessness. There's President Clinton's failure to pursue Iran-Contra, Al Gore's failure to protest a Supreme Court coup, John Kerry's failure to protest apparent election fraud in Ohio, etc.

A less partisan and less contemporary context might include Nixon's phony pro-peace election campaign with those of Woodrow Wilson, Franklin Roosevelt, and other presidents elected to stay out of wars that they promptly jumped into. And that pattern might include candidate Obama's innumerable campaign-rally promises to end the war in Iraq, which as president he kept going for years, attempted to prolong further, and has begun trying to restart now that an opportunity has presented itself—meanwhile having tripled troop levels in Afghanistan, attacked Libya, created a new kind of war with drones in multiple nations, and pushed the U.S. military into a greater and more active presence in numerous African and Asian countries.

It's almost universally maintained by those who have expressed any opinion on the matter that if the public had known about Nixon's treason while he was president, all hell would have broken loose. Are we really such idiots that we've now slipped into routinely acknowledging the truth of the matter but raising no hell whatsoever? Do we really care so much about personalities and vengeance that Nixon's crime means nothing if Nixon is dead? Isn't the need to end wars and spying and government secrets, to make diplomacy public and nonviolent, a need that presses itself fiercely upon us regardless of how many decades it will take before we learn every offensive thing our current top officials are up to?

## *Local Police and Much Else Will Be Militarized As Long As Federal Government Is*

*"Groups on the ground in St. Louis are calling for* nationwide solidarity actions[65] *in support of Justice for Mike Brown and the end of police and extrajudicial killings everywhere."*

---

65 https://actionnetwork.org/groups/solidarity-actions-for-mike-brown

As they should. And we should all join in[66].

But "nationwide" and "everywhere" are odd terms to equate when discussing police militarization. Are we against extrajudicial killings (otherwise known as murder) by U.S. government employees and U.S. weapons in Pakistan? Yemen? Iraq? Gaza? And literally *everywhere* they occur? The militarization of local police in the United States is related to the militarization of U.S. foreign policy, which has now reached the point that bombing and "doing nothing" are generally conceived[67] as the only two choices available. Local police are being militarized as a result of these factors:

A culture glorifying militarization and justifying it as global policing.

A federal government that directs roughly $1 trillion every year into the U.S. military, depriving virtually everything else of needed resources.

A federal government that still manages to find resources to offer free military weapons to local police in the U.S. and elsewhere.

Weapons profiteers that eat up local subsidies as well as federal contracts while funding election campaigns, threatening job elimination in Congressional districts, and pushing for the unloading of weapons by the U.S. military on local police as one means of creating the demand for more.

---

66 https://www.facebook.com/events/312628798897146/
67 http://davidswanson.org/node/4486

The use of permanent wartime fears to justify the removal of citizens' rights, gradually allowing local police to begin viewing the people they were supposed to protect as low-level threats, potential terrorists, and enemies of law and order in particular when they exercise their former rights to speech and assembly. Police "excesses" like war "excesses" are not apologized for, as one does not apologize to an enemy.

The further funding of abusive policing through asset forfeitures and SWAT raids.

The further conflation of military and police through the militarization of borders, especially the Mexican border, the combined efforts of federal and local forces in fusion centers, the military's engagement in "exercises" in the U.S., and the growth of the drone industry with the military, among others, flying drones in U.S. skies and piloting drones abroad from U.S. land.

The growth of the profit-driven prison industry and mass incarceration, which dehumanize people in the minds of participants just as boot camp and the nightly news do to war targets.

Economically driven disproportionate participation in, and therefore identification with, the military by the very communities most suffering from its destruction of resources, rights, and lives.

But policing is not the only thing militarized by what President Eisenhower called the "total influence — economic, political, even spiritual" of the military industrial complex. Our morality is militarized, our entertainment is militarized, our natural world is militarized, and our education system is militarized. "Unwarranted influence, whether sought or unsought, by the military industrial complex" is not easily opposed while maintaining the military industrial complex. When Congress Members lend their support to a new war in Iraq while proposing that the U.S. Post Office and a dozen other decent things not be defunded, they are speaking out of both sides of their mouths. The United States cannot live like other wealthy nations while dumping $1 trillion a year into a killing machine.

The way out of this cycle of madness in which we spend more just on *recruiting* someone into the military or on *locking them up* behind bars than we spend on educating them is to confront in a unified and coherent manner what Martin Luther King Jr. called the evils of racism, extreme materialism, and militarism. Not racism, extreme materialism, and what the military does to the local police. Not racism, extreme materialism, and what the military does to weapons testing sites. Not racism, extreme materialism, and what the military does to the people of Honduras causing them to flee to a land that then welcomes them with an attitude of militarism. Not any of these partial steps alone, but the whole package of interlocking evils of attitude and mindset.

There is a no-fly-zone[68] over Ferguson, Missouri, because people in the U.S. government view the people of the United States increasingly as they view the people of other countries: as best

---

68    http://thinkprogress.org/justice/2014/08/12/3470567/why-theres-a-no-fly-zone-over-ferguson-missouri

controlled from the air. Notes the War Resister League[69],

> "Vigils and protests in Ferguson – a community facing
> persistent racist profiling[70] and police brutality – have
> been attacked by tear gas, rubber bullets, police in fully-
> armored SWAT gear, and tank-like personnel carriers. This
> underscores not only the dangers of being young, Black,
> and male in the US[71], but also the fear of mobilization and
> rebellion from within racialized communities facing the
> violence of austerity and criminalization.

> "The parallels between the Israeli Defense Forces in Palestine,
> the Military Police of Rio de Janeiro, the Indian police in
> Kashmir, the array of oppressive armed forces in Iraq, and
> the LAPD in Skid Row could not be any clearer. . . .

> "This is not happening by accident. What is growing the
> capacity of local police agencies to exercise this force are
> police militarization programs explicitly designed to do so.
> As St. Louis writer Jamala Rogers wrote in an article on the
> militarization of St. Louis Police this past April[72], 'It became
> clear that SWAT was designed as a response to the social
> unrest of the 1960s, particularly the anti-war and black
> liberation movements.' Federal programs such as DoD 1033
> and 1122, and the Urban Areas Security Initiative (UASI),

69 http://facingteargas.org/p/126/solidarity-occupied-ferguson
70 http://ago.mo.gov/VehicleStops/2013/reports/161.pdf
71              https://www.facebook.com/resistwar/photos/pb.171910856163140.-
2207520000.1407953190./594458753908346/?type=3&theater
72        http://www.stlamerican.com/news/columnists/jamala/article_4181a88c-
c580-11e3-ad04-001a4bcf887a.html

*in which St. Louis Police are active participants[73], provide*
*weapons and training to police departments across the*
*country, directly from the Pentagon. Commenting on the*
*ominous growth of the phenomenon, Rogers continues: 'and*
*now, Police Chief [of St. Louis Police] Sam Dotson wants to*
*add drones to his arsenal.'*

*"The events in Ferguson over these last few days demonstrate*
*that the violence of policing and militarism are inextricably*
*bound. To realize justice and freedom as a condition for*
*peace, we must work together to end police militarization*
*and violence."*

The War Resisters League is organizing[74] against Urban Shield,
an expo of military weapons for police and training event planned
for Oakland, Calif., this September 4-8. The Week of Education
and Action will take place in Oakland from August 30-September
5. Read all about it here[75].

## On Killing Trayvons

This Wednesday is a day of action that some are calling a national
day of action against police brutality, with others adding "and mass
incarceration," and I'd like to add "and war" and make it global
rather than national. This Tuesday, the Governor of Pennsylvania
is expected to sign a bill that will silence prisoners' speech, and

73 http://www.stl-starrs.org/aboutus/aboutus.htm
74 https://docs.google.com/forms/d/1bSOkctYzZf5NbZcNktEgryZuU25jZ47kj
NVpe9k0Yuc/viewform
75 http://www.facingteargas.org/stop-urban-shield-oakland

people are pushing back[76]. A movement is coalescing around reforming police procedures[77] and taking away their military weapons[78]. And a powerful book has just been published called Killing Trayvons: An Anthology of American Violence[79].

Saving Trayvon Martin would have required systemic reforms or cultural reforms beyond putting cameras on police officers. This young man walking back from a store with candy was spotted by an armed man in an SUV who got out of his vehicle to pursue Trayvon despite having been told not to when he called the police. George Zimmerman was not a police officer, though he wanted to be one. He'd lost a job as a security guard for being too aggressive. He'd been arrested for battery on a police officer. He had left Manassas, Va., and its climate of hatred for Latinos in which he participated, for Florida, where he was a one-man volunteer neighborhood watch group in a gated neighborhood. He'd phoned the police on 46 previous occasions. He apparently expressed his contempt for Trayvon Martin in racist terms. When the police arrived, they let Zimmerman ride in the front seat (no handcuffs, of course) and never tested him for drugs, testing instead the dead black boy he'd murdered. When public outrage finally put Zimmerman on trial, his defense displayed a photo of a white woman living in the neighborhood who had nothing to do with the incident but who was used to represent what Zimmerman had been "defending." He was found innocent.

76      http://act.rootsaction.org/p/dia/action3/common/public/?action_KEY=10521
77 http://www.popularresistance.org/uniting-to-transform-us-policing/
78      http://act.rootsaction.org/p/dia/action3/common/public/?action_KEY=10264
79 http://store.counterpunch.org/product/killing-trayvons/

*Killing Trayvons* is a rich anthology, including police records, trial transcripts, statements by President Obama, accounts of numerous similar cases, essays, poetry, and history and analysis of how we got here . . . and how we might get the hell out of here.

Recently I was playing a game with my little boy that must have looked to any observer like I was secretly spying on people. I found myself thinking that it was a good thing I wasn't black or I'd risk someone reporting me to the police, and I'd find myself struggling to explain the situation to them rather than yelling at them, and they wouldn't listen. "What do I tell my son," wrote Talib Kweli, "He's 5 years old and he's still thinking cops are cool / How do I break the news that when he gets some size / He'll be perceived as a threat and see the fear in their eyes." I remember a character of James Baldwin's explaining to a younger brother on the streets of New York that when walking in the rich part of town you must always keep your hands in your pockets so as not to be accused of touching a white woman. But a set of rules devised by Etan Thomas in *Killing Trayvons* includes: "Keep your hands visible. Avoid putting them in your pockets." Opposite advice, same injustice. I can recall how offended I was when, as a young white man, I became old enough for a strange woman in a deserted place to hurry away from me in panic. Maybe if I'd been black someone would have prepared me for that. Maybe I'd have experienced it a lot earlier. Maybe I'd have experienced it as racist. Maybe it would have been. But would I have come around to the conclusion, as I have, that there's nothing I have a right to be indignant about, that people's fear—wherever it comes from—is more important to reduce than other people's annoyance?

But what about fear that leads to murder? What about white fear of black violence that leads to the killing of so many African Americans—and many of them women, suggesting that fear isn't all there is to it? Police and security guards kill hundreds of African Americans each year, most of them unarmed. In most cases, the killers claim to have felt threatened. In most cases they escape any accountability. Clearly this is a case of fear to be doubted and treated with appropriate skepticism, fear to be understood and sympathized with where real, but fear never to be respected as reasonable or justified.

We need a combination of addressing the fear through enlightenment and impeding the violence with application of the rule of law in a manner that does not treat murdering black kids as what any reasonable person would do. We need to rein in and hold accountable individuals and institutions—groups like the NRA and ALEC that push racist policies on us. Police and neighbors should not see a black boy as an intruder in his own house[80] when his foster parents are white. They also shouldn't spray chemical weapons in someone's face before asking him questions (or after).

The editors of *Killing Trayvons*, Kevin Alexander Gray, Jeffrey St. Clair, and JoAnn Wypijewski put killing in context. What if Trayvon actually got into a fight with his stalker superhero? Would that have been a good reason to kill him? "It takes a jacked-up disdain for proportionality to conclude the execution is a reasonable response to a fistfight. And yet . . . high or low, power teaches such disdain every day. Lose two towers; destroy two countries. Lose

80        http://www.blacknews.com/news/black-teen-with-white-foster-parents-mistaken-for-burglar-neighbors-called-police-and-had-him-arrested101.html#.VEV0BYf2eGE

three Israelis; kill a couple thousand Palestinians. Sell some dope; three strikes, you're out. Sell a loosey; choke, you're dead. Reach for your wallet; bang, you're dead. Got a beef; bang, you're dead."

This is exactly the problem. High and low includes supreme courts that kill black men like Troy Davis, and presidents who kill dark-skinned Muslim foreigners (some of them U.S. citizens) with drones, leading Vijay Prashad to call Zimmerman a domestic drone and Cornel West to call President Obama a global Zimmerman. Two bizarre varieties of murder have been legalized at the same time in the United States. One is Stand-Your-Ground killing justified by fear and applied on a consistently racist basis. The other is drone missile killing justified by fear and applied on a consistently racist basis. Both types of murder are much more obviously murder than other instances that have not been given blanket legalization.

Stand-your-ground murders are facilitated by racism; and racist propaganda that blames the victims protects the killers after the fact. Drone murders are driven by profit, politics, power lust, and racism; and the guilt of President Obama is sheltered by the prevalence of racist hatred for him—which comes from generally the same group of people who support stand-your-ground laws. (How can Obama be guilty of any wrong in overseeing a global kill list, when racists hate him?) Millions of Americans think of themselves as above the ignorant whites who fear every black person they see, and yet have swallowed such a fear of ISIS that even giving ISIS a war it wants and benefits from seems justified. After all, ISIS is barbaric. If it were civilized, ISIS wouldn't behead people; it would have its hostages commit suicide while handcuffed in the backseat of police cars.

## How Is a Prison Like a War?

The similarities between mass incarceration and mass murder have been haunting me for a while, and I now find myself inspired by Maya Schenwar's excellent new book *Locked Down, Locked Out: Why Prison Doesn't Work and How We Can Do Better.* This is one of three books everyone should read right away. The others are *The New Jim Crow* and *Burning Down the House*, the former with a focus on racism in incarceration, the latter with a focus on the incarceration of youth. Schenwar's is an overview of incarceration in all its absurd and unfathomable evil—as well as being a spotlight leading away from this brutal institution.

*Locked Down, Locked Out* is both an incomparably put together report incorporating statistics and studies with individual quotations and anecdotes, and a personal story of how incarceration has impacted the author's own family and how the author has thought through the complex issues.

Yes, I did recently write an article specifically criticizing the widespread habit of calling everything a "war," and I do still want to see that practice ended—but not because the linguistic quirk offends me, rather because we make so many things, to one degree or another, actually be like wars. As far as I have seen, no other practice bears remotely as much similarity to war as does prison. How so? Let me count the ways.

1. Both are distinctly American. No other nation spends as much on its military or its prisons, engages in as many wars or locks up as many people.

2. Both are seemingly simple and easy solutions that don't solve anything, but seek to hide it away at a distance. Wars are waged thousands of miles from home. Prisoners are stored out-of-sight hundreds or thousands of miles from home.

3. Both are fundamentally violent and dependent upon the notion that a state "monopoly" on violence prevents violence by others, even while the evidence suggests that it actually encourages violence by others.

4. Both rely on the same process of dehumanizing and demonizing people, either enemies in a war or criminals in a prison. Never mind that most of the people killed by bombs had nothing to do with the squabble used as motivation for the war. Never mind that most of the prisoners had nothing to do with the sort of behavior used to demonize them. Both populations must be labeled as non-human or both institutions collapse.

5. Both are hugely profitable and promoted by the profiteers, who constitute a small clique, the broader society actually being drained economically by both enterprises. Weapons factories and prisons produce jobs, but they produce fewer and lower-paying jobs than other investments, and they do so with less economic benefit and more destructive side-effects.

6. Both are driven by fear. Without the fear-induced irrational urge to lash out at the source of our troubles, we'd be able to think through, calmly and clearly, far superior answers to foreign and domestic relations.

7. Both peculiar institutions are themselves worse than anything they claim to address. War is a leading cause of death, injury, trauma, loss of home, environmental destruction, instability, and lasting cycles of violence. It's not a solution to genocide, but its wellspring and its big brother. U.S. prisons lock up over 2 million, control and monitor some 7 million, and ruin the lives of many millions more in the form of family members impacted. From there the damage spreads and the numbers skyrocket as communities are weakened. No damage that incarcerated people could have done if left alone, much less handled with a more humane system, could rival the damage done by the prison industry itself.

8. Both are default practices despite being demonstrably counter-productive by anybody's measure, including on their own terms. Wars are not won, do not build nations, do not halt cruelty, do not spread democracy, do not benefit humanity, do not protect or expand freedom. Rather, freedoms are consistently stripped away in the name of wars that predictably endanger those in whose name they are waged. The nation waging the most wars generates the most enemies, thus requiring more wars, just as the nation with the most prisoners also has the most recidivists. Almost all prisoners are eventually released, and over 40% of them return to prison. Kids who commit crimes and are left alone are—as many studies have clearly and uncontroversially documented—less likely to commit more crimes than kids who are put in juvenile prison.

9. Both are classist and racist enterprises. A poverty draft has replaced ordinary conscription, while wars are waged only on poor nations rich in natural resources and darkish in skin tone. Meanwhile African Americans are, for reasons of racism and accounting for all other factors, far more likely than whites to be reported to the police, charged by the police, charged with higher offenses, sentenced to longer imprisonment, refused parole, and held to be violating probation. The poor are at the mercy of the police and the courts. The wealthy have lawyers.

10. The majority of the casualties, in both cases, are not those directly and most severely harmed. Injuries outnumber deaths in war, refugees outnumber the injured, and traumatized and orphaned children outnumber the refugees. Prisoners' lives are ruined, but so are the greater number of lives from which theirs have been viciously removed. A humane person might imagine some leniency for the convict who has children. On the contrary, the majority of U.S. prisoners have children.

11. Both institutions seem logical until one imagines alternatives. Both seem inevitable and are upheld by well-meaning people who haven't imagined their way around them. Both appear justifiable as defensive measures against inscrutable evil until one thinks through how much of that evil is generated by optional policies and how extremely rare to nonexistent is the sort of evil dominating the thinking behind massive industries designed for a whole different scale of combat.

12. Both war and prisons begin with shock and awe. A SWAT team invades a home to arrest a suspect, leaving an entire family

afraid to go to sleep for years afterward. An air force flattens whole sections of a city, leaving huge numbers of people traumatized for life. Another word for these practices is terrorism.

13. Both institutions include extreme measures that are as counterproductive as the whole. Suicidal prisoners put into solitary confinement as punishment for being suicidal are rendered more suicidal, not less. Burning villages or murdering households with gunfire exacerbate the process of making the aggressor more hated, more resented, and less likely to know peace.

14. Both institutions hurt the aggressor. An attacking nation suffers morally, economically, civilly, environmentally; and its soldiers and their families suffer very much as prisoners and prison guards suffer. Even crime victims suffer the lack of apology or restitution or reconciliation that comes with an adversarial justice system that treats the courtroom as a civilized war.

15. Both horrors create alternative realities to which people sometimes long to return. Prisoners unable to find work or support or friendship or family sometimes return to prison on purpose. Soldiers unable to adapt to life back home have been known to choose a return to war despite suffering horrifically from a previous combat experience. The top killer of U.S. soldiers is suicide. Suicide is not uncommon among prisoners who have recently been released. Neither members of the military nor prisoners are provided serious preparation for reintegrating into a society in which everything that has been helping them survive will tend to harm them.

16. Both war and prisons generate vicious cycles. Crime victims are more likely to become criminals. Those imprisoned are more likely to commit crimes. Children effectively orphaned by incarceration are more likely to become criminals and be incarcerated. Nations that have been at war are more likely to be at war again. Solving Libya's problems three years ago by bombing it predictably created violent chaos that even spilled into other nations. Launching wars on Iraq to address the violence created by previous wars on Iraq has become routine.

17. Both institutions are sometimes supported by their victims. An endangered family can prefer incarceration of a violent or drug-addicted loved one to nothing, in the absence of alternatives. Members of the military and their families can believe it is their duty to support wars and proposals for new wars. Prisoners themselves can see prison as preferable to starving under a bridge.

18. Both institutions are disproportionately male in terms of guards and soldiers. But the victims of war are not. And, when families are considered, as Schenwar's book considers them so well, the victims of incarceration are not.

19. Both institutions have buried within them rare stories of success, soldiers who matured and grew wise and heroic, prisoners who reformed and learned their lessons. No doubt the same is true of slavery or the holocaust or teaching math by the method of applying a stick to a child's hands.

20. Both institutions are often partially questioned without the

possibility of questioning the whole ever arising. When Maya Schenwar's sister gives birth in prison and then remains in prison, separated from her baby, people ask Schenwar "What's the point? How is Kayla being in prison helping anyone?" But Schenwar thinks to herself: "How is *anyone* being in prison helping anyone?" Candidate Barack Obama opposed dumb wars, while supporting massive war preparations, eventually finding himself in several wars, all of them dumb, and one of them the very same war (or at least a new war in the very same nation) he had earlier described in those terms.

21. Both institutions churn along with the help of thousands of well-meaning people who try to mitigate the damage but who are incapable of redeeming fundamentally flawed systems. Reforms that strengthen the system as a whole tend not to help, while actions that shrink, limit, or weaken support for the whole machinery of injustice deserve encouragement.

22. Both are 19th century inventions. Some form of war and of slavery may go back 10,000 years, but only in the 19th century did it begin to resemble current war and incarceration. Changes through the 20th and early 21st centuries expanded on the damage without fundamentally altering the thinking involved.

23. Both include state-approved murder (the death penalty and the killing in war) and both include state-sanctioned torture. In fact much of the torture that has made the news in war prisons began in domestic prisons. A current war enemy, ISIS, had its leadership developed in the cauldron of brutal U.S. war prisons.

Again, the aggressors, the torturers, and their whole society are not unharmed.

24. Crime victims are used to justify an institution that results in more people being victimized by crime. Victims of warlike abuse by others are used to justify wars likely to harm them and others further.

25. Prisoners and veterans often leave those worlds without the sort of education valued in the other world, the "free world" the prisoners dream of and soldiers fantasize that they are defending. A criminal record is usually a bar to employment. A military record can be an advantage but in other cases is a disadvantage as well in seeking employment.

26. Beyond all the damage done by war and prisons, by far the greatest damage is done through the trade-off in resources. The money invested in war could pay for the elimination of poverty and various diseases worldwide. A war-making nation could make itself loved for far less expense than what it takes to make itself hated. It could hang onto a much smaller, more legitimately defensive military like those of other nations while attempting such an experiment. The money spent on prisons could pay for drug treatment, childcare, education, and restorative justice programs. A nation could go on locking up violent recidivists while attempting such a change.

27. Restorative justice is the essence of the solution to both war and prison. Diplomacy and moderated reconciliation are answers

to the common problem of writing an enemy off as unreachable through words.

I might go on, but I imagine you get the idea. Huge numbers of Americans are being made seriously worse citizens, and almost all of them will be back out of prison trying to survive. And, if that doesn't do it for you, consider this: when incarceration is this widespread, there's every possibility that it will someday include you. What if you're falsely accused of a crime? What if somebody puts a link on a website to illegal pornography and you—or someone using your computer—clicks it? Or you urinate in public? Or you use marijuana in a state that legalized it, but the feds disagree? Or you blow the whistle on some abuse in some branch of the government that you work for? Or you witness something and don't report it? Or you work so hard that you fall asleep driving your car? An injustice to one is an injustice to all, and injustice on this scale is potentially injustice to every one.

What to do?

Californians just voted on their ballots to reduce prison sentences. Get that on your ballot. For the first time ever, this week, a prosecutor was sent to prison for falsely convicting an innocent person. We need a whole reworking of the rewards and incentives for prosecutors who have long believed that locking people up was the path to success. We need activist resistance to prison expansion, divestment from for-profit prison companies, and educational efforts to begin changing our culture as well as our laws. *Locked Down, Locked Out* provides a terrific list of organizations to support, including those that can help you become a prisoner's pen-pal. Schenwar explains that there is nothing prisoners need more, as long as they are locked up. Those *not* receiving mail are seen as the easiest targets for abuse by guards and other prisoners. And our receiving their letters may be the best way for us to learn about the hidden world in our midst.

## *Torturer on the Ballot*

Michigan's First Congressional District is cold enough to freeze spit. Half of it is disconnected from the rest of Michigan and tacked onto the top of Wisconsin. A bit of it is further north than that, but rumored to be inhabited nonetheless.

In the recent Congressional elections, incumbent Republican Congressman Dan Benishek was reelected to his third term with 52 percent of the votes. Benishek is a climate-change denier and committed to limiting himself to three terms, a pair of positions that may end up working well together.

Benishek's predecessor in Congress was a Democrat, and a Democrat took 45 percent of the vote this year. Will that Democrat run again in 2016? Some would argue that if he does it should be from prison. Before he ran for office, Jerry Cannon ran the U.S. death camp at Guantanamo and, according to a witness, was personally responsible for ordering torture.

Green Party candidate Ellis Boal took 1 percent of the vote in

Michigan's First, after apparently failing to interest corporate media outlets in his campaign, and by his own account failing utterly to interest them in what he managed to learn about Cannon, who also "served" in the war in Iraq.

Now, Congress is jam-packed with members of both major parties who have effectively condoned and covered up torture for years. Both parties have elected numerous veterans of recent wars who have participated in *killing* in wars that they themselves, in some cases, denounce as misguided. And we've read about[81] the Bush White House overseeing torture in real time from afar. But it still breaks new ground for the party of the President who has claimed to be trying to close Guantanamo for six years to put up as a candidate a man who ran the place, and a man whose role in torture was not entirely from his air-conditioned office.

I would also venture to say that it breaks new media ground for the news outlets covering the recent election nationally and locally in Michigan's First District to not only miss this story but actively refuse to cover it when Boal held it in their faces and screamed. "Despite many attempts," Boal says, "I have been unable to interest any media in it, save for a small newspaper in Traverse City (near me) which gave it cursory attention."

Boal sent out an offer to any reporter willing to take an interest: "I located a witness, a former detainee now cleared and back home in Bosnia, who can testify of an instance of torture visited on him in early 2004, ordered and supervised by Cannon. I can put you in touch with him through his attorney. The details of the incident

81 http://abcnews.go.com/TheLaw/LawPolitics/story?id=4583256

are here[82]. . . . Without success I tried to make it a campaign issue."

Jerry Cannon, according to both Wikipedia[83] and his own website[84], first "served" in the war that killed three to four million Vietnamese. He was commander of the Joint Detention Operations Group Joint Task Force Guantanamo from 2003 to 2004. He was Deputy Commanding General responsible for developing Iraqi police forces in Iraq from 2008 to 2009, and U.S. Forces-Iraq Provost Marshal General and Deputy Commanding General for Detention Operations in Iraq from 2010 to 2011. Boy, everything this guy touches turns out golden!

Boal has collected evidence of torture during Cannon's time at Guantanamo, from the Red Cross, the Center for Constitutional Rights, the U.S. Senate, and public reports including in the *New York Times,* here[85].

Boal focuses on Mustafa Ait Idir, a former prisoner of Guantanamo who, like most, has been widely written about, and who, like most, has been found innocent of any wrong-doing and been released (in November 2008 after years of wrongful imprisonment).

Mustafa Ait Idir says that soldiers at Guantanamo threw him down on rocks and jumped on him, causing injuries including a broken finger, dislocated knuckles, and half his face paralyzed; they sprayed chemicals in his face, squeezed his testicles, and

82 http://ellisboal.org/pages/guant%C3%A1namoBay.shtml
83 http://en.wikipedia.org/wiki/Jerry_Cannon
84 http://www.jerrycannon.com/why-im-running
85 http://ellisboal.org/pages/guant%C3%A1namoBay.shtml

slammed his head on the floor and jumped on him. They bent his fingers back to cause pain, and broke one of them in the process. They stuck his head in a toilet and flushed it. They stuck a hose in his mouth and forced water down his throat. They refused him medical attention.

Boal communicated with Idir through Idir's lawyer, and Idir identified Cannon from photos and a video as the man who had threatened him with punishment if he did not hand over his pants. (Prisoners who believed they needed pants in order to pray were being stripped of their pants as a means of humiliation and abuse.) Idir refused to give up his pants unless he could have them back to wear for praying. Consequently, he was "enhanced interrogated."

Torture and complicity in torture are felonies under U.S. law, a fact that the entire U.S. political establishment has gone to great lengths to obscure.

I shared the information above with Rebecca Gordon, author of *Mainstreaming Torture*, and she replied:

> *"Torture is a 'non-partisan' practice in this country. It's beyond disgraceful that the Democratic Party would run Jerry Cannon for Congress. Sadly, while most (but clearly not all!) Dems have repudiated torture in words, their deeds have been more ambiguous. Five years after President Obama took office, the prison at Guantánamo remains open, and torture continues there. The Senate Intelligence Committee report on CIA torture has yet to be released. (Perhaps lame duck senator Mark Udall will be persuaded*

*to read the whole thing into the Congressional Record, as some of us are hoping.) We have yet to get a full accounting, not only of the CIA's activities, but of all U.S. torture in the 'war on terror.' Equally important, President Obama made it clear at the beginning of his first term that no one would be held accountable for torture. 'Nothing will be gained,' he said 'by spending our time and energy laying blame for the past.' But we know this is not true. When high government officials know that they can torture with impunity, torture will continue."*

Noting Cannon's resume post-Guantanamo, Gordon said, "Under the al-Maliki government, the Iraqi police force, and in particular the detention centers operated by the Iraqi Special Police Commandos, routinely abused members of Iraq's Sunni communities, thereby further inflaming the political and social enmity between Sunnis and Shias in Iraq. When the so-called Islamic State began operating in Iraq, they found willing collaborators in Sunni communities whose members had been tortured by the al-Maliki government's police. When Jerry Cannon went to Guantánamo, he went as an Army reservist. In civilian life he was Sheriff of Kalkaska County in Michigan. Cannon's abusive practices and contemptuous attitudes towards detainees did not originate in Guantánamo. He brought them with him from the United States. Similarly, in civilian life, the members of the reservist unit responsible for the famous outrages at Abu Ghraib were prison guards from West Virginia. Their ringleader, Specialist Charles Graner, famously wrote home to friends about his activities at Abu Ghraib, 'The Christian in me says it's wrong, but the corrections officer in me says, "I love to make a grown man piss himself."' In fact, if you want to find torture hidden in plain sight, look no farther than the jails and prisons of this country."

The mystery of where torture came from turns out to be no mystery at all. It came from the prison industrial complex. And it's now been so mainstreamed that it's no bar to running for public office. But here's another mystery: Why is President Obama going to such lengths to cover up his predecessor's torture, including insisting on redactions in the Senate report on CIA torture that even Senator Dianne Feinstein claims not to want censored? Surely it's not because of all the gratitude Obama's receiving from former President Bush or his supporters! Actually, it's no mystery at all. As Gordon points out: the torture is ongoing.

"Look at the current situation," Obama said in 2013, "where we are force-feeding detainees who are being held on a hunger strike . . . Is this who we are?" Those retaining some sense of decency are currently urging[86] the Obama administration to go easy in its punishment of a nurse who refused to participate in the force-feeding, who in fact insisted on being "who we are."

86      http://www.nytimes.com/2014/11/20/health/nurses-urge-leniency-over-refusal-to-force-feed-at-guantnamo-bay.html?_r=0

# Syria

## They Never Announce When You Prevent a War

There exists, I suppose, some slight chance of this one making it into the State of the Union address, no doubt in a distorted, bellicose, and xenophobic disguise. Typically, there's no chance of any announcement at all.

**We're stopping another war.**

There are a million qualifications that need to be put on that statement. None of them render it false. A bill looked likely to move through Congress that would have imposed new sanctions on Iran, shredded the negotiated agreement with Iran, and committed the United States to join in any Israeli war on Iran. This would be a step toward war and has become understood as such by large numbers of people. Efforts to sell sanctions as an alternative to war failed. Tons of pushback has come, and is still coming[87], from the public, including from numerous organizations not always known for their opposition to war. And the bill, for the moment, seems much less likely to pass.

This is no time to let up, but to recognize our power and press harder for peace.

Pushback against the sanctions bill has come from the White House, from within the military, and from elsewhere within the

87 http://act.rootsaction.org/p/dia/action3/common/public/?action_KEY=9091

government. But this bill was something the warmongers wanted, AIPAC wanted, a majority of U.S. senators wanted, and corporate media outlets were happy to support. The underlying pretense that Iran has a nuclear weapons program that endangers the world had the support of the White House and most other opponents of the March-to-War bill. That pretense has been successfully sold to much of the public. The additional supporting pretense that sanctions have helped, rather than hindered, diplomacy has similar widespread backing. But when it comes to a measure understood as a step into *war,* the public is saying no, and that public response is a factor in the likely outcome.

In this instance, President Obama has been on the right side of the debate. I've never known that to actually be true before. But there's been a whole infrastructure of activism set up and fine-tuned for five years now, all based around the pretense that Obama was right on various points and Congress wrong. So, when that actually happened to be true, numerous organizations knew exactly what to do with it. War opposition and Obama-following merged. But let's remember back to August and September. That was a different situation in which . . .

**We stopped another war.**

Raytheon's stock was soaring. The corporate media wanted those missiles to hit Syria. Obama and the leadership of both parties wanted those missiles to hit Syria. The missiles didn't fly.

Public pressure led the British Parliament to refuse a prime minister's demand for war for the first time since the surrender at

Yorktown, and the U.S. Congress followed suit by making clear to the U.S. president that his proposed authorization for war on Syria would not pass through either the Senate or the House. Numerous Congress members, from both houses and both parties, said they heard more from the public against this war than ever before on any issue. It helped that Congress was on break and holding town hall meetings. It helped that it was Jewish holidays and AIPAC wasn't around.

And there were other factors. After the public pushed Congress to demand a say, Obama agreed to that. Perhaps he wanted something so controversial—something being talked about as "the next Iraq"—to go to Congress. Perhaps he expected Congress would probably say No. In such a scenario, the decisive factor would remain the past decade of growing public sentiment against wars. But I don't think that's what happened. Obama and Kerry were pushing hard and publicly for those missiles to fly. When they couldn't get the "intelligence" agencies to back their fraudulent case, they announced it anyway. Those lies are just being exposed now[88], in a very different context from that in which the Iraq war lies[89] or the Afghanistan[90] or Libya[91] war lies have been exposed. Obama told us to watch videos of children suffering and dying in Syria and to choose between war and inaction. We rejected that choice, opposed war, and supported humanitarian aid (which hasn't happened on remotely the necessary scale).

In the space of a day, discussions in Washington, D.C., shifted

88  http://davidswanson.org/node/4283
89  http://warisacrime.org/iraq
90 http://worldbeyondwar.org/node/45
91 http://worldbeyondwar.org/node/46

from the supposed necessity of war to the clear desirability of avoiding war. The Russians' proposal to eliminate Syria's chemical weapons had already been known to the White House but was being rejected. When Kerry publicly suggested that Syria could avoid a war by handing over its chemical weapons, everyone knew he didn't mean it. In fact, when Russia called his bluff and Syria immediately agreed, Kerry's staff put out this statement: "Secretary Kerry was making a rhetorical argument about the impossibility and unlikelihood of Assad turning over chemical weapons he has denied he used. His point was that this brutal dictator with a history of playing fast and loose with the facts cannot be trusted to turn over chemical weapons, otherwise he would have done so long ago. That's why the world faces this moment." In other words: stop getting in the way of our war! By the next day, however, with Congress rejecting war, Kerry was claiming to have meant his remark quite seriously and to believe the process had a good chance of succeeding, as of course it did. Diplomatic solutions are always available. What compelled Obama to accept diplomacy as the last resort was the public's and Congress's refusal to allow war.

These victories are limited and tentative. The machinery that pushes for war hasn't gone away. The arms are still flowing into Syria. Efforts to negotiate peace there seem less than wholehearted. The U.S. puppeteer has stuck its arm up the rear end of the United Nations and uninvited Iran from the talks. The people of Syria and Iran are no better off.

But they're also no worse off. No U.S. bombs are falling from their skies.

There could be other proposals for wars that we'll find much harder to prevent. That's precisely why we must recognize the possibility of stopping those proposals too, a possibility established by the examples above, from which we should stop fleeing in panic as if the possibility that everything we do might have some point to it horrifies us.

Any war can be stopped. Any pretended necessity to hurry up and kill large numbers of people can be transformed into a negotiation at a table using words rather than missiles. And if we come to understand that, we'll be able to start dismantling the weaponry, which in turn will make the tendency to think of war as the first option less likely. By steps we can move to a world in which our government doesn't propose bombing someone new every few months but instead proposes helping someone new.

If we can stop one war, if we can stop two wars, why can't we stop them all and put our resources into protection rather than destruction? Why can't we move to a world beyond war[92]?

## Oppose Force to Save Starving Syrians

I've been asked to debate Danny Postel on the question of Syria, and so have read the op-ed he co-authored with Nader Hashemi, "Use Force to Save Starving Syrians."[93] Excellent responses

---

92 http://WorldBeyondWar.org
93     http://www.nytimes.com/2014/02/11/opinion/use-force-to-save-starving-syrians.html?_r=0

have been published by Coleen Rowley[94] and Rob Prince[95] and probably others. And my basic thinking on Syria has not changed fundamentally since I wrote down my top 10 reasons not to attack Syria[96] and lots and lots of other writing[97] on Syria over the years. But replying to Postel's op-ed might be helpful to people who've read it and found it convincing or at least disturbing. It might also allow Postel to most efficiently find out where I'm coming from prior to our debate.

So, here's where I'm coming from. Postel's op-ed proposes the use of force as if force hadn't been tried yet, as if force were not in fact the very problem waiting to be solved. What he is proposing is *increased* force. The arming and funding and training of one side in Syria by the CIA, Saudi Arabia, et al, and the other side by Russia, et al, is not enough; more is needed, Postel believes. But "force" is a very non-descriptive term, as are all the other terms Postel uses to refer to what he wants: "air cover," "coercive measures," "Mr. Assad ... [should] be left behind."

I find it hard to imagine people on the ground while NATO dropped thousands of bombs on Libya pointing to the sky and remarking "Check out the air cover!"

Or this: "What happened to your children, Ma'am?" "They experienced some coercive measures."

94 http://fpif.org/calls-u-s-military-intervention-syria-re-surfacing-2/
95 http://fpif.org/military-humanitarian-intervention-shock-doctrine-applied-syria/
96 http://davidswanson.org/node/4130
97 http://davidswanson.org/taxonomy/term/14

Or this: "What became of Gadaffi?" "Oh, him? He was left behind."

When people who experience modern wars that wealthy nations launch against poor ones talk about them, they describe detailed horror, terror, and trauma. They recount what it's like to try to hold a loved one's guts into their mutilated body as they gasp their last. Even the accounts of recovering and regretful drone pilots in the U.S. have much more humanity and reality in them than do Postel's euphemisms.

I'm not questioning the sincerity of Postel's belief that, despite it's long record of abysmal failure, humanitarian war would find success in a nation as divided as Syria, of all unlikely places. But Postel should trust his readers to share his conclusion after being presented with the full facts of the case. If Postel believes that the people whose lives would be ended or devastated by "air cover" are out-weighed by the people who he believes would be thereby saved from starvation, he should say so. He should at the very least acknowledge that people would be killed in the process and guesstimate how many they would be.

Postel claims Somalia as a past example of a "humanitarian intervention," without dwelling on the chaos and violence aggravated and ongoing there. This seems another shortcoming to me. If you are going to make a moral decision, not only should it include the negative side of the ledger, but it should include the likely medium-term and long-term results, good and bad. Looking at Somalia with a broader view hurts Postel's case, but so does looking at Libya, Afghanistan, or Iraq. Studies by Erica Chenoweth and others have documented that violent solutions to oppression and tyranny are not only less likely to succeed, but if they succeed their success is shorter lived. Violence breeds violence. "Force," translated into the reality of killing people's loved ones, breeds resentment, not reconciliation.

So, I think Postel's case for dropping tons of deadly "coercive measures" on Syria would be a weak one even were it likely to resemble his outline. Sadly, it isn't. The war on Libya three years ago was sold as an emergency use of "force" to protect supposedly threatened people in Benghazi. It was immediately, illegally, predictably, cynically, and disastrously turned into a campaign of bombing the nation to overthrow its government—a government that, like Syria's, had long been on a Pentagon list to be overthrown for anything but humanitarian reasons. Postel presents a quick and antiseptic "leaving behind" operation to provide food to the starving, but surely he knows that is not what it would remain for any longer than it takes to say "R2P." Why else does Postel refer so vaguely to leaving Assad behind?

It may be worth noting that it's not aid workers advocating for "coercion" strikes on Syria. I spoke with a U.S. government aid worker in Syria some months back who had this to say:

> *"Before we contemplate military strikes against the Syrian regime, we would do well to carefully consider what impact such strikes would have on our ongoing humanitarian programs, both those funded by the U.S. and by other countries and international organizations. These programs*

*currently reach hundreds of thousands of vulnerable people throughout Syria, in areas controlled both by the regime and the opposition. We know from past military interventions, such as in Yugoslavia and Iraq, that airstrikes launched for humanitarian reasons often result in the unintended deaths of many civilians. The destruction of roads, bridges, and other infrastructure, which such airstrikes may entail, would significantly hamper the delivery of humanitarian aid in Syria.*

*"The provision of this assistance in regime controlled areas requires the agreement, and in many cases the cooperation, of the Asad government. Were the Asad regime, in response to U.S. military operations, to suspend this cooperation, and prohibit the UN and Nongovernmental Organizations from operating in territory under its control, hundreds of thousands of Syrian civilians would be denied access to food, shelter, and medical care. In such a scenario, we would be sacrificing programs of proven effectiveness in helping the people of Syria, in favor of ill considered actions that may or may not prevent the future use of chemical weapons, or otherwise contribute to U.S. objectives in any meaningful way."*

Let's grant that the crisis has continued for months and worsened. It remains the fact that it is advocates of war advocating war, not aid workers advocating war. The option of ceasing to arm both sides, and of pursuing a negotiated settlement, is simply ignored by the war advocates. The option of nonviolent efforts to deliver aid is avoided entirely. The failure to provide adequate aid to refugees who *can* be reached seems far less pressing than the failure to provide aid where that failure can become a justification for an escalated war.

"Humanitarian interventions," Postel writes, "typically occur when moral principles overlap with political interests." This seems to be an acknowledgment that political interests are something other than moral. So, there's no cry for "humanitarian intervention" in Bahrain or Palestine or Egypt because it doesn't fit "political interests." That seems like an accurate analysis. And presumably some interventions that do fit political interests are not moral and humanitarian. The question is which are which. Postel believes there have been enough humanitarian interventions to describe something as being typical of them, but he doesn't list them. In fact, the record of U.S. military and CIA interventions is a unbroken string of anti-humanitarian horrors. And in most cases, if not every case, actual aid would have served humanity better than guns and bombs, and so would have ceasing pre-existing involvement rather than escalating it and calling that an intervention.

But once you've accepted that the tool of war should be encouraged in certain cases, even though it's misused in other cases, then something else has to be added to your moral calculation, namely the propagation of war and preparations for war. Those of us who cannot find a single war worth supporting differ only slightly perhaps from those who find one war in a hundred worth backing. But it's a difference that shifts opposition to support for an investment that costs the world some $2 trillion a year. The United Nations believes that $30 billion a year could end serious starvation around the world. Imagine what, say, $300 billion could do for food, water, medicine, education, and green energy. Imagine if the United States were to offer that kind of aid to every nation able to peacefully and democratically accept it. Would polls continue to find the U.S. viewed as the greatest threat to peace on earth? Would the title of most beloved nation on earth begin to look plausible?

Members of the nonviolent peaceforce, Nobel peace laureate Mairead Maguire, and other advocates of de-escalation in Syria traveled freely around Syria some months back. How were they able to do that? What might trainers in creative nonviolent action offer Syria that CIA and military trainers aren't offering? The alternative is never even considered by advocates of war-or-nothing. Postel wants to back "democratically oriented" rebel groups, but is violence clearly democratically oriented? Turning our eyes back on ourselves suggests a rather disturbing answer. In September 2013, President Obama gave us the hard sell. Watch these videos of suffering children, he said, and support striking their nation with missiles or support their ongoing suffering. And a huge majority in the U.S. rejected the idea that those were the only two choices. A majority opposed the strikes. An even larger majority opposed arming the rebels. And a large majority favored humanitarian aid. There is a case to be made that democracy would be better spread by example than by defying the will of the U.S. people in order to bomb yet another nation in democracy's name.

Postel, to his credit, calls the "Responsibility to Protect" a "principle." Some have called it a "law." But it cannot undo the U.N.

Charter. War being illegal, its use damages the rule of law. That result must also be factored into a full moral calculation of how to act. Act we must, as Postel says repeatedly. The question is how. Rob Prince presents a useful plan of action in the article linked above.

Postel's most persuasive argument is probably, for many readers, his contention that only threatening to act will save the day. He claims that Syria has responded positively to threats of force. But this is not true. Syria was always willing to give up its chemical weapons and had long since proposed a WMD-free Middle East—a proposal that ran up against the lack of "political interest" in eliminating Israel's illegal weapons. Also false, of course, were claims by the Obama administration to know that Assad had used chemical weapons. See Coleen Rowley's summary of how that case has collapsed in the article linked above.

Granted, there can be a good honest case for an action for which misguided, false, and fraudulent cases have been offered. But I haven't seen such a case yet for taking an action in Syria that would, to be sure, dramatically declare that action was being taken, release a lot of pent-up tension, and enrich Raytheon's owners, but almost certainly leave Syrians, Americans, and the world worse off.

# Afghanistan

## Everybody's Got Afghanistan Wrong

This goes deeper than the usual war lies.

We've had plenty of those. We weren't told the Taliban was willing to turn bin Laden over to a neutral nation to stand trial. We weren't told the Taliban was a reluctant tolerator of al Qaeda, and a completely distinct group. We weren't told the 911 attacks had also been planned in Germany and Maryland and various other places not marked for bombing. We weren't told that most of the people who would die in Afghanistan, many more than died on 911, not only didn't support 911 but never heard of it. We weren't told our government would kill large numbers of civilians, imprison people without trial, hang people by their feet and whip them until they were dead. We weren't told how this illegal war would advance the acceptability of illegal wars or how it would make the United States hated in much of the world. We weren't given the background of how the U.S. interfered in Afghanistan and provoked a Soviet invasion and armed resistance to the Soviets and left the people to the tender mercies of that armed resistance once the Soviets left. We weren't told that Tony Blair wanted Afghanistan first before he'd get the UK to help destroy Iraq. We certainly weren't told that bin Laden had been an ally of the U.S. government, that the 911 hijackers were mostly Saudi, or that there might be anything at all amiss with the government of Saudi Arabia. And nobody mentioned the trillions of dollars we'd waste or the civil liberties we'd have to lose at home or the severe damage that would be inflicted on the natural environment. Even *birds* don't go to Afghanistan anymore.

OK. That's all sort of par-for-the-course, war-marketing bullshit. People who pay attention know all of that. People who don't want to know any of that are the last great hope of military recruiters everywhere. And don't let the past tense fool you. The White House is trying to keep the occupation of Afghanistan going for TEN MORE YEARS ("and beyond"), and articles have been popping up this week about sending U.S. troops back into Iraq. But there's something more.

I've just read an excellent new book by Anand Gopal called *No Good Men Among the Living: America, the Taliban, and the War Through Afghan Eyes.* Gopal has spent years in Afghanistan, learned local languages, interviewed people in depth, researched their stories, and produced a true-crime book more gripping, as well as more accurate, than anything Truman Capote came up with. Gopal's book is like a novel that interweaves the stories of a number of characters—stories that occasionally overlap. It's the kind of book that makes me worry I'll spoil it if I say too much about the fate of the characters, so I'll be careful not to.

The characters include Americans, Afghans allied with the U.S. occupation, Afghans fighting the U.S. occupation, and men and women trying to survive—including by shifting their loyalties toward whichever party seems least likely in that moment to imprison or kill them. What we discover from this is not just that enemies, too, are human beings. We discover that the same human beings switch from one category to another quite easily. The blunder of the U.S. occupation's de-Baathification policy in Iraq has been widely discussed. Throwing all the skilled and armed killers out of work turned out not to be the most brilliant move. But think about what motivated it: the idea that whoever had supported the evil regime was irredeemably evil (even though Ronald Reagan and Donald Rumsfeld had supported the evil regime too—OK, bad example, but you see what I mean). In Afghanistan the same cartoonish thinking, the same falling for one's own propaganda, went on.

People in Afghanistan whose personal stories are recounted here sided with or against Pakistan, with or against the USSR, with or against the Taliban, with or against the U.S. and NATO, as the tides of fortune turned. Some tried to make a living at peaceful employment when that possibility seemed to open up, including early-on in the U.S. occupation. The Taliban was very swiftly destroyed in 2001 through a combination of overwhelming killing power and desertion. The U.S. then began hunting for anyone who had once been a member of the Taliban. But these included many of the people now leading the support of the U.S. regime—and many such allied leaders were killed and captured despite *not* having been Taliban as well, through sheer stupidity and corruption. We've often heard how dangling $5000 rewards in front of poor people produced false-accusations that landed their rivals in Bagram or Guantanamo. But Gopal's book recounts how the removal of these often key figures devastated communities, and turned communities against the United States that had previously been inclined to support it. Add to this the vicious and insulting abuse of whole families, including women and children captured and harassed by U.S. troops, and the revival of the Taliban under the U.S. occupation begins to become clear. The lie we've been told to explain it is that the U.S. became distracted by Iraq. Gopal documents, however, that the Taliban revived precisely where U.S. troops were imposing a rule of violence and not where other internationals were negotiating compromises using, you know, *words*.

We find here a story of a bumbling oblivious and un-comprehending foreign occupation torturing and murdering a lot of its own strongest allies, shipping some of them off to Gitmo—even shipping to Gitmo young boys whose only offense had been being the sexual assault victims of U.S. allies. The danger in this type of narrative that dives deep into the crushing Kafkan horror of rule by brute ignorant force is that a reader will think: Let's do the next war better. If occupations can't work, let's just blow shit up and leave. To which I respond: Yeah, how are things working out in Libya? The lesson for us to learn is not that wars are badly managed, but that human beings are not Good Guys or Bad Guys. And here's the hard part: That includes Russians.

Want to do something useful for Afghanistan? Go here[98]. Or here[99].

---

98    http://warisacrime.org/content/most-trusted-man-afghanistan-accepting-donations-mudslide-victims

99 http://ourjourneytosmile.com/blog/borderfree-blue-scarf/

# *First 13 Years in Afghanistan Big Success, Next 10 Promise Joy and Prosperity*

Here comes another October 7th, time once again for celebrating the International Day of Wars-Start-Easy-But-They're-a-Bitch-to-End. That is, if we can spare a few moments away from celebrating the new wars we're starting.

On this date 13 years ago, the United States attacked Afghanistan, which the U.S. President saw primarily as a step[100] toward attacking Iraq, although — in fairness — God had told[101] him to attack both countries. I asked God about that recently and he said, "You want to see regrets. Oh my God, you should talk to the Nobel Committee about that peace laureate." I didn't have to ask which one, and I didn't ask who his God was, fearing an endless discussion loop.

Way back yonder in 2001 before presidents openly spied on everything, launched wars without a pretense of legality, imprisoned without charge, assassinated at will, and kept enough secrets to have outraged Richard Nixon, the general public wasn't given quite all the information by its beloved televisions. We weren't told the Taliban was willing to turn bin Laden over to a neutral nation to stand trial. We weren't told the Taliban was a reluctant tolerator of al Qaeda, and a completely distinct group. We weren't told the 911 attacks had also been planned in Germany and Maryland and various other places not marked for bombing. We weren't told that most of the people who would die in Afghanistan, many more than died on 911, not only didn't support 911 but never heard of

100 http://www.theguardian.com/politics/2004/apr/04/iraq.iraq
101 http://www.theguardian.com/world/2005/oct/07/iraq.usa

it. We weren't told our government would kill large numbers of civilians, imprison people without trial, hang people by their feet and whip them until they were dead.

We weren't told how this illegal war would advance the acceptability of illegal wars or how it would make the United States hated in much of the world. We weren't given the background of how the U.S. interfered in Afghanistan and provoked a Soviet invasion and armed resistance to the Soviets and left the people to the tender mercies of that armed resistance once the Soviets left. We weren't told that Tony Blair wanted Afghanistan first before he'd get the UK to help destroy Iraq. We certainly weren't told that bin Laden had been an ally of the U.S. government, that the 911 hijackers were mostly Saudi, or that there might be anything at all amiss with the government of Saudi Arabia. And nobody mentioned the trillions of dollars we'd waste or the civil liberties we'd have to lose at home or the severe damage that would be inflicted on the natural environment. Even *birds* don't go to Afghanistan anymore.

The Taliban was very swiftly destroyed in 2001 through a combination of overwhelming killing power and desertion. The U.S. then began hunting for anyone who had once been a member of the Taliban. But these included many of the people now leading the support of the U.S. regime — and many such allied leaders were killed and captured despite *not* having been Taliban as well, through sheer stupidity and corruption. Dangling $5,000 rewards in front of poor people produced false-accusations that landed their rivals in Bagram or Guantanamo, and the removal of these often key figures devastated communities, and turned communities against the United States that had previously been inclined to support it. Add to this the vicious and insulting abuse of whole families, including women and children captured and harassed by U.S. troops, and the revival of the Taliban under the U.S. occupation begins to become clear. The lie we've been told to explain it is that the U.S. became distracted by Iraq, but the Taliban revived precisely where U.S. troops were imposing a rule of violence and not where other internationals were negotiating compromises using, you know, *words*.

This has been a bumbling oblivious and uncomprehending foreign occupation (as they always are) torturing and murdering a lot of its own strongest allies, shipping some of them off to Gitmo — even shipping to Gitmo young boys whose only offense had been being the sexual assault victims of U.S. allies

When Barack Obama became president, there were 32,000 U.S. troops in Afghanistan. He escalated to over 100,000 troops, plus contractors, and has been celebrated for ending the war ever since. Five years have been spent discussing the "drawdown." The U.S. public has been telling pollsters we want all U.S. troops out of Afghanistan "as soon as possible" for years and years. Endless speeches have bragged about ending wars that Obama supposedly "inherited." And yet, there are now 33,000 U.S. troops in Afghanistan, more than when Obama became president. Several NATO allies have wisely departed, but that's the extent of the "drawdown." Measured death and destruction or financial cost, Afghanistan is much more President Obama's war than President Bush's.

Now, Obama has managed to get a new Afghan president to agree to U.S. troops remaining in Afghanistan with immunity from any criminal prosecution, until "2024 and beyond." Obama claims he'll reduce troop levels to 9,800 this year, 6,000 next year, and 1,000 the following year — at which point he'll still be guarding Afghanistan's new president better than he guards the White House.

This has been Obama's plan from Day 1. He's never actually said he would ever end the war; he's just been given endless credit for doing so. But there's a bit of rightwing nonsense in the air these days that, combined with the sheer number of U.S. wars, distracts people from the outrageousness of keeping the war on Afghanistan going for another decade "and beyond." The bit of nonsense is the idea that Iraq has gone to hell because U.S. troops left. In fact, Iraq was a worse hell when U.S. troops were there, and it was the hard work of the U.S. troops and their allies over several years that put Iraq on the path to the hell it now is. Even Obama, who tried desperately to get criminal immunity for U.S. troops in order to leave them in Iraq three years ago, admits that having left them there would have done no good. But surely this bit of counterfactual lunacy — the idea that the troops *leaving* broke Iraq — helps to stifle our protests and outrage at the latest news from Vietghanistan.

Obama used to be a proud member of the Let's Stop Killing Iraqis and Kill More Afghans Club. Now he's back in Iraq plus Syria killing so many civilians that he's announced that rules for minimizing civilian deaths don't apply. I've got a scheme to help him bamboozle his antiwar supporters back into adoring him. It's easy. It's cheap. It's an unexpected reversal. And at least half the country already thinks he's done it anyway: Get the U.S. Military Out of Afghanistan. Now. Entirely. No Strings Attached.

# Ukraine

## So, I Asked the Russian Ambassador What He Thinks of NATO

The Russian Ambassador to the United States, Sergey Ivanovich Kislyak, spoke at the University of Virginia on Tuesday evening, in an event organized by the Center for Politics[102], which no doubt has video of the proceedings. Kislyak was once ambassador to Belgium and to NATO.

Kislyak spoke to a packed auditorium and took, I think, well over an hour of questions. He spoke frankly, and the questions he was asked by students, professors, and other participants were polite and for the most part far more intelligent than he would have been asked on, for example, *Meet the Press*.

He told the audience that Russia had known there were no WMDs in Iraq, and had known that attacking Iraq would bring "great difficulties" to that country. "And look what is happening today," he said. He made the same comment about Libya. He spoke of the U.S. and Russia working together to successfully remove

102 http://centerforpolitics.org

chemical weapons from the Syrian government. But he warned against attacking Syria now.

There will be no new Cold War, Kislyak said, but there is now a greater divide in some ways than during the Cold War. Back then, he said, the U.S. Congress sent delegations over to meet with legislators, and the Supreme Court likewise. Now there is no contact. It's easy in the U.S. to be anti-Russian, he said, and hard to defend Russia. He complained about U.S. economic sanctions against Russia intended to "suffocate" Russian agriculture.

Asked about "annexing" Crimea, Kislyak rejected that characterization, pointed to the armed overthrow of the Ukrainian government, and insisted that Kiev must stop bombing its own people and instead talk about federalism within Ukraine.

There were remarkably few questions put to the ambassador that seemed informed by U.S. television "news." One was from a politics professor who insisted that Kislyak assign blame to Russia over Ukraine. Kislyak didn't.

I always sit in the back, thinking I might leave, but Kislyak was only taking questions from the front. So I moved up and was finally called on for the last question of the evening. For an hour and a half, Kislyak had addressed war and peace and Russian-U.S. relations, but he'd never blamed the U.S. for anything in Ukraine any more than Russia. No one had uttered the word "NATO."

So I pointed out the upcoming NATO protests[103]. I recalled

103 http://nonatonewport.org

the history of Russia being told that NATO would not expand eastward. I asked Kislyak whether NATO ought to be disbanded.

The ambassador said that he had been the first Russian to "present his credentials" to NATO, and that he had "overestimated" NATO's ability to work with Russia. He'd been disappointed by NATO actions in Serbia, he said, and Libya, by the expansion eastward, by NATO pressure on Ukraine and Poland, and by the pretense that Russia might be about to attack Poland.

"We were promised," Kislyak said, that NATO would not expand eastward at all upon the reunification of Germany. "And now look." NATO has declared that Ukraine and Georgia will join NATO, Kislyak pointed out, and NATO says this even while a majority of the people in Ukraine say they're opposed.

The ambassador used the word "disappointed" a few times.

"We'll have to take measures to assure our defense," he said, "but we would have preferred to build on a situation with decreased presence and decreased readiness."

Wouldn't we all. Join the campaign to shut down NATO[104]. Sign a petition[105] for an independent investigation into the airplane crash in Ukraine. Send a note to the Russian Embassy[106] to let them know you're against a new Cold War too.

---

104 http://nonatonewport.org
105      http://diy.rootsaction.org/petitions/call-for-independent-inquiry-of-the-airplane-crash-in-ukraine-and-its-catastrophic-aftermath
106 http://russianembassy.org

# Iraq Has WMDs and Russia Has Invaded!

How did they imagine they'd get away with it, claiming that Iraq had vast stockpiles of chemical and biological weapons and even nuclear weapons?

Defectors had made clear the chemical and biological weapons (some of them provided by the United States) had been destroyed. Inspectors had searched almost every inch of Iraq and said they'd get to the last few inches if given a few more days. Iraq was screaming that it had no such weapons. Numerous nations around the world were agreeing with Iraq. Colin Powell's own staff warned him that his claims would not be deemed plausible.

And yet, they got away with it to such an extent that most well-intentioned people in the United States to this day maintain that nobody can possibly be sure that Bush, Cheney, et alia, knew their statements were false when they made them.

> *"All this was inspired by the principle—which is quite true within itself—that in the big lie there is always a certain force of credibility; because the broad masses of a nation are always more easily corrupted in the deeper strata of their emotional nature than consciously or voluntarily; and thus in the primitive simplicity of their minds they more readily fall victims to the big lie than the small lie, since they themselves often tell small lies in little matters but would be ashamed to resort to large-scale falsehoods." —Adolf Hitler*

The U.S. media has repeatedly been claiming that Russia has invaded Ukraine. They claim it for a while, and there's obviously been no invasion, so they pause. Then they claim it again. Or they claim that a convoy of aid trucks constitutes an invasion. But the aid trucks look like aid trucks in all the photographs, and yet nobody has taken similar photographs of any invasion. When Ukrainian tanks rolled into eastern Ukraine and were surrounded by civilians, we saw photographs and videos. Now there's just a Colin-Powellesque satellite photo from NATO supposedly showing Russian artillery in Ukraine.

The major Russian invasion that apparently comes complete with some sort of muggle-and-photographer-repellant charm is said to consist of 1,000 troops—or roughly as many troops as the U.S. has now sent back into Iraq in no sort of invasion to worry about whatsoever.

But where are the 1,000 Russian troops invading Ukraine? Ukraine claims to have captured 10 of them, but the captured troops don't seem to have agreed to the story. And what happened to the other 990? How did someone get close enough to capture 10 but not photograph the other 990?

Meanwhile Russia says it's all lies and publicly urges the United States to engage with Ukraine diplomatically and urge the Ukrainian government to stop bombing its own citizens and work out a federalist system that represents everyone within its borders.

But NATO is busy announcing a counter-invasion to the invisible Russian invasion.

How do they imagine they'll get away with it? Well, let's see. Not a single individual responsible for the lies that launched the destruction of Iraq and the death of some million people and the predictable and predicted chaos now tormenting Iraq's whole region has been held accountable in any way.

The lie that Gadaffi was about to slaughter innocents, the lie that facilitated the attack on Libya and the hell that has now been established there—No one has been held accountable for that lie in any way whatsoever.

The lie that the White House had proof that Assad had used chemical weapons—No one has been held accountable. No one has even had to recant as they switch targets and propose bombing Assad's enemies.

The lie that drone strikes don't kill innocents and don't kill those who could easily have been arrested instead—No one has been held accountable.

The lie that the United States had proof Russia had shot down an airplane over Ukraine—No one has been held accountable, and the United States is opposing an independent investigation.

The lie that torture makes us safe, a lie that led to the United States torturing some folks—No one at the level of air-conditioned office work has been held responsible at all. Why do they think they can get away with it?

Because you let them. Because you don't want to believe they commit such atrocities. Because you don't want to believe they tell big lies.

You know, some people feel like idiots for having believed the Iraq lies. Imagine how they're going to feel when they find out they believed a nation had been invaded when it hadn't.

# Drones

## Why I Don't Want to See the Drone Memo

*And when the people saw that Moses delayed to come down out of the mount, the people gathered themselves together unto Aaron, and said unto him, Up, make us a secret memo that gets us out of the bit about Thou-shalt-not-kill.*

And, lo, as I was driving home from the committee hearing I was pulled over for speeding, and I said unto the officer, "I've got a memo that lets me speed. Would you like to see it?" and he said, "No thank you, and not your grocery list or your diary either."

Transparency in drone murders has been a demand pushed by

U.N. lawyers and pre-vetted Congressional witnesses, and not by the victims' families. Nobody asks for transparency in child abuse or rape. "Oh, have you got a memo that explains how aliens commanded you to kill and eat those people? Oh, well that's all right then."

Seriously, what the filibuster?

I don't want to see the memo that David Barron wrote "legalizing" the killing of U.S. citizens with drone strikes, after which (or is it beforehand?) I'll decide whether he should be a federal judge.

Laws don't work that way. A law is a public document, known to or knowable to all, and enforced equally on all. If a president can instruct a lawyer to write a memo legalizing murder, what can a president not instruct a lawyer to legalize? What's left of legality?

Let's assume that the memo argues with great obfuscation that, in essence, killing people with drones is part of a war and therefore legal, will we better off or worse off after watching all the human rights groups and lawyers bow down before that idol?

Just because Amnesty International and Human Rights Watch don't recognize the U.N. Charter or the Kellogg Briand Pact is not a reason for us not to. Laws don't work that way. Laws remain law until they are repealed. These laws have not been. If a memo can make a murder part of a war and therefore legal, we are obliged to ask: What makes the war legal?

The answer is not the U.S. government, not the pretense that the president can declare war, and not the pretense that Congress has declared eternal war everywhere. The U.S. government is in violation of the U.N. Charter and of the Kellogg Briand Pact.

Or let's assume the memo says something else. The point is not what it says but its purported power to say it. The law against murder in Pakistan and the law against murder in Yemen don't cease to exist in Pakistan and Yemen because a new Jay Bybee, willing to say whatever's needed to become a judge, writes a secret memo—or a public memo.

And, as this conversation plays out, think what it will have U.S. editorial pages all silently assuming about the legality of murdering non-U.S. citizens. If a memo is needed to kill U.S. citizens, what about the other 99% of drone victims? That, too, is not how actual laws work. The laws against war don't prevent war only on U.S. citizens. The laws of Pakistan don't protect only U.S. citizens. The amendments in the U.S. bill of rights, for that matter, don't apply only to U.S. citizens.

Now, the memo is likely to describe people who are an imminent threat to the United States. And our newspapers are likely to remind us that President Obama made a speech claiming that one of the four U.S. citizens known to have been killed under this program was such a threat. It will be tempting to point out that Anwar al Awlaki, on the contrary, was already on the kill list prior to the incident that Obama claims justified putting him there. It will be tempting to point out that nobody's made even a blatantly false argument to justify killing the other three U.S. citizens, much less the thousands of other human beings.

We shouldn't fall for those traps. A president is not legally allowed to invent criteria for killing people. Never mind that he doesn't meet his own criteria. We should not be so indecent or so lawless as to engage in such a conversation. We should not want to see the blood-soaked memo.

## So That's Why They Kept the Drone Kill Memo Secret

Now that the U.S. government has released parts of its We-Can-Kill-People-With-Drones memo[107], it's hard to miss why it was kept secret until now.

Liberal professors and human rights groups and the United Nations were claiming an inability to know whether drone murders were legal or not because they hadn't seen the memo that the White House said legalized them. Some may continue to claim that the redactions in the memo make judgment impossible.

I expect most, however, will now be willing to drop the pretense that ANY memo could possibly legalize murder. Oh, and yall can stop telling me not to use the impolite term "murder" to describe the, you know, murders—since "murder" is precisely the term used by the no-longer secret memo.

---

107 http://pdfserver.amlaw.com/nlj/usca2-olc-memo-6232014.pdf

The memo considers a section[108] of the U.S. code dealing with the murder of a U.S. citizen by another U.S. citizen abroad, drawing on another section that defines murder as "the unlawful killing of a human being with malice aforethought."

David Barron, the memo's author, needed a loophole to make murder-by-missile a *lawful* killing rather than an unlawful killing, so he pulls out the "public authority justification" under which the government gets to use force to enforce a law. It's a novel twist, though, for the government to get to use force to violate the law, claiming the violation is legal on the Nixonian basis that it is the government doing it.

Alternatively, Barron suggests, a government gets to use force if doing so is part of a war. This, of course, ignores the U.N. Charter and the Kellogg Briand Pact and the illegality of wars, as well as the novelty of claiming that a war exists everywhere on earth forever and ever. (None of Barron's arguments justify governmental murder on U.S. soil any less than off U.S. soil.)

In essence, Barron seems to argue, the people who wrote the laws were thinking about private citizens and terrorists, not the government (which, somehow, cannot be a terrorist), and therefore it's OK for the government to violate the laws.

Then there's the problem of Congressional authorization of war, or lack thereof, which Barron gets around by pretending that the Authorization for the Use of Military Force was as broad as the White House pretends rather than worded to allow targeting only

---

108 http://www.law.cornell.edu/uscode/text/18/1119

those responsible for the 911 attacks. Then there are the facts of the matter in the case of Anwar al Awlaki, who was targeted for murder prior in time to the actions that President Obama has claimed justified that targeting. Then there are the facts in the other cases of U.S. killings of U.S. citizens, which aren't even redacted, as they're never considered. Then there are the vastly more numerous killings of non-U.S. citizens, which the memo does not even attempt to excuse.

In the end, the memo admits that calling something a war isn't good enough; the targeted victim has to have been an imminent threat to the United States. But who gets to decide whether he or she was that? Why, whoever does the killing of course. And what happens if nobody ever even makes an unsupported assertion to that effect? Nothing, of course.

This is not the rule of law. This is savage brute force in minimal disguise. I don't want to see any more of these memos. I want to see the video footage of the drone murders on a television. I want to see law professors and revolving-door State Department / human rights group hacks argue that dead children fall under the public authority justification.

# Pay No Attention to the Apocalypse Behind the Curtain

Remarks in London, England, July 2, 2014.

Thank you to Bruce Kent and the Movement for the Abolition of War and to Veterans For Peace and the Campaign for Nuclear

Disarmament. Thank you to the Stop the War Coalition and everyone else for helping spread the word.

In 8 days, on July 10th Mary Ann Grady-Flores, a grandmother from Ithaca, NY, is scheduled to be sentenced to up to one year in prison. Her crime is violating an order of protection, which is a legal tool to protect a particular person from the violence of another particular person. In this case, the commander of Hancock Air Base has been legally protected from dedicated nonviolent protesters, despite the protection of commanding his own military base, and despite the protesters having no idea who the guy is. That's how badly the people in charge of the flying killer robots we call drones want to avoid any questioning of their activity entering the minds of the drone pilots.

Last Thursday a place in the U.S. called the Stimson Center released a report on the new U.S. habit of murdering people with missiles from drones. The Stimson Center is named for Henry Stimson, the U.S. Secretary of War who, prior to the Japanese attack on Pearl Harbor wrote in his diary, following a meeting with President Roosevelt: "The question was how we should maneuver them into the position of firing the first shot without allowing too much danger to ourselves. It was a difficult proposition." (Four months earlier, Churchill had told his cabinet at 10 Downing Street that U.S. policy toward Japan consisted of this: "Everything was to be done to force an incident.") This was the same Henry Stimson who later forbid dropping the first nuclear bomb on Kyoto, because he'd once been to Kyoto. He'd never visited Hiroshima, much to the misfortune of the people of Hiroshima.

I know there's a big celebration of World War I going on over here (as well as big resistance to it), but in the United States there's been an ongoing celebration of World War II for 70 years. In fact, one might even suggest that World War II has continued in a certain way and on a lesser scale for 70 years (and on a greater scale in particular times and places like Korea and Vietnam and Iraq). The United States has never returned to pre-World War II levels of taxes or military spending, never left Japan or Germany, has engaged in some 200 military actions abroad during the so-called post-war era, has never stopped expanding its military presence abroad, and now has troops permanently stationed in almost every country on earth. Two exceptions, Iran and Syria, are regularly threatened.

So it is altogether appropriate, I think, that it was the Stimson Center that released this report, by former military officials and military-friendly lawyers, a report that included this rather significant statement: "The increasing use of lethal UAVs may create a slippery slope leading to continual or wider wars." At least that sounds significant to me. Continual wars? That's a pretty bad thing, right?

Also last week, the U.S. government made public a memo in which it claims the right to legally murder a U.S. citizen (never mind anybody else) as part of a war that has no limit in time or space. Call me crazy, but this seems serious. What if this war goes on long enough to generate significant enemies?

Last year the United Nations released a report that stated that drones were making war the norm rather than the exception. Wow.

That could be a problem for a species of creatures who prefer not being bombed, don't you think? The United Nations, created to rid the world of war, mentions in passing that war is becoming the norm rather than the exception.

Surely the response to such a grave development should be equally significant.

We've grown habituated, I think, to reading reports that say things like "If we don't leave 80% of known fossil fuels in the ground we're all going to die, and lots of other species with us," and then experts recommend that we use more efficient light bulbs and grow our own tomatoes. I mean we've become used to the response not remotely fitting the crisis at hand.

Such is the case with the UN, the Stimson Center, and a good crowd of humanitarian law experts, as far as I can tell.

The Stimson Center says of murders by drone, they should be "neither glorified not demonized." Nor, apparently, should they be stopped. Instead, the Stimson Center recommends reviews and transparency and robust studies. I'm willing to bet that if you or I threatened massive continual or widening death and destruction we'd be demonized. I'm willing to bet the idea of our being glorified wouldn't even come up for consideration.

The United Nations, too, thinks transparency is the answer. Just let us know whom you're murdering and why. We'll get you the forms to do a monthly report. As other nations get in on this game we'll compile their reports and create some real international transparency.

That's some people's idea of progress.

Drones are, of course, not the only way or—thus far—the most deadly way the U.S. and its allies wage wars. But there is this minimal pretense of ethical discussion about drones because drone murders look like murders to a lot of people. The U.S. president goes through a list of men, women, and children on Tuesdays, picks whom to murder, and has them and anyone standing too close to them murdered—although he also often targets people without knowing their name. Bombing Libya or anywhere else looks less like murder to many people, especially if—like Stimson in Hiroshima—they've never been to Libya, and if numerous bombs are all supposedly aimed at one evil person whom the U.S. government has turned against. So, the United States goes through something like the 2011 war on Libya that has left that nation in such a fine state without it occurring to any military-friendly think tanks that there's an ethical question to be pondered.

How, I wonder, would we talk about drones or bombs or so-called non-combat advisors if we were trying to eliminate war rather than ameliorate it? Well, I think that if we saw the complete abolition of war as even our very distant goal, we'd talk very differently about every type of war today. I think we'd stop encouraging the idea that any memo could possibly legalize murder, whether or not we'd seen the memo. I think we'd reject the human rights groups' position that the U.N. Charter and the Kellogg-Briand Pact should be ignored. Rather than considering the illegality of tactics during a war, we'd object to the illegality of the war itself. We wouldn't speak positively of the United States and Iran possibly joining hands in friendship if the basis for such a proposed alliance was to be a joint effort to kill Iraqis.

In the U.S. it's not unusual for peace groups to focus on 4,000 dead Americans and the financial costs of the war on Iraq, and to steadfastly refuse to mention a half-million to a million and a half Iraqis killed, which silence has contributed to most Americans not knowing what happened. But that's the strategy of opponents of some wars, not opponents of all wars. Depicting a particular war as costly to the aggressor doesn't move people against war preparations or rid them of the fantasy that there could be a good and just war in the days ahead.

It's common in Washington to argue against military waste, such as weapons that don't work or that the Pentagon didn't even ask Congress for, or to argue against bad wars that leave the military less prepared for other possible wars. If our project was aimed ultimately at war's elimination, we'd be against military efficiency more than military waste and in favor of an ill-prepared military unable to launch more wars. We'd also be as focused on keeping young people out of the military and militarism out of school books as we are on preventing a particular batch of missiles from flying. It's routine to profess loyalty to soldiers while opposing their commanders' policies, but once you've praised soldiers for their supposed service, you've accepted that they must have provided one. Celebrating World War I resisters, as I know some of you have been doing recently, is the sort of thing that ought to replace honoring war participants.

We may need to not just change our conversation from opposing specific war after specific war to discussing the ending of the whole institution. We may also need to alter at least subtly every part of the conversation along the way.

Instead of proposing that veterans in particular have earned our gratitude and should receive healthcare and retirement (which one hears all the time in the U.S.), we may want to propose that all people—including veterans—have human rights, and that one of our chief duties is to cease creating any more veterans.

Instead of objecting to troops urinating on corpses, we may want to object to the creation of the corpses. Instead of trying to eliminate torture and rape and lawless imprisonment from an operation of mass-murder, we may want to focus on the cause. We can't go on putting $2 trillion a year globally, and half of that just in the United States, into getting ready for wars and not expect wars to result.

With other addictions we're told to go after the biggest dealers of the drug or to go after the demand by the users. The dealers of the drug of war are those funding the military with our grandchildren's unearned pay and dumping buckets of money into propaganda about Vietnam and World War I. They know the lies about past wars are even more important than the lies about new wars. And we know that the institution of war could not survive people learning the truth about it to such an extent that some people begin to act on that knowledge.

U.S. public opinion has moved against wars. When Parliament and Congress said no to missiles into Syria, public pressure of the past decade played a big role. The same is true of stopping a horrible bill on Iran in Congress earlier this year, and of resistance to a new war on Iraq. Congress members are worried about voting for another war like Iraq, whether in Iraq or elsewhere. Her vote to attack Iraq 12 years ago is the only thing that has kept us thus far from seeing Hillary Clinton in the White House. People don't want to vote for someone who voted for that. And, let's get this said early to our dear friends at the Nobel Committee: another peace prize will not help things. The United States doesn't need another peace prize for a war maker, it needs what Bruce and so many of you have been working on over here: a popular movement for the abolition of war!

A number of peace activists have started up a new effort called World Beyond War at http://WorldBeyondWar.org aimed at bringing more people into peace activism. People and organizations in at least 58 countries so far have signed the Declaration of Peace at WorldBeyondWar.org. Our hope is that, by bringing more people and groups into the movement, we can strengthen and enlarge, rather than compete against, existing peace organizations. We hope that we can support the work of groups like the Movement for the Abolition of War, and that we can, as groups and individuals, work globally.

The website at WorldBeyondWar.org is intended to provide educational tools: videos, maps, reports, talking points. We make the case against the idea that war protects us—an outrageous idea, given that the nations that engage in the most war face the most hostility as a result. A poll at the start of this year of people in 65 nations found the U.S. in a huge lead as the nation considered the greatest threat to peace in the world. U.S. veterans are killing themselves in record numbers, in part over what they've done to Iraq and Afghanistan. Our humanitarian wars are a leading cause of suffering and death for humanity. And so we also refute the idea that war can benefit the people where it is waged.

We also lay out the arguments that war is deeply immoral, a first-cousin of and frequent cause of, not alternative to, genocide; that war destroys our natural environment, that war erodes our civil liberties, and that just transferring a bit of what we spend on war to something useful would make us beloved rather than feared around the world. One and a half percent of what the world spends on war could be spent to end starvation on earth. War has taken 200 million lives over the past century, but the good that could be done with the resources dumped into war far outstrips the evil that could be avoided by ending war. For one thing, if we quickly redirected war's resources we'd have our best shot at doing something to protect the climate of the planet. That our concept of "defense" doesn't include that illustrates how far we've gone toward accepting the inevitability of what is after all the perfectly avoidable and perfectly horrible and completely indefensible institution of war.

Having accepted war, we try for cheaper wars, better wars, even more one-sided wars, and what do we get? We get warnings from respectable war supporters that we're beginning to make war the norm and risking continual warfare.

On the one hand this is a case of unintended consequences to rival those who sought the truth about god's creation and ended up with the guy who's on the money around here, Charles Darwin. On the other hand it's not unintended at all. A professor at Stanford University has just put out a book arguing that war is so good for us that we must always keep it going. That strain of thought courses through the veins of our military funded academia and activism.

But that kind of thinking is increasingly unpopular, and this may be the moment in which to expose it, denounce it, and crystallize into action the growing popular sentiment against war, and the realization into which we've stumbled that particular wars can be prevented, and if particular wars can be prevented then each and every one of them can be prevented. I look forward to working on that project, with the urgency it demands, and together with all of you.

# *Palestine*

## *The Story of Gaza*

Young authors of fiction from Gaza, some of whom say they are finding Palestine on the internet while unable to see it exist in reality, have just published a collection[109] of stories, written in English, marking the five-year anniversary of the 23 days from December 27, 2008, until Obama's inauguration, during which Israel bombed the people of Gaza far more heavily than usual. They're publishing a new excerpt of the book each of these 23 days on their FaceBook page[110]. You can talk with them in an upcoming Google Hangout[111].

For five years, the world—just like Obama—has overwhelmingly been "looking forward" when it comes to crimes committed by nations aligned with the U.S. government. But the crimes in Gaza then and now, and in other countries, have been exposed to unprecedented "looking present" through immediate real-time blogging available to those actively looking, even in the places responsible for the far-away terrorism-too-big-to-call-by-that-name. If everyone turned off their television and searched on a computer for news about their own country as reported in other countries, injustice, rather than our natural environment, would be endangered.

---

109 http://justworldbooks.com
110 https://www.facebook.com/GazaWritesBack
111    http://salsa3.salsalabs.com/o/50601/p/salsa/event/common/public/?event_KEY=75346

The telling of truer-than-news stories by these young Gazans has the potential to reach many more minds, and to set an example that just might scare off the next "humanitarian war" no matter where it's targeted. If victims of military benevolence can have their stories read by people who matter, or who could matter if they acted, and if those stories inevitably effect understanding of the obvious-but-always-denied fact that *they* are like *we*, that those people are people just like these people, that something has "brought out their humanity," then the shock and awe might have to move from its fictional location in the streets of non-humans' cities to a real existence in the offices of Lockheed Martin.

The stories in this book are of childhood and family, love and loss, soccer and toothaches. As with any story, people are placed in particularly special circumstances. A visit to the doctor is a visit to someone making decisions of triage: Will your father be sent to a specialist to be saved, or will this baby who has a better chance at living be sent instead? Two farmers, a Gazan and an Israeli unknowingly stand just inches or feet away from each other, separated by an impenetrable wall. A Gazan and an Israeli are perhaps attracted to each other, but blocked by a wall that needs no physical presence. A child is listening to a bedtime story when a missile strikes the house. Who will live? And who will be traumatized? Or was everyone pre-traumatized already?

*"I spent that night thinking of Thaer's home, of the distant life in Mama's eyes. I kept wondering what's more torturous: the awful buzz of the drone outside or the sounds of some tough questions inside. I guess I eventually slept with no*

*answer, thanking the drone for not giving my inner uproar any chance to abate."*

Children in Gaza know the names of books, of toys, of movies, of trees, and of deadly flying aircraft. Some of the latter are called "Apaches," named after a people marched, and imprisoned, and slaughtered by the U.S. military, people kept in camps that inspired the Nazis', whose camps in turn inspired what the nation of Israel now does to non-Jewish African immigrants. How long will it be before little children in China are pointing to the sky in fear of a swarm of "Gazas"?

These stories are of people and of land, and of efforts to understand other people on the land. Understanding is a challenge:

*"If a Palestinian bulldozer were ever invented (Haha, I know!) and I were given the chance to be in an orchard, in Haifa for instance, I would never uproot a tree an Israeli planted. No Palestinian would. To Palestinians, the tree is sacred, and so is the Land bearing it."*

Gazans try to imagine what goes on in the minds of Israeli soldiers, particularly those soldiers who have killed their family members. One story tells the tale of an Israeli soldier's regret (or what we like to clinically and cleanly call PTSD), and of the soldier's wife's efforts to ease his pain:

"Honey, you were doing your job to follow orders. It's alright." These words come as kind words of comfort, spoken to a man beyond the point of being able to hear them. And at the same time they come as an articulation of an ongoing horror of immense proportions. The contrast of these multiple meanings might make us all stop and question what we hear too often without thinking. Here in the United States, for example, any soldier in uniform gets on any airplane first and is thanked for his or her "service." Surely not thanking someone for their service would be impolite. But those who flip the switch on our prisons' electric chairs aren't thanked. Those who risk their lives to put out fires are not thanked. Only those who kill in war, even as their largest current killing operation—in Afghanistan—has the support of 17% in the U.S. and polling around the globe finds a consensus that the United States is the leading threat to peace on earth.

The stories from Gaza are not essays. They do not address the inevitable "What about the Gazans' own violence?" One need not misunderstand the nature of the occupation, the slow genocide, the international injustice, the vastly disproportionate violence and suffering imposed on one side of this so-called conflict in order to believe that "What about the Gazans' own violence?" is a reasonable question. Nor need one be a Gazan or an inexcusably arrogant and unsympathetic fool to have the right to disagree with the usual answer. The stories come with an introduction from the editor in which he expresses support for this well-known concept: "by any means necessary." I prefer this phrasing: "by any means effective." Means that most easily express rage are sometimes misinterpreted as necessary, while means that have the best chance of succeeding are rejected for not having a greater chance than they do.

The stories themselves don't actually take up that debate. Rather they depict the struggle merely to survive, the bravery that we may in fact all need everywhere if the earth's climate goes the way scientists expect. These young people from Gaza may become leaders in a movement to create peace and justice before madness and disaster-imperialism overtake the comfortable and the forgotten alike. I wonder if, and hope, they know the Afghan Peace Volunteers[112], and the people of No Dal Molin[113] in Italy, and of Gangjeong Village[114] on Jeju Island, and I hope they will join a new worldwide movement to end war[115] that will be launching next year.

Sending Love to Gaza: http://youtu.be/VrqZLLFWxWA

## *This is the Israeli Military Calling: Civilizing War Has Failed*

Probably the biggest news story of 1928 was the war-making nations of the world coming together on August 27th and legally outlawing war. It's a story that's not told in our history books, but it's not secret CIA history. There was no CIA. There was virtually no weapons industry as we know it. There weren't two political parties in the United States uniting in support of war after war. In fact, the four biggest political parties in the United States all backed abolishing war.

---

112 http://ourjourneytosmile.com/blog/
113 http://www.nodalmolin.it/
114 http://savejejunow.org/
115 http://worldbeyondwar.org

Cue whining, polysyllabic screech: *"But it didn't wooooooooork!"*

I wouldn't be bothering with it if it had. In its defense, the Kellogg-Briand Pact (look it up or read my book[116]) was used to prosecute the makers of war on the losing sides following World War II (an historic first), and—for whatever combination of reasons (nukes? enlightenment? luck?)—the armed nations of the world have not waged war on each other since, preferring to slaughter the world's poor instead. Significant compliance following the very first prosecution is a record that almost no other law can claim.

The Kellogg-Briand Pact has two chief values, as I see it. First, it's the law of the land in 85 nations including the United States, and it bans all war-making. For those who claim that the U.S. Constitution sanctions or requires wars regardless of treaty obligations, the Peace Pact is no more relevant than the U.N. Charter or the Geneva Conventions or the Anti-Torture Convention or any other treaty. But for those who read the laws as they are written, beginning to comply with the Kellogg-Briand Pact makes far more sense than legalizing drone murders or torture or bribery or corporate personhood or imprisonment without trial or any of the other lovely practices we've been "legalizing" on the flimsiest of legal arguments. I'm not against new national or international laws against war; ban it 1,000 times, by all means, if there's the slightest chance that one of them will stick. But there is, for what it's worth, already a law on the books if we care to acknowledge it.

Second, the movement that created the Pact of Paris grew out of a widespread mainstream international understanding that war must

116 http://davidswanson.org/outlawry

be abolished, as slavery and blood feuds and duelling and other institutions were being abolished. While advocates of outlawing war believed other steps would be required: a change in the culture, demilitarization, the establishment of international authorities and nonviolent forms of conflict resolution, prosecutions and targeted sanctions against war-makers; while most believed this would be the work of generations; while the forces leading toward World War II were understood and protested against for decades; the explicit and successful intention was to make a start of it by outlawing and formally renouncing and rendering illegitimate all war, not aggressive war or unsanctioned war or inappropriate war, but war.

In the never-ending aftermath of World War II, the U.N. Charter has formalized and popularized a very different conception of war's legality. I've just interviewed Ben Ferencz, aged 94, the last living Nuremberg prosecutor, for an upcoming edition of Talk Nation Radio[117]. He describes the Nuremberg prosecutions as happening under the framework of the U.N. Charter, or something identical to it, despite the chronological problem. He believes that the U.S. invasion of Iraq was illegal. But he claims not to know whether the U.S. invasion and ongoing over-12-year war on Afghanistan is legal or not. Why? Not because it fits either of the two gaping loopholes opened up by the U.N. Charter, that is: not because it is U.N.-authorized or defensive, but—as far as I can make out—just because those loopholes exist and therefore wars might be legal and it's unpleasant to acknowledge that the wars waged by one's own nation are not.

Of course, plenty of people thought more or less like that in the

117 http://talknationradio.org

1920s and 1930s, but plenty of people also did not. In the era of the United Nations, NATO, the CIA, and Lockheed Martin we have seen steady progress in the doomed attempt, not to eliminate war, but to civilize it. The United States leads the way in arming the rest of the world, maintaining a military presence in most of the world, and launching wars. Western allies and nations armed, free-of-charge, by the United States, including Israel, advance war-making and war-civilizing, not war-abolition. The notion that war can be eliminated using the tool of war, making war on war-makers in order to teach them not to make war, has had a far longer run than the Kellogg-Briand Pact had prior to its supposed failure and the Truman Administration's remaking of the U.S. government into a permanent war machine in the cause of progress.

Civilizing war for the benefit of the world has been an abysmal failure. We now have wars launched on unarmed defenseless people thousands of miles away in the name of "defense." We now have wars depicted as U.N.-authorized because the U.N. once passed a resolution related to the nation being destroyed. And just seconds before the Israeli military blows up your house in Gaza, they ring you up on the telephone to give you a proper warning.

I remember a comedy sketch from Steve Martin mocking the phony politeness of Los Angeles: a line of people waited their turn to withdraw cash from a bank machine, while a line of armed robbers waited their turn in a separate line to politely ask for and steal each person's money. War is past the point of such parody. There is no space left for satire. Governments are phoning families to tell them they're about to be slaughtered, and then bombing the shelters they flee to if they manage to flee.

Is mass-murder acceptable if done without rape or torture or excessive targeting of children or the use of particular types of chemical weapons, as long as the victims are telephoned first or the murderers are associated with a group of people harmed by war several decades back?

Here's a new initiative that says No, the abolition of the greatest evil needs a renaissance and completion: WorldBeyondWar.org.

# The Palestinian Right and the American Left

Chris Hedges says[118] that Palestinians have the right to self-defense in the form of rockets, without including any consideration of whether the rockets make the Palestinians more or less defended. There is, after all, a reasonable argument that the rockets are counter-productive and endangering, rather than protecting, Palestine.

Legally, if we ignore the Kellogg-Briand Pact and stick to the U.N. Charter, much less its frequent abuse by the powerful nations of the world, there is no doubt that Hedges is correct. If demolishing Iraqi or Afghan or Libyan or Pakistani or Yemeni homes is "defense" of the United States, then surely the people of Gaza, under actual attack, have the legal right to shoot rockets at Israel. That's just basic Western consensus with the hypocrisy removed.

---

118      http://www.truthdig.com/report/item/the_palestinians_right_to_self-defense_20140723

"[M]any Palestinians, especially young men trapped in overcrowded hovels where they have no work and little dignity," writes Hedges, "will risk immediate death to defy the slow, humiliating death of occupation. I cannot blame them."

Here are the false choices framed: either we blame the victims of Israel's vicious and massive assault on a trapped population, blame them for reacting as virtually anyone else in the so-called developed world would, or we advocate for the right to fight defensive wars— regardless of whether it helps or hurts the situation. Those are not the only options.

I'm not sure I can prove that the rockets hurt the situation, but to render the question inadmissible seems fatally flawed. The justification that the U.S. Congress and White House use for arming Israel and seeking to shelter Israel from legal consequences is always and exclusively the rockets. The justification that Israeli spokespeople use on television is likewise almost entirely the rockets. In a world without the rockets, would other excuses prove successful? It's hard to say for sure. But the rockets provide the public packaging for Israeli war-making, accomplish virtually nothing in military terms, and almost certainly do more to frighten and enrage the people of Israel than to bring Israelis around to sympathizing with the plight of their government's victims.

I've just spoken by phone with a smart writer in Gaza named Sarah Ali for an upcoming edition of Talk Nation Radio[119]. She explained to me quite eloquently how Israeli attacks on Gaza were generating support for Hamas and violence against Israel.

119 http://talknationradio.org

She described the emotional need to fight back. So, I asked her if rocket attacks on Israel weren't likewise counterproductive. No, she said, she imagined that Israelis saw the rockets and began to understand the point of view of Palestinians. In the absence of any evidence of that phenomenon, I can only say that I'll believe it when I see it. In every case I'm aware of in which one nation has militarily attacked another, it has done far more to enrage than to stimulate sympathy in the people coming under attack.

Of course, I have no right to tell the people of Gaza what to do or not do from the comfort of my home in the heart of the imperial monster that is funding their apocalypse. Of course I cannot know the situation as they know it. But it's not clear to me that every Gazan has as deep a familiarity with Israelis or every Israeli with Gazans as one might imagine from their geographic vicinity. The division between these two societies is extreme. How else could Israelis imagine children as their enemies? And how else could those children's parents imagine that firing rockets would win over hearts and minds?

## Should Israel Teach the Holocaust Less?

Humans almost invariably imagine humans to be far more imaginative and original than they are. But most of our ideas come from (often imperfect and improvised) imitation. And even more powerful than our tendency to imitate is our inability to refrain from imitating, to shake an idea out of our heads once it's there, to "not think of an elephant."

Anthropologists have found cultures whose members cannot conceive of killing. "Why won't you shoot an arrow at those slave raiders?" "Because it would kill them."

In Western culture, children hear of killing in fairy tales, cartoons, Harry Potter books, video games, the TV news, the newspaper, the games played in the park. It's everywhere. Usually it's frowned upon, although often a distinction is made between bad killing by bad guys and good killing by good guys, or inexplicable random killing and killing justified and sanctified by bitter revenge.

But even when a behavior is frowned upon, the listener or viewer has now heard of that behavior. There have been studies of children's responses to stories and television dramas in which fictional children misbehave for three-quarters of the episode and then learn an important moral lesson at the end. Guess what? Kids don't retroactively view the whole story as a package and wipe the bad behavior out of their minds. Instead they display a tendency to try out the behavior demonstrated to them in so many of the isolated moments that they lived while watching or listening to the story.

Humans also almost invariably imagine humans to be far kinder and far more selfless than they are. Most of us very much want others to be kind to us, and we try our best to be kind to others. So, when we see behaviors and institutions that cause horrendous suffering, we like to imagine there is a rational cause, a greater good, or that the explanation is incompetence or stupidity—anything other than the most obvious explanation: vicious, evil sadism.

We are often encouraged to picture vicious cruelty and irrational evil in certain foreign groups of humans. But usually this perspective is intended to help us avoid seeing cruelty in those who are supposedly like ourselves.

These thoughts arise as I'm confronted by the polling[120] showing that 95% of Israelis deem the slaughter of Gazans to be just, and the realization that for many in Israel "just" is a rather disgusting euphemism for "satisfyingly sadistic." People are sitting on hills watching the missiles hit the homes, some of them telling cameras they want everyone killed, and then explaining that their thoughts are "a little bit fascist."[121]

This week we'll be remembering Harry Truman's bombing of Japan with nuclear weapons, and we'll be told that he must have believed those acts of mass murder would help end the war, even though the evidence shows he knew otherwise. Truman had earlier advocated aiding the Russians or the Germans, whoever was losing, so that as many people as possible would die, he said. Top U.S. military officials wanted Japan cleansed of all human life. The most likely explanation for the nukes, namely that Truman viewed killing lots of Japanese as an advantage to be weighed along with impressing the Russians and so forth, is too ugly, so we turn away. We even have to turn away from his own statement on the occasion, which justified the bombing in terms of revenge, not in terms of ending the war.

---

120        http://www.washingtonpost.com/world/middle_east/israelis-support-netanyahu-and-gaza-war-despite-rising-deaths-on-both-sides/2014/07/29/0d562c44-1748-11e4-9349-84d4a85be981_story.html
121 https://www.youtube.com/watch?v=Vg59Xf53GLk

Also this week we'll mark 50 years since the Gulf of Tonkin fraud. We like to imagine such incidents, even when they result in the deaths of 4 million foreigners, as misunderstandings. But during the course of the savagery that followed, how was progress gauged? That's right: by body counts.

Examples of evil policies, in one's own or other parts of the world, flood in the moment you begin to look for them. The evidence is clear that locking kids up in juvenile prisons makes them more likely, not less likely, to grow into criminals. But we just go on locking them up for other motives we don't care to examine too closely. We've learned what it's impolite to mention. Support for wars in Afghanistan or Iraq is discussed on television in terms of "strategic interests" and other such blather, but the counter-demonstrators across the street from a peace rally sometimes have different desires, including the death of foreigners—and of the peace activists with them.

Courageous peace activists in Israel have been facing hostile counter-demonstrations from those in their society who have moved in a different direction.[122]

There are many reasons why I shouldn't make any observation on Israeli society, beginning with the fact that I know very little about it. But when a nation is continually engaging in the most horrific and massive crimes, using weapons and criminal immunity provided by my nation, and protests are raging around the earth, when the news is packed with information, analysis, propaganda,

---

122        http://www.amazon.com/Goliath-Life-Loathing-Greater-Israel/dp/1568586345

and poisonous pontificating, when the peace meetings I go to discuss the matter at great length, when the guests on my radio show and the books I read and Israelis I meet begin to inform me a little, and when the problem appears enormous and glaring but guarded by a protection of intimidation and obedience, then I think tossing an idea into the mix may be justified, despite being dramatically more impolite by U.S. standards than criticizing Harry Truman or LBJ.

Israel is a nation where children[123] grow up[124] learning about[125] the holocaust[126], marking the holocaust with holidays, planning trips to Germany to visit the camps. U.S. children dress up as Pilgrims and Indians, but nobody tells them that the Pilgrims ended up murdering the Indians, or what it was like to be an Indian child preparing to be murdered or watching your loved ones murdered. The U.S. origin story is, appropriately enough, one of feasting, not one of genocide. I'm speaking of how it is told, of course, rather than what actually happened.

To criticize the Israeli government for its wars, even though I also criticize every other government for their wars, generates inevitable and truly stupid accusations of anti-Semitism. But criticizing the teaching of the holocaust, which I've never done before, seems likely to go beyond that into an area of accusations of holocaust denial. I have, of course, been there. I've been accused of denying

123        http://www.tikkun.org/tikkundaily/2014/04/23/the-crisis-in-israels-holocaust-education/
124        http://www.myjewishlearning.com/holidays/Jewish_Holidays/Modern_Holidays/Yom_Hashoah/Teaching_the_Holocaust.shtml
125 http://www.haaretz.com/jewish-world/jewish-world-features/1.587655
126        http://www.theguardian.com/world/2013/nov/10/israel-plans-holocaust-lessons-for-five-year-olds

the holocaust for opposing bombing Iran because someone in Iran supposedly denied the holocaust. I've been accused of denying the holocaust for criticizing World War II, even though the actions I express a wish had been taken include opposing fascism in its early years instead of waiting, defunding the Nazis rather than supporting them as preferable to Communists, and finding homes for Jewish refugees when they needed them, rather than turning them away. But this is all ridiculously dumb: denying the holocaust and flooding society with its ubiquitous presence are not the only two choices, any more than leveling people's homes in Gaza and "doing nothing" are the only two choices.

To say that people are behaving like Nazis is not to say that they are exactly identical to Nazis, any more than to say that your child's piano playing is exactly like Mozart. Without question, Nazism is a source of imitation for rightwingers around the world, including in Israel. Might a lesser focus on its significance be helpful? Would a greater emphasis on peace studies do any harm?

## Guess Who Cheers When Cease-Fires Collapse

Among those who cheer when a cease-fire ends and killing resumes are those who want more Palestinians slaughtered as a form of mass punishment for fictional offenses. Also among those cheering are certain mainstream U.S. newspaper columnists. In fact, at least one person is clearly in both of the above categories.

My local newspaper in Charlottesville, Va., printed a column on Friday from Thomas Sowell, distributed by Creators Syndicate but actually written for the right-wing Jewish World Review. Sowell writes:

> "It is understandable that today many people in many lands just want the fighting between the Israelis and the Palestinians to stop. Calls for a cease-fire are ringing out from the United Nations and from Washington, as well as from ordinary people in many places around the world. According to the New York Times, Secretary of State John Kerry is hoping for a cease-fire to 'open the door to Israeli and Palestinian negotiations for a long-term solution.' President Obama has urged Israeli Prime Minister Benjamin Netanyahu to have an 'immediate, unconditional humanitarian cease-fire'—again, with the idea of pursuing some long-lasting agreement."

Here is where Sowell might logically object to Washington shipping Israel more weaponry in the midst of proposing cease-fires and mumbling quietly about the inappropriateness of particular bits of the mass-murder underway. John Kerry doesn't hope for a long-term solution any more than he knew Syria used chemical weapons or Putin shot down a plane or Iraq deserved to be destroyed before it didn't but after it did. John Kerry knows the U.S. provides the weaponry and the criminal immunity to a nation intent on completing the process of eliminating its native peoples, as Kerry's own nation effectively did long ago. There's no solution possible in that context other than a Final Solution for Palestinians. But this is not what Sowell goes on to say.

*"If this was the first outbreak of violence between the Palestinians and the Israelis, such hopes might make sense. But where have the U.N., Kerry and Obama been during all these decades of endlessly repeated Middle East carnage?"*

Well, the same place all of their Republican and Democratic predecessors have been, supporting endless armaments for Israel and most of its neighbors, and vetoing any U.N. resolutions that would impose any consequences for Israel's occupation, blockade, and Apartheid repression on the basis of religion and race.

*"The Middle East must lead the world in cease-fires. If cease-fires were the road to peace, the Middle East would easily be the most peaceful place on the planet."*

Stop for a moment and appreciate the unfathomable stupidity of that remark. One might as well say the Middle East must lead the world in U.S. weapons imports or the Middle East must lead the world in wars. If these were paths to peace, the Middle East would easily be the most peaceful place on the planet. One might also just as easily say the Middle East must lead the world in the brevity of its cease-fires, with cease-fires elsewhere lasting longer, and with as many broken agreements lying in the sand of the Middle East as anywhere since the last big batch of promises made to Native Americans. One might even just as easily say the Middle East must lead the world in resumptions of fighting, rather than in halts to fighting. But that's not where Sowell is headed. He's out to reverse Benjamin Franklin's notion that there has never been a good war or a bad peace.

> "'Cease-fire' and 'negotiations' are magic words to 'the international community.' But just what do cease-fires actually accomplish? In the short run, they save some lives. But in the long run they cost far more lives, by lowering the cost of aggression."

Here it comes. Just as the Jewish World Review wants to make poor people "self-sufficient" by denying them any assistance, Sowell wants to teach the people of Palestine a lesson for their own good. Of course people dispossessed of their land, made refugees, entrapped and blockaded, and targeted with missiles that level their homes and explode in their schools and hospitals and shelters are unusual suspects to accuse of aggression. And for those who shoot rockets, so ineffectively and counter-productively, into Israel, the lesson Sowell wants to teach through mass slaughter is demonstrably not taught. Everyone in Gaza will tell you that Israeli violence increases support for Palestinian violence. Not every Palestinian understands that the reverse is also true, that the rockets fuel Israeli attacks, but that hardly justifies their murder or creates a lesson where Sowell imagines Israeli missiles teaching one.

> "At one time, launching a military attack on another nation risked not only retaliation but annihilation. When Carthage attacked Rome, that was the end of Carthage."

Ah, the good old days, when any colony or challenger that stepped out of line could be wiped out, starved out, and cleansed from the earth.

*"But when Hamas or some other terrorist group launches an attack on Israel, they know in advance that whatever Israel does in response will be limited by calls for a cease-fire, backed by political and economic pressures from the United States."*

The political pressure of Kerry groveling before Netanyahu? Of Susan Rice explaining to the world that Kerry never meant to negotiate and has always been 100% in Israel's camp? Of Obama joining Sowell in blaming the victims? The economic pressure of the free weapons continuing to flow from the U.S. to Israel? What sort of fantasy is this? One possibility is that it's a fantasy of racism or culturalism. Americans are rational beings in this fantasy. It would only make sense to apply obvious points of pressure for a cease-fire once you've proposed one. Arming the Middle East for peace would be insanity. So, Sowell perhaps fantasizes that sanity and rationality prevail. Except in places like Palestine or Iran:

*"Those who say that we can contain a nuclear Iran, as we contained a nuclear Soviet Union, are acting as if they are discussing abstract people in an abstract world. Whatever the Soviets were, they were not suicidal fanatics, ready to see their own cities destroyed in order to destroy ours. . . . Even if the Israelis were all saints—and sainthood is not common in any branch of the human race—the cold fact is that they are far more advanced than their neighbors, and groups that cannot tolerate even subordinate Christian minorities can hardly be expected to tolerate an independent, and more advanced, Jewish state that is a daily rebuke to their egos."*

Since when does Iran not tolerate minorities? Since when is it populated by 76 million suicidal fanatics?

You see, not only do the Gazans want to die, in the view of Sowell and so many others we've been hearing from via our so-called public airwaves, because it makes good footage, because they have a culture of martyrdom—you've heard all the explanations for Gazans stubbornly remaining in their homes and hospitals rather than swimming to Cyprus as normal people would do—but the source of Gazans' irrational aggression against the benevolent power that stole their land and starves their children and bans the importation of books is—wait for it—jealousy. It's wounded egos. Just as poor Americans are jealous of the success of those with the wisdom and fortitude to be born into the families of billionaires, so Palestinians resent the superiority, the Ubermenschness of the people who have been clever enough to get born into Pentagon subsidies.

As a contrasting view of the world to Sowell's allow me to offer this new Willie Nelson video: http://youtu.be/MezGqmMCrwo

## If a Genocide Falls in the Forest

There's a wide and mysterious chasm between the stated intentions of the Israeli government as depicted by the U.S. media and what the Israeli government has been doing in Gaza, even as recounted in the U.S. media.

With the morgues full, Gazans are packing freezers with their dead children. Meanwhile, the worst images to be found in Israel depict fear, not death and suffering. Why the contrast? If the Israeli intent is defensive, why are 97% of the deaths Gazan, not Israeli? If the targets are fighters, why are whole families being slaughtered and their houses leveled? Why are schools and hospitals and children playing on the beach targeted? Why target water and electricity if the goal is not to attack an entire population?

The mystery melts away if you look at the stated intentions of the Israeli government as *not* depicted by the U.S. media but readily available in Israeli media and online.

On August 1st, the Deputy Speaker of Israel's Parliament posted on his FaceBook page a plan[127] for the complete destruction of the people of Gaza using concentration camps. He had laid out a somewhat similar plan in a July 15th column[128].

Another member of the Israeli Parliament, Ayelet Shaked, called for[129] genocide in Gaza at the start of the current war, writing: "Behind every terrorist stand dozens of men and women, without whom he could not engage in terrorism. They are all enemy combatants, and their blood shall be on all their heads. Now this also includes the mothers of the martyrs, who send them to hell with flowers and kisses. They should follow their sons, nothing would be more just. They should go, as should the physical homes

127          http://electronicintifada.net/blogs/ali-abunimah/concentrate-and-exterminate-israel-parliament-deputy-speakers-gaza-genocide-plan
128          http://www.israelnationalnews.com/Articles/Article.aspx/15326#.U-GoGUjc3YM
129          http://electronicintifada.net/blogs/ali-abunimah/israeli-lawmakers-call-genocide-palestinians-gets-thousands-facebook-likes

in which they raised the snakes. Otherwise, more little snakes will be raised there."

Taking a slightly different approach, Middle East scholar Dr. Mordechai Kedar of Bar-Ilan University has been widely quoted[130] in Israeli media saying, "The only thing that can deter [Gazans] is the knowledge that their sister or their mother will be raped."

The *Times of Israel* published a column[131] on August 1st, and later unpublished it, with the headline "When Genocide Is Permissible." The answer turned out to be: now.

On August 5th, Giora Eiland, former head of Israel's National Security Council, published a column[132] with the headline "In Gaza, There Is No Such Thing as 'Innocent Civilians.'" Eiland wrote: "We should have declared war against the state of Gaza (rather than against the Hamas organization). . . . [T]he right thing to do is to shut down the crossings, prevent the entry of any goods, including food, and definitely prevent the supply of gas and electricity."

It's all part of putting Gaza "on a diet," in the grotesque wording[133] of an advisor to a former Israeli Prime Minister.

If it were common among members of the Iranian or Russian government to speak in favor of genocide, you'd better believe the U.S. media would notice. Why does this phenomenon go unremarked in the case of Israel? Noticing it is bound to get you

130 http://www.haaretz.com/news/national/.premium-1.606542
131 https://archive.today/RPf3M
132 http://www.ynetnews.com/articles/0,7340,L-4554583,00.html
133 http://electronicintifada.net/content/israels-starvation-diet-gaza/11810

called an anti-Semite, but that's hardly a concern worthy of notice while children are being killed by the hundreds.

Another explanation is U.S. complicity. The weapons Israel is using are given to it, free-of-charge, by the U.S. government, which also leads efforts to provide Israel immunity for its crimes. Check out this revealing map[134] of which nations recognize the nation of Palestine.

A third explanation is that looking too closely at what Israel's doing could lead to someone looking closely at what the U.S. has done and is doing. Roughly 97% of the deaths in the 2003-2011 war on Iraq were Iraqi. Things U.S. soldiers and military leaders said about Iraqis were shameful and genocidal.

War is the biggest U.S. investment, and contemporary war is almost always a one-sided slaughter of civilians. If seeing the horror of it in Israeli actions allow us to begin seeing the same in U.S. actions, an important step will have been taken toward war's elimination.

> Yes, how many times can a man turn his head
> Pretending he just doesn't see?
> The answer my friend is blowin' in the wind
> The answer is blowin' in the wind.

---

134    http://upload.wikimedia.org/wikipedia/commons/thumb/0/08/Palestine_recognition_only.svg/1376px-Palestine_recognition_only.svg.png

# Israeli Chooses "Honorable Life" Over Joining Military

Danielle Yaor is 19, Israeli, and refusing to take part in the Israeli military. She is one of 150 who have committed themselves, thus far, to this position[135]:

> We, citizens of the state of Israel, are designated for army service. We appeal to the readers of this letter to set aside what has always been taken for granted and to reconsider the implications of military service.

> We, the undersigned, intend to refuse to serve in the army and the main reason for this refusal is our opposition to the military occupation of Palestinian territories. Palestinians in the occupied territories live under Israeli rule though they did not choose to do so, and have no legal recourse to influence this regime or its decision-making processes. This is neither egalitarian nor just. In these territories, human rights are violated, and acts defined under international law as war-crimes are perpetuated on a daily basis. These include assassinations (extrajudicial killings), the construction of settlements on occupied lands, administrative detentions, torture, collective punishment and the unequal allocation of resources such as electricity and water. Any form of military service reinforces this status quo, and, therefore, in accordance with our conscience, we cannot take part in a system that perpetrates the above-mentioned acts.

---

135 https://www.facebook.com/refusingIDF

*The problem with the army does not begin or end with the damage it inflicts on Palestinian society. It infiltrates everyday life in Israeli society too: it shapes the educational system, our workforce opportunities, while fostering racism, violence and ethnic, national and gender-based discrimination.*

*We refuse to aid the military system in promoting and perpetuating male dominance. In our opinion, the army encourages a violent and militaristic masculine ideal whereby 'might is right'. This ideal is detrimental to everyone, especially those who do not fit it. Furthermore, we oppose the oppressive, discriminatory, and heavily gendered power structures within the army itself.*

*We refuse to forsake our principles as a condition to being accepted in our society. We have thought about our refusal deeply and we stand by our decisions.*

*We appeal to our peers, to those currently serving in the army and/or reserve duty, and to the Israeli public at large, to reconsider their stance on the occupation, the army, and the role of the military in civil society. We believe in the power and ability of civilians to change reality for the better by creating a more fair and just society. Our refusal expresses this belief.*

Only a few of the 150 or so resisters are in prison. Danielle says that going to prison helps to make a statement. In fact, here's[136]

136 http://edition.cnn.com/2014/08/18/world/meast/israel-refusers/

one of her fellow refuseniks on CNN because he went to prison. But going to prison is essentially optional, Danielle says, because the military (IDF) has to pay 250 Shekels a day ($66, cheap by U.S. standards) to keep someone in prison and has little interest in doing so. Instead, many claim mental illness, says Yaor, with the military well-aware that what they're really claiming is an unwillingness to be part of the military. The IDF gives men more trouble than women, she says, and mostly uses men in the occupation of Gaza. To go to prison, you need a supportive family, and Danielle says her own family does not support her decision to refuse.

Why refuse something your family and society expect of you? Danielle Yaor says that most Israelis do not know about the suffering of Palestinians. She knows and chooses not to be a part of it. "I have to refuse to take part in the war crimes that my country does," she says. "Israel has become a very fascist country that doesn't accept others. Since I was young we've been trained to be these masculine soldiers who solve problems by violence. I want to use peace to make the world better."

Yaor is touring the United States[137], speaking at events together with a Palestinian. She describes the events thus far as "amazing" and says that people "are very supportive." Stopping the hatred and violence is "everyone's responsibility," she says — "all the people of the world."

In November she'll be back in Israel, speaking and demonstrating. With what goal?

---

137 http://www.tolef.org/

One state, not two. "There's not enough space anymore for two states. There can be one state of Israel-Palestine, based on peace and love and people living together." How can we get there?

As people become aware of Palestinians' suffering, says Danielle, they should support BDS (boycotts, divestments, and sanctions). The U.S. government should end its financial support for Israel and its occupation.

Since the latest attacks on Gaza, Israel has moved further to the right, she says, and it has become harder to "encourage youth not to be part of the brainwashing that is part of the education system." The letter above was published "everywhere possible" and was the first many had ever heard that there was a choice available other than the military.

> *"We want the occupation to end," says Danielle Yaor, "so that we can all live an honorable life in which all of our rights will be respected."*

Learn more[138].

---

138 https://www.facebook.com/refusingIDF

# *Iraq*

## *A Brief History of Iraq for Westerners*

Iraq was saved from ignorant subhuman barbarism by a gentlewoman named Gertrude[139] at the time that the civilized nations of the world were, in a quite advanced and sophisticated manner, slaughtering their young men in a project now called the First World War.

Because the Arabs were too backward to be allowed to govern themselves, or even to contemplate creating a world war, and because tribes and ethnicities and religions never really garner much loyalty or support that can't be wiped away with a good cup of tea or a few clouds of poison gas, and because the French were too dumb to know where the oil was, it became necessary for the British to install an Iraqi leader who wasn't Iraqi, through a democratic election with one candidate running.

The great Winston Churchill explained the governance of Iraq and the new civilizing technique of bombing civilians thusly: "I am strongly in favor of using poison gas against uncivilized tribes." Others failed to see the wisdom, and the Royal Air Force used[140] *non-chemical* "terror bombing, night bombing, heavy bombers, [and] delayed action bombs (particularly lethal against children)" to police disobedient Iraqis. Only by developing these techniques on Iraqis were the world's civilizers prepared to use them on Nazis

139    http://www.thedailybeast.com/articles/2014/06/17/gertrude-of-arabia-the-woman-who-invented-iraq.html

140 http://www.theguardian.com/world/2003/apr/19/iraq.arts

when the time came to level German cities in the name of defeating Nazis, which of course also places the rest of this paper beyond the reach of moral criticism.

Iraqis, from the formation of Iraq by Gertrude to this day, were never quite able to create a democracy for the CIA to overthrow as in neighboring Iran. But the idea that Iraqis have been violent or resistant to control because of lack of representation misses the central fact that people in the Middle East enjoy killing each other over sectarian differences. Of course it's hard to find evidence of significant sectarian fighting in Iraq prior to 2003 and some say[141] there wasn't any. There was violent looting of Jewish neighborhoods in 1941, but the British government keeps all information on that event secret. There was bombing of synagogues in Baghdad in 1950-51 but that turned out to have been done by Zionists trying to convince Jews to come to Israel. And "until the 1970s nearly all Iraq's political organisations were secular, attracting people from all religions and none." But what was simmering just below the surface waiting to burst out at the slightest scratching?

Think how little it took[142]. Supporting and arming a brutal dictator in Saddam Hussein and his catastrophic war against Iran, then bombing Iraq and imposing the most murderous sanctions in history, and then newly bombing Iraq and occupying it for 8 years while arming and training death squads and torturers and imposing sectarian segregation, creating 5 million refugees, and killing a half-million to a million-and-a-half people, while

141    http://stopwar.org.uk/news/the-sectarian-myth-of-iraq-peddled-by-the-west-is-a-recipe-for-endless-war#.U6Gagajc3YN
142 http://warisacrime.org/iraq

devastating the nation's infrastructure, and then imposing a puppet government loyal to one sect and one neighboring nation. That, plus arming the new government for vicious attacks on its own people, while arming mad killers in neighboring Syria, some of whom want to combine parts of Syria and Iraq: that was *all* it took, and suddenly, out of nowhere, ignorant Arabs are killing each other, just out of pure irrationality, just like in Palestine.

During the 8 years of U.S.-led occupation people mistook purely irrational violence that had been bubbling under the surface for centuries for resistance to the occupiers, and now some imagine that part of the violence against the puppet government is motivated by grievances against that government. But this misses the fundamental truths here, which are:

1. Shock and Awe was meant to put people at ease and make them comfortable.

2. The plan to rid Iraq of weapons it was about to use against those of us who matter was successful beyond the wildest expectations, working retroactively by a decade.

3. Our great leaders, Bush and Cheney, meant well in giving Iraqis freedom even if they weren't ready for it.

4. The election of Maliki was even more legitimate than the election of Faisal.

5. When the Bush-Maliki treaty ended the U.S. military presence

in Iraq, that was thanks to President Obama who is way smarter than Bush but couldn't get Iraq to let U.S. troops stay with immunity for crimes—crimes of course being necessary for policing, just ask Winnie.

6. When Iraq remained a disaster, that was President Obama's fault for focusing too much on murdering people in Afghanistan and Pakistan and Yemen, and never Iraq—as if we just don't care about Iraq any more.

7. The U.S. weapons being seized and used against the U.S. puppet government in Iraq are no match for the vast stockpiles of weapons of mass destruction that we can and must ship into Iraq now to be seized and redirected later on down the road.

8. The few people getting rich from all of this misery mean well.

## *The Democratic Push to Bomb Iraq Again*

People forget the extent to which Democrats, who controlled the U.S. Senate at the time, pushed for and supported the 2003 attack on Iraq. Remember them or not, theeeeeeeeey're back!

The Center for American Progress, the head of whose "action fund," former Democratic Congressman from Virginia's Fifth District Tom Perriello, slipped through the revolving door into a

State Department job in February, is now pushing for "principled"[143] bombings of Iraq.

Principled or not, the Center for American Progress is funded by[144] Lockheed Martin and other huge war profiteers. C.A.P. has just put out a report[145] recommending that air strikes be considered. For that to happen, many other things need to not be considered:

1. The views of the U.S. public, which opposes more wars and some of whom here in the fifth district of Virginia fantasized they'd elected an antiwar candidate in Perriello several years back.

2. The views of the Iraqi public, who have been nonviolently and violently protesting an illegitimate government installed by the U.S.-led occupation.

3. The rule of law, which bans wars (under both the U.N. Charter and the Kellogg-Briand Pact) even in places where the U.S. has recently fought wars in blatant violation of the law without any legal consequences.

4. The U.S. Constitution, which required that wars be authorized by Congress even before Article VI came to encompass the aforementioned treaties.

5. The 100-year history of foreign military interference consistently making things worse in Iraq.

143  http://www.thedailybeast.com/articles/2014/06/17/obama-s-favorite-think-tank-we-should-prepare-to-bomb-iraq.html
144       http://www.thenation.com/article/174437/secret-donors-behind-center-american-progress-and-other-think-tanks-updated-524
145  http://www.scribd.com/doc/230080299/IraqISISBrief-1

6. The 11-year history of foreign military interference making things dramatically worse in Iraq to the point where it is no exaggeration to say that the nation has been destroyed.[146]

7. The record suicide rate among U.S. war veterans, many of whom are realizing the role they played in destroying Iraq.

8. The liberties we keep losing as long as the wars for "freedom" role on.

9. The environmental destruction of our largest consumer of petroleum and greatest poisoner of land masses, the U.S. military.

10. The financial cost of trillion-dollar wars when tens of billions in reparations and actual aid could make a world of difference.

11. The history of small numbers of "advisors" in Vietnam and many other wars mushrooming into devastating occupations and millions of murders.

12. The need people have to imagine that Democrats are fundamentally different from Republicans. Think of the damage being done to that already tenuous pretense. Spare those tender souls any troubled thoughts if you can't spare the lives of Iraqis for their own sake.

---

146 http://warisacrime.org/iraq

# *Back in Iraq, Jack!*

President Obama may want us to sympathize[147] with patriotic torturers, he may turn on[148] whistleblowers like a flesh-eating zombie, he may have lost[149] all ability to think an authentic thought, but I will say this for him: He knows how to mark the 50th anniversary of the Gulf of Tonkin fraud like a champion.

It's back in Iraq, Jack! Yackety yack! Obama says the United States has fired missiles and dropped food in Iraq—enough food to feed 8,000, enough missiles to kill an unknown number (presumably 7,500 or fewer keeps this a "humanitarian" effort). The White House told reporters on a phone call[150] following the President's Thursday night speech that it is expediting weapons to Iraq, producing Hellfire missiles and ammunition around the clock, and shipping those off to a nation where Obama swears there is no military solution and only reconciliation can help. Hellfire missiles are famous for helping people reconcile.

Obama went straight into laying out his excuses for this latest war, before speaking against war and in favor of everything he invests no energy in. First, the illegitimate government of Iraq asked him to do it. Second, ISIS is to blame for the hell that the United States created in Iraq. Third, there are still lots of places in the world that Obama has not yet bombed. Oh, and this is not

147    http://www.whitehouse.gov/the-press-office/2014/08/01/press-conference-president

148    http://www.theguardian.com/commentisfree/2013/aug/06/obama-abuse-espionage-act-mccarthyism

149    http://news.yahoo.com/russia-says-confused-obamas-accusations-over-malaysian-jet-103734988.html

150 https://twitter.com/JasonLeopold

really a war but just protection of U.S. personnel, combined with a rescue mission for victims of a possible massacre on a scale we all need to try to understand.

Wow! We need to understand the scale of killing in Iraq? This is the United States you're talking to, the people who paid for the slaughter of 0.5 to 1.5 million Iraqis this decade. Either we're experts on the scale of mass killings or we're hopelessly incapable of understanding such matters.

Completing the deja vu all over again Thursday evening, the substitute host of the Rachel Maddow Show seemed eager for a new war on Iraq, all of his colleagues approved of anything Obama said, and I heard "Will troops be sent?" asked by several "journalists," but never heard a single one ask "Will families be killed?"

Pro-war veteran Democratic congressman elected by war opponents Patrick Murphy cheered for Obama supposedly drawing a red line for war. Murphy spoke of Congress without seeming aware that less than two weeks ago the House voted to deny the President any new war on Iraq. There are some 199 members of the House who may be having a hard time remembering that right now.

Pro-war veteran Paul Rieckhoff added that any new veterans created would be heroes, and—given what a "mess" Iraq is now—Rieckhoff advocated "looking forward." The past has such an extreme antiwar bias.

Rounding out the reunion of predictable pro-war platitudes and prevarications, Nancy Pelosi immediately quoted the bits of Obama's speech that suggested he was against the war he was starting. Can Friedman Units and benchmarks be far behind?

Obama promises no combat troops will be sent back to Iraq. No doubt. Instead it'll be planes, drones, helicopters, and "non-combat" troops. "America is coming to help" finally just sounded as evil as Reagan meant it to, but it was in Obama's voice. The ironies exploded like Iraqi houses on Thursday. While the United States locks Honduran refugee children in cages, it proposes to bomb Iraq for refugees. While Gaza starves and Detroit lacks water, Obama bombs Iraq to stop people from starving. While the U.S. ships weapons to Israel to commit genocide, and to Syria for allies of ISIS, it is rushing more weapons into Iraq to supposedly prevent genocide on a mountaintop—also to add to the weapons supplies[151] already looted by ISIS.

Of course, it's also for "U.S. interests," but if that means U.S. people, why not pull them out? If it means something else, why not admit as much in the light of day and let the argument die of shame?

Let me add a word to the U.N. Office for the Coordination of Humanitarian Affairs spokesman David Swanson, who is not me and whom I do not know: Please do keep pushing for actual humanitarian aid. But if you spoke against the missiles that are coming with the food, the reporters left that bit out. You have to

151          http://act.rootsaction.org/p/dia/action3/common/public/?action_
KEY=10169

fit it into the same sentence with the food and water if you want it quoted. I hope there is an internal U.N. lobby for adoption by the U.N. of the U.N. Charter, and if there is I wish it all the luck in the world.

# Top Nine Reasons to Stop Bombing Iraq

**1. It's not a rescue mission.** The U.S. personnel could be evacuated without the 500-pound bombs. The persecuted minorities could be supplied, moved, or their enemy dissuaded, or all three, without the 500-pound bombs or the hundreds of "advisors" (trained and armed to kill, and never instructed in how to give advice—Have you ever tried taking urgent advice from 430 people?). The boy who cried rescue mission should not be allowed to get away with it after the documented deception in Libya where a fictional threat to civilians was used to launch an all-out aggressive attack that has left that nation in ruins. Not to mention the false claims about Syrian chemical weapons and the false claim that missiles were the only option left for Syria—the latter claims being exposed when the former weren't believed, the missiles didn't launch, and less violent but perfectly obvious alternative courses of action were recognized. If the U.S. government were driven by a desire to rescue the innocent, why would it be arming Israel, Egypt, Jordan, Bahrain? The U.S. government destroyed the nation of Iraq between 2003 and 2011, with results including the near elimination of various minority groups. If preventing genocide were a dominant U.S. interest, it could have halted its participation in and aggravation of that war at any time, a war in which 97% of the dead were on one side, just as in Gaza this month—the distinction between war and genocide being one of perspective, not proportions. Or, of course, the U.S. could have left well alone. Ever since President Carter declared that the U.S. would kill for Iraqi oil, each of his successors has believed that course of action justified, and each has made matters significantly worse.

**2. It's going to make things worse, again.** This bombing will aggravate the Sunni-Shia divide, increase support for ISIS, and create a lasting legacy of hostility and violence. President Obama says there is no military solution, only reconciliation. But bombs don't reconcile. They harden hearts and breed murderers. Numerous top U.S. officials admit that much of what the U.S. military does generates more enemies than it kills. When you continue down a path that is counterproductive on its own terms, the honesty of those terms has to be doubted. If this war is not for peace, is it perhaps—like every other war we've seen the U.S. wage in the area—for resources, profits, domination, and sadism? The leader of ISIS learned his hatred in a U.S. prison in Iraq. U.S. media report that fact as if it is just part of the standard portrait of a new Enemy #1, but the irony is not mere coincidence. Violence is created. It doesn't arise out of irrational and inscrutable foreignness. It is planted by those great gardeners in the sky: planes, drones, and helicopters. A bombing campaign justified as protecting people actually endangers them, and those around them, and many others, including those of us living in the imperial Homeland.

**3. Bombs kill.** Big bombs kill a lot of people. Massive bombing campaigns slaughter huge numbers of people, including those fighting in the hell the U.S. helped to create, and including those not fighting—men, women, children, grandparents, infants. Defenders of the bombing know this, but ignore it, and make no effort to calculate whether more people are supposedly being saved than are being killed. This indifference exposes the humanitarian pretensions of the operation. If some humans are of no value to you, humanitarianism is not what's driving your decisions. The U.S. war on Iraq '03-'11 killed a half million to a million-and-a-half Iraqis and 4,000 Americans. A war that puts fewer Americans on the ground and uses more planes and drones is thought of as involving less death only if our concern is narrowly limited to U.S. deaths. From the vantage point of the ground, an air war is the deadliest form of war there is.

**4. There are other options.** The choice between bombing and doing nothing is as false now as it was in September. If you can drop food on some people, why can't you drop food on everyone? It would cost a tiny fraction of dropping bombs on them. It would confuse the hell out of them, too—like Robin Williams' version of God high on pot and inventing the platypus. Of course, I now sound crazy because I'm talking about people who've been demonized (and personified in a killer straight out of a U.S. prison). It's not as if these are human beings with whom you can lament the death of Robin Williams. They're not like you and me. Etc. Yadda. Yadda. But in fact ISIS fighters were sharing their appreciation of Williams on Twitter on Tuesday. The United States could talk about other matters with ISIS as well, including a ceasefire, including a unilateral commitment to cease arming the Iraqi government even while trying to organize its ouster, including an offer to provide real humanitarian aid with no nasty strings attached, but with encouragement of civil liberties and democratic decision making. It's amazing how long minority ethnic groups in Iraq survived and thrived prior to the U.S. bringing democracy, and prior to the U.S. existing. The U.S. could do some good but must first do no harm.

**5. There are now enough weapons already there to practically justify one of Colin Powell's slides retroactively.** The U.S. accounts for 79% of foreign weapons transfers to Western Asia (the Middle East). The war on Libya had identical U.S. weapons on both sides. ISIS almost certainly has weapons supplied by the U.S. in Syria, and certainly has weapons taken from Iraq. So, what is the U.S. doing? It's rushing more weapons to Iraq as fast as possible. Americans like to think of the Middle East as backward and violent, but the tools of the violence trade are manufactured in the United States. Yes, the United States does still manufacture something, it's just not something that serves any useful purpose or about which most of us can manage to feel very proud. Weapons making also wastes money rather than creating it, because unaccountable profits are the single biggest product manufactured.

**6. This is going to cost a fortune.** Bombing Iraq is depicted as a measure of great restraint and forbearance. Meanwhile building schools and hospitals and green energy infrastructure in Iraq would be viewed as madness if anyone dared propose it. But the latter would cost a lot less money—a consideration that is usually a top priority in U.S. politics whenever killing large numbers of people is not involved. The world spend $2 trillion and the U.S.

$1 trillion (half the total) on war and war preparations every year. Three percent of U.S. military spending could end starvation on earth. The wonders that could be done with a fraction of military money are almost unimaginable and include actual defense against the actual danger of climate change.

**7. Bombs are environmental disasters.** If someone photographs a big oil fire, some will give a thought to the environmental damage. But a bombing campaign is, rather than an environmental accident, an intentional environmental catastrophe. The poisoned ground and water, and the disease epidemics, will reach the United States primarily through moral regret, depression, and suicide.

**8. There go our civil liberties.** Discussions of torture, imprisonment, assassination, surveillance, and denial of fair trials are severely damaged by wartime postures. After all, war is for "freedom," and who wouldn't be willing to surrender all of their freedoms for that?

**9. War is illegal.** It doesn't matter if the illegitimate government that you're trying to dump invited you to bomb its country. How can anyone take that seriously, while the U.S. installed that government and has armed it for years, as it has attacked its people? War is illegal under the Kellogg Briand Pact and the United Nations Charter, and pretending otherwise endangers the world. Domestically, under U.S. law, the president cannot launch a war. While the Senate has been silent, the U.S. House voted two weeks ago to ban any new presidential war on Iraq. Offering Congress a slap in the face, Obama waited for it to go on break, and then attacked Iraq.

# *What to Do About ISIS*

John Horgan asked me for a paragraph on what to do about ISIS. I sent him this:

I'd say start by recognizing where ISIS came from. The U.S. and its junior partners destroyed Iraq, left a sectarian division, poverty, desperation, and an illegitimate government in Baghdad that did not represent Sunnis or other groups. Then the U.S. armed and trained ISIS and allied groups in Syria, while continuing to prop up the Baghdad government, providing Hellfire missiles with which to attack Iraqis in Fallujah and elsewhere. ISIS has religious adherents but also opportunistic supporters who see it as the force resisting an unwanted rule from Baghdad and who increasingly see it as resisting the United States. It is in possession of U.S. weaponry provided directly to it in Syria and seized from the Iraqi government. At last count by the U.S. government, 79% of weapons transferred to Middle Eastern governments come from the United States, not counting transfers to groups like ISIS, and not counting weapons in the possession of the United States. So, the first thing to do differently going forward: stop bombing nations into ruins, and stop shipping weapons into the area you've left in chaos. Libya is of course another example of the disasters that U.S. wars leave behind them—a war, by the way, with U.S. weapons used on both sides, and a war launched on the pretext of a claim well documented to have been false that Gadaffi was threatening to massacre civilians. So, here's the next thing to do: be very skeptical of humanitarian claims. The U.S. bombing around Erbil to protect Kurdish and U.S. oil interests was initially justified as bombing to protect people on a mountain. But most of those people on the mountain were in no need of rescue, and that justification has now been set aside, just as Benghazi was. Recall also that Obama was forced to withdraw U.S. troops from Iraq when he couldn't get the Iraqi government to give them immunity for crimes they commit. He has now obtained that immunity and back in they go, the crimes preceding them in the form of 500 pound bombs. While trying to rescue hostages and discovering an empty house, and racing to a mountain to save 30,000 people but finding 3,000 and most of those not wanting to leave, the U.S. claims to know exactly whom the 500-pound bombs are killing. But whoever they are killing, they are generating more enemies, and they are building support for ISIS, not diminishing it. So, now the U.S. finds itself on the opposite side of the war in Syria, so what does it do? Flip sides! Now the great moral imperative is not to bomb Assad but to bomb in defense of Assad, the only consistent point being that "something must be done" and the only conceivable something is to pick some party and bomb it. But why is that the only conceivable thing to be done? I can think of some others:

1. Apologize for brutalizing the leader of ISIS in Abu Ghraib and to every other prisoner victimized under U.S. occupation.

2. Apologize for destroying the nation of Iraq and to every family there.

3. Begin making restitution by delivering aid (not "military aid" but actual aid, food, medicine) to the entire nation of Iraq.

4. Apologize for role in war in Syria.

5. Begin making restitution by delivering actual aid to Syria.

6. Announce a commitment not to provide weapons to Iraq or Syria or Israel or Jordan or Egypt or Bahrain or any other nation anywhere on earth and to begin withdrawing U.S. troops from foreign territories and seas, including Afghanistan. (The U.S. Coast Guard in the Persian Gulf has clearly forgotten where the coast of the U.S. is!)

7. Announce a commitment to invest heavily in solar, wind, and other green energy and to provide the same to democratic representative governments.

8. Begin providing Iran with free wind and solar technologies— at much lower cost of course than what it is costing the U.S. and Israel to threaten Iran over a nonexistent nuclear weapons program.

9. End economic sanctions.

10. Send diplomats to Baghdad and Damascus to negotiate aid and to encourage serious reforms.

11. Send journalists, aid workers, peaceworkers, human shields, and negotiators into crisis zones, understanding that this means risking lives, but fewer lives than further militarization risks.

12. Empower people with agricultural assistance, education,

cameras, and internet access.

13. Launch a communications campaign in the United States to replace military recruitment campaigns, focused on building sympathy and desire to serve as critical aid workers, persuading doctors and engineers to volunteer their time to travel to and visit these areas of crisis.

14. Work through the United Nations on all of this.

15. Sign the United States on to the International Criminal Court and voluntarily propose the prosecution of top U.S. officials of this and the preceding regimes for their crimes.

## *Warning to War Supporters*

I know you mean well. I know you think you've found a bargain that nobody else noticed hidden in a back corner of the used car lot. Let me warn you: it's a clunker. Here, I'll list the defects. You can have your own mechanic check them out:

1. If you want to bomb a country every time an evil group murders people in a gruesome manner, you'll have to bomb a lot of countries including our own. ISIS draws its strength in Iraq from resentment of the Iraqi government, which bombs its own cities[152] using U.S. weapons, and which beheads people[153], albeit in grainier footage

---

152      http://www.democracynow.org/2014/1/9/as_us_rushes_weapons_to_iraq?autostart=true

153 http://www.brussellstribunal.org/article_view.asp?id=1774#.VBBKQeff5rd

with lower production values. Allies in the region, including allies that support ISIS[154], including allies armed by the United States[155] (some of which arms end up in the hands of ISIS[156]), themselves behead[157] people regularly. But is that worse than other types of killing? When President Barack Obama blew up a 16 year old American boy[158] whom nobody had ever accused of so much as jaywalking, and blew up six other kids who were too close to him at the time, do you imagine his head remained on his body?

As with most drone strikes, that boy could have been arrested and questioned. Had he been, though, gruesome death would have remained a possibility. In April, the United States injected[159] a man with chemicals that made him writhe in excruciating pain for 43 minutes and die. Last week in the United States a man facing a similar fate on death row[160] was proven innocent and freed. The prosecutor who had put him there 30 years earlier showed zero remorse[161]. Now I'm not proposing that we bomb North Carolina because I'm angry at that prosecutor. I'm not even angry at that prosecutor. I am suggesting that there are evil killers all over the

154      http://www.independent.co.uk/voices/comment/iraq-crisis-how-saudi-arabia-helped-isis-take-over-the-north-of-the-country-9602312.html

155  http://online.wsj.com/articles/SB10001424052748704621204575488361149625050

156      http://www.theguardian.com/world/2014/sep/08/isis-jihadis-using-arms-troop-carriers-supplied-by-us-saudi-arabia

157      http://www.independent.co.uk/news/world/middle-east/saudi-arabia-executes-19-during-half-of-august-in-disturbing-surge-of-beheadings-9686063.html

158      http://www.nytimes.com/2013/07/18/opinion/the-drone-that-killed-my-grandson.html?_r=0

159      http://www.washingtonpost.com/news/morning-mix/wp/2014/04/30/botched-oklahoma-execution-reignites-death-penalty-debate/

160      http://www.cbsnews.com/news/exonerated-north-carolina-men-freed-from-prison/

161      http://www.nytimes.com/2014/09/08/us/as-2-go-free-joe-freeman-britt-a-dogged-ex-prosecutor-digs-in.html

place, some wearing Western suits and ties, some wearing military uniforms. Bombs, which mostly kill innocent people who had nothing to do with it, won't help.

2. The bombs will mostly kill innocent people who had nothing to do with it, and will only make the crisis worse. Most people who die in wars are civilians[162] by everyone's definition. People still use words like "battlefield" as if wars were waged in a field the way a football game is played. They couldn't play football on our streets and sidewalks because grandparents and baby strollers would end up tackled and crushed. Well, wars are waged on people's streets and sidewalks, even when one side is only present in the sky above in the form of unmanned robot death planes. The slow-moving die first: the very old and the very young. And when anyone dies, according to top U.S. officials[163], more enemies are created in greater numbers. Thus, the operation is counterproductive on its own terms, making us less safe rather than safer. This is why President Obama is always saying "There is no military solution" just before proposing to use the military to seek a solution. When he proposes bombing Iraq for three more years, that number has no basis in military calculation whatsoever. I challenge you to find a general who says otherwise. It is a number almost certainly based on the U.S. election schedule, aimed at convincing us to accept a war without question until a date after the next presidential election. When Obama says[164] he's going to get a good government in place in Iraq this week and then make a speech, he's delusional

162 http://www.worldbeyondwar.org/public-health-experts-identify-militarism-threat/
163 http://warisacrime.org/lesssafe
164 http://www.nbcnews.com/meet-the-press/president-barack-obamas-full-interview-nbcs-chuck-todd-n197616

or enjoying toying with your gullibility, but he's also pointing to the actual problem: a nation destroyed by 24 years of wars and sanctions and lacking a legitimate governing system.

3. Bombing is crazy, and bombing for three years is certifiable. Bombing strengthens[165] ISIS. Three years is longer than most U.S. wars have taken from beginning to end. The U.S. Constitution, which did not foresee a permanent standing army, much less one permanently standing in most other nations on earth, did not permit—and does not permit—creating and funding one for a longer period than two years at a time (Article I. Section 8.). But of course nothing guarantees that the bombing will stop after three years and not go on for thirty more. And nothing guarantees that this war will involve only bombing. Already Obama has sent over 1,100 troops, and is promising[166] to send some number less than 100,000. Read that twice please, slowly. Obama wants[167] Congress to debate his war plans but not vote on them. Why not? Because Congress might be compelled by you and me to vote no, if not on this war then on the next one. Obama wants himself and all future presidents free to launch wars without Congress, exactly what he campaigned[168] for office opposing.

*"The President does not have power under the Constitution to unilaterally authorize a military attack in a situation*

---

165        http://www.democracynow.org/2014/9/3/journalist_indiscriminate_bombing_of_civilians_by

166        http://www.nbcnews.com/meet-the-press/president-barack-obamas-full-interview-nbcs-chuck-todd-n197616

167        http://www.nbcnews.com/meet-the-press/president-barack-obamas-full-interview-nbcs-chuck-todd-n197616

168        http://www.buzzfeed.com/andrewkaczynski/obama-and-biden-have-said-military-action-without-congressio#zloaio

*that does not involve stopping an actual or imminent threat*
*to the nation." —Senator Barack Obama.*

The U.S. "intelligence" agencies, by the way, deem ISIS no threat to the United States. Apart from trashing the Constitution and really the one thing its framers got right, President Obama is trashing the U.N. Charter and the Kellogg Briand Pact, laws that forbid war.

4. The fact that it's Obama doesn't make it OK[169]. A majority of you supported attacking Afghanistan and within a couple of years a majority of you said Afghanistan should not have been attacked. Why not? Not because there weren't evil people in Afghanistan, but because bombing the country made everything worse, not better. You kept telling pollsters it was a bad idea for over another decade, but the war rolled on, and still rolls on. Iraq is a similar story, although you were even faster to change your mind. And the occupation ended when President Bush and Prime Minister Maliki signed an agreement for three more years of that war, and then the three years ran out. At that point, President Obama tried to win approval from the Iraqi government to keep U.S. troops in Iraq longer, but with immunity for any crimes they might commit. Failing at that, Obama withdrew the troops. Having won that concession now, he's sending them back in. Does the fact that it's Obama doing it, rather than Bush, make it OK? Remember the massive protests when Bush proposed a war on Iraq? Obama just put the band back together in Wales, and you're squealing with delight that he visited Stonehenge, or you're busy coloring in your "I'm Ready for Hillary" posters.

169 https://www.youtube.com/watch?v=z-sdO6pwVHQ

The nation of Iraq was utterly destroyed[170] last time. The place is in total chaos: violence, hatred, poverty, illness, desperation, fanaticism. Dumping gasoline on that fire is worse now than before, not better. And now we have NATO toying with a nuclear confrontation with Russia, drone wars generating violence and terrorism in Yemen, Pakistan, and Somalia, the U.S. Navy poking China in the eye with a stick, troops heading into a dozen new parts of Africa—How is starting a war this time better than last time, which you came to view as a mistake by 2004, elected a Congress to end in 2006, thought you were voting against again in 2008, and cheered for the eventual ending of in 2011? Observers have called this[171] the most dangerous moment since World War II. Please don't tell me you trust Obama, believed the fraudulent threat[172] to Benghazi and are now unaware of the disaster[173] he created in Libya, where France has just proposed yet another war to fix the damage of the last war. Please don't tell me you believed the disproven claims of evidence that Assad used chemical weapons or Russia shot down an airplane. This is a government that lies about possible grounds for war and possible outcomes of war, just like its predecessors.

5. The enemy of your enemy is your *other* weapons customer. Public pressure was instrumental[174] last year in halting proposed attacks on Syria, the plans[175] for which involved massive death and

---

170 http://warisacrime.org/iraq
171 http://davidswanson.org/node/4515
172 http://www.worldbeyondwar.org/libya/
173 http://www.nytimes.com/2014/09/02/world/africa/militias-seize-control-of-libyan-capital.html
174 http://www.worldbeyondwar.org/syria/
175 http://www.lrb.co.uk/v36/n08/seymour-m-hersh/the-red-line-and-the-rat-line

destruction. But the White House and CIA went right ahead and armed and trained one side in that war, the ISIS side. ISIS now has weapons provided directly to it and indirectly to it by the United States, including those seized from the Iraqi government. ISIS has troops trained by the United States and "radicalized" (enraged) by the United States in its brutal prisons in Iraq, as well as troops previously in the Iraqi military who were thrown out of work in 2003 by the U.S. occupation. Last year, the evil to be confronted was Assad, at all costs. To your great credit you didn't fall for it. Why not? Not because Assad doesn't do evil things, but because you understood that more war would make things even worse.

Now you're being told that Assad's enemies must be attacked at all cost, and you're falling for it, to your great discredit. With supposed surgical precision the "moderate" beheaders will be spared, in order to blow up only the "extremist" beheaders. Don't believe it. Six months ago the great Satan was Iran. Now you're on Iran's side. Were you aware of that? You're stirring up trouble to the ultimate benefit of only one group: the weapons makers. You think of the Middle East as a violent place, but 80% of the weapons come from the United States. Imagine how much less violent the Middle East could be if it only had 20% of the weapons. We're not talking about stockpiles. These weapons get used.

6. There are other options. Try telling a four-year-old he has only two choices: eat the broccoli or eat the lima beans. He'll throw another 18 alternatives at you in less than a minute, beginning with eating ice cream. Try telling a non-American adult about the current state of disaster in Iraq, and they'll begin by opposing making it

worse, and then start discussing a variety of steps to make it better, from humanitarian aid to diplomacy to disarmament to emergency U.N. police forces, etc. But tell a U.S. adult that Iraq must be bombed or we must do nothing other than sit back and revel in our evil state of ISIS-loving, and your befuddled manipulated subject will shout "Bomb em! Bomb em!" Why?

Last year we were told that we had to bomb Syria or love the poisoning of children with chemical weapons. We did not accept that those were the only two choices. Why not? Because we were thinking straight. We hadn't been frightened into blind stupidity by high-quality videos of beheadings and threats that we might be next. Nobody thinks well when they're scared. That's why the government likes to scare you. That's why you're hearing all this nonsense about ISIS coming to your neighborhood. The more the U.S. keeps bombing people, the more some of those people will want to fight back. Did you ever wonder why nations that spend 2% what the U.S. does on its military feel so much safer than you do? Part of it is the reality that war generates enemies rather than removing them, but mostly it's a culture of cowardice that we're living in. Here are 15 things we could do about ISIS instead of bombing[176].

7. We don't have time for this barbaric insanity. War is sucking our resources[177] and energy and attention away from where they are needed, namely on a massive campaign to protect the climate of the earth. Imagine a proposal to dump untold trillions of dollars and every ounce of energy into that project! Would Congress

176 http://www.worldbeyondwar.org/isis/
177 http://www.worldbeyondwar.org/2trillion/

step aside and allow it? It would benefit[178] even your short-term economic interests, but would you permit it? Would you demand it? Would you join with me in insisting that we stop the wars and save the climate?[179]

UPDATE: *Newsweek* says ISIS is intentionally manipulating you into attacking it.[180]

UPDATE 2: Matt Hoh Says the Beheadings Are Bait.[181]

## James Foley Is Not a War Ad

To the extent that the U.S. public is newly, and probably momentarily, accepting of war—an extent that is wildly exaggerated[182], but still real—it is because of videos of beheadings of James Foley and Steven Sotloff.

When 9-11 victims were used as a justification to kill hundreds of times the number of people killed on 9-11, some of the victims' relatives pushed back[183].

Now James Foley is pushing back from the grave.

---

178 http://www.worldbeyondwar.org/impoverishes/
179 http://www.worldbeyondwar.org/eventsforWBW/
180     http://www.newsweek.com/isiss-enemy-list-10-reasons-islamic-state-doomed-268953
181 http://www.huffingtonpost.com/matthew-hoh/isis-beheadings_b_5766542.html
182     https://www.youtube.com/watch?v=TI9izR6KvOk&list=UUh_HwmAnbMJZ9JbOOJgIA0A
183 http://peacefultomorrows.org/

Here is video[184] of Foley talking about the lies that are needed to launch wars, including the manipulation of people into thinking of foreigners as less than human. Foley's killers may have thought of him as less than human. He may not have viewed them the same way.

The video shows Foley in Chicago helping Haskell Wexler with his film Four Days in Chicago[185]—a film about the last NATO protest before the recent one in Wales. I was there in Chicago for the march and rally against NATO and war. And I've met Wexler who has tried unsuccessfully to find funding for a film version of my book War Is A Lie[186].

Watch Foley in the video discussing the limitations of embedded reporting, the power of veteran resistance, veterans he met at Occupy, the absence of a good justification for the wars, the dehumanization needed before people can be killed, the shallowness of media coverage—watch all of that and then try to imagine James Foley cheering like a weapons-maker or a Congress member for President Obama's announcement of more war. Try to imagine Foley accepting the use of his killing as propaganda for more fighting.

You can't do it. He's not an ad for war any more than the WMDs were a justification for war. His absence as a war justification has been exposed even faster than the absence of the WMDs was.

---

184          http://www.democracynow.org/2014/9/12/james_foley_on_the_dehumanization_of
185 http://www.fourdaysinchicago.com/
186 http://warisalie.org

While ISIS may have purchased Sotloff, if not Foley, from another group, when Foley's mother sought to ransom him, the U.S. government repeatedly threatened her with prosecution. So, instead of Foley's mother paying a relatively small amount and possibly saving her son, ISIS goes on getting its funding from oil sales and supporters in the Gulf and free weapons from, among elsewhere, the United States and its allies. And we're going to collectively spend millions, probably billions, and likely trillions of dollars furthering the cycle of violence that Foley risked his life to expose.

The Coalition of the Willing is already crumbling[187]. What if people in the United States were to watch the video[188] of Foley when he was alive and speaking and laughing, not the one when he was a prop in a piece of propaganda almost certainly aimed at provoking the violence that Obama has just obligingly announced? Foley said he believed his responsibility was to the truth. It didn't set him free. Is it perhaps not too late for the rest of us?

## If ISIS Were Really a Movie

ISIS has created a movie preview[189] for the coming war, a war it eagerly wants Washington to take part in. The White House and

187     http://www.nytimes.com/2014/09/12/world/middleeast/arabs-give-tepid-support-to-us-fight-against-isis.html?hp&action=click&pgtype=Homepage&version=LedeSum&module=first-column-region&region=top-news&WT.nav=top-news

188           http://www.democracynow.org/2014/9/12/james_foley_on_the_dehumanization_of

189     http://www.nytimes.com/2014/09/17/world/middleeast/isis-issues-video-riposte-to-obama.html?hp&action=click&pgtype=Homepage&version=HpHeadline&module=first-column-region&region=top-news&WT.nav=top-news

Congress would like to oblige, as long as the movie can be a short one, on the model of Libya. Here's the plot: Evil force arises out of nowhere; United States destroys it; credits roll. If Libya-The-Movie had begun with years of support for Gadaffi or ended with the disaster left behind, the critics would have hated it. Framing is everything.

Kathy Kelly published an article[190] on Wednesday describing her visit some years back to a U.S. prison camp in Iraq where Awwad Ibrahim Ali al-Badri al-Samarrai spent four years under the name Abu Bakr Al-Baghdadi before becoming the leader of ISIS.

Imagine a Hollywood-like movie that began in that camp. An opening scene might show Baghdadi and his fellow prisoners paraded naked in front of female soldiers and forced to say "I love George Bush" before they could get their food rations. We'd see them sleeping on the ground in the cold, cursing their captors and swearing every last drop of energy and instant of remaining life to that highest of all Hollywood values: violent revenge.

Cut to the present and a scene in a small house in Iraq with 500-pound U.S. bombs exploding just outside. Baghdadi and his gang of loveable heroes look horrified, but—with a twinkle in his eye—Baghdadi gathers the others to him and begins to smile. Then he begins to laugh. His comrades look bewildered. Then they start to catch on. "You wanted this, didn't you?" exclaims Sexy Female Rebel. "This was your plan, wasn't it!"

"Hand me the ultimate weapon," Baghdadi says, turning to a

190 http://warisacrime.org/content/lessons-learned-bucca-camp

future nominee for best male supporting actor. BMSA grins and pulls out a video camera. Baghdadi raises the camera over his head with one hand. Turning to Sexy Female Rebel he says "Go on the roof and look north. Tell me what you see coming."

Cut to view through binoculars as music swells to high enthusiasm. Countless oceans of people on foot are making their way over the land with burning U.S. flags on sticks leading the way.

Of course, even Hollywood, which made *Avatar*, wouldn't make exactly THIS movie. The White House is going to have to make it. But who's directing? President Obama is hunting around for a name for this war, while ISIS has already released one in its video preview. Even the U.S. public seems increasingly interested in the full-length feature. "How does this end?" they want to know. "This was begun by Bush" they say, depending on their partisanship.

What if the script were flipped, not to portray the Iraqi as protagonist, but to abandon the religion of violent revenge? What if Washington were to say to ISIS this:

*We see that you want a war with us. We understand that you would gain local support because of how deeply we are hated. We're tired of being hated. We're tired of taking direction from criminals like you. We're not going to play along. We're going to make ourselves loved rather than hated. We're going to apologize for our occupations and bombings and prisons and torture. We're going to make restitution. We're going to provide aid to the entire region. It'll cost us a lot less to do that than to keep dropping bombs on you, so you can forget the plan to bankrupt us. We're going to save trillions of dollars in fact by ceasing to arm ourselves and the rest of the world to the teeth. We're going to announce a ban on shipping weapons to the Middle East. And since we ship 80% of them, not even counting our own military's, we're already off to a huge start. We're going to prosecute any oil company or country that does business with your organization. But we're going to hold no grudges against anyone who abandons your organization and seeks peace, just as we ask you to do what you can toward overcoming grudges against our past barbarity.*

What would happen? You might be surprised. Gandhi-The-Movie brought in over $50 million in 1982.

## *Killed by Congressional Cowardice*

We tend to think of war as resulting from an excess of aggression or disorderliness or rebellion. Western academics hunt in the genes of foreigners and study chimpanzees to find the root of the nastiness.

But one would be hard press to count the number of people who have lost their lives to an excess of cowardice in the halls of the United States Congress. "This chamber reeks of blood," said Senator George McGovern, who would have been shocked anew this week.

On Constitution Day, the House of Representatives—followed the next day by the Senate—decided to put off until after the next U.S. elections in November any possible consideration of the new

U.S. war already underway in Iraq and Syria, but voted in the meantime to approve of shipping weapons over to Syria to fuel the violence.

Here's a website[191] that tells you how your Representative and Senators voted and lets you send them an appropriate message with one click.

Said Congressman Jim McDermott, who voted No: "This amendment, which is valid only through early December, serves as nothing more than a faux authorization designed to get Congress through the election season. Moreover, it addresses only one aspect of the strategy the President outlined last week. That is not a responsible way to conduct public policy."

So, the President announced a three-year war, based on no timetable anyone has produced other than that of U.S. presidential elections. And Congress declared that it would consider looking into the matter after the next Congressional election. But it's not as if we don't all know that they are allowing the war to go on and worsen each and every day. Numerous Congress members denounce[192] Congress for what they themselves call a shameful act of cowardice. But which of them are protesting their "leadership"? Which of them are moving a discharge petition to force a vote? Which of them are using the War Powers Resolution to compel a vote regardless of what the "leadership" wants?

---

191          http://act.rootsaction.org/p/dia/action3/common/public/?action_
KEY=10398
192          http://www.huffingtonpost.com/2014/09/18/congress-war-authorization-
isis_n_5831408.html

Back on the 25th of July the House overwhelmingly passed the McGovern-Jones-Lee resolution which required the President to seek Congressional authorization before sending troops to Iraq. The President went ahead and ignored that. Will Congress cut off the funding? Censure? Impeach? Nope. Congress voted to approve weapons and training for Syrians who are closely allied with the forces Obama is already waging an air and ground war against in Iraq.

Senator Tim Kaine had been leading the charge to demand that Congress vote before any new war. (As noted, the House did, and the Senate did not follow suit.) Now Kaine says a discussion of that following the U.S. Congressional elections will be sufficient. Until then, the United States will fuel the violence on both sides of a complex war, while repeating incessantly "There is no military solution" and deploying the military and military weaponry in a counterproductive effort to find a solution.

Remarked Congresswoman Barbara Lee, who voted No on weapons to Syria: "The consequences of this vote will be a further expansion of a war currently taking place and our further involvement in a sectarian war. . . . What is missing from this debate is the political, economic, diplomatic and regionally-led solutions that will ultimately be the tools for security in the region and for any potential future threats to the United States."

Also missing was an organized opposition. Republicans voted yes and no, as did Democrats, as did the so-called Progressive Caucus, as did the Black Caucus. These people need to hear the message that cowardice is not a campaign strategy. They must be confronted with the demand that they stop this war, just as they were a year ago, when scary ISIS videos weren't manipulating Americans into once again doing the bidding of terrorists who gain strength from U.S. attacks. A year ago we spoke up. We confronted Congress members at town hall meetings. We stopped them.

Now they've literally cut and run. They're taking a two-month vacation in order to pretend they have nothing to do with the escalating violence. They need to hear from us in person. But we can start by sending them a note[193] to let them know what we think.

Remember, their duty is not to vote approval for a new war, which will then somehow make everything OK. Their duty is to uphold the Kellogg-Briand Pact, the U.N. Charter, the wisdom of most of the world, the lessons of the past decade, and basic common decency by stopping the war.

## ISIS, Weapons Makers, Thugs Benefit from This Crime

President Obama is bombing the opposite side in Syria from the side he swore we needed to attack one year ago, and those pleased by this declare that he is "doing something."

U.S. polls suggest that the same people recognize that this

---

193          http://act.rootsaction.org/p/dia/action3/common/public/?action_
KEY=10398

*something* will make the U.S. more likely[194] to be attacked and nonetheless favor this action. This is unthinking fear produced by slick beheading videos for audiences too distracted to notice that the Iraqi government, Saudi government and numerous other U.S. friends and allies behead. And are we to imagine that when Obama kills a 16 year old American and the 6 kids near him his head remains intact? Should we pretend that the people being killed by U.S. missiles right now aren't losing their heads?

This action is illegal under the UN Charter, Kellogg-Briand Pact, and U.S. Constitution. This action is immoral as it fuels violence that needs to be reduced. This action is knowingly, maddeningly counterproductive, guaranteed to build hostility to the United States, which is already so hated that ISIS openly advocates for a U.S. attack on it. This action by this White House is what ISIS wants and what weapons makers want. It is not what the people of Syria or Iraq or the world want. It further shreds the rule of law while dumping gasoline on a fire of U.S. creation.

What's needed is, contrary to what your television suggests, not to "do nothing" or love beheadings. What's needed is an arms embargo. The U.S. ships 79% of the weapons shipped to the Middle East, not counting the weapons of the U.S. military. An arms embargo could be 79% successful with just one country participating, and others could certainly be brought to do so.

What's needed is actual aid[195] on a massive scale, restitution to the people of the region for the crimes of the U.S. government. An

194 http://www.worldbeyondwar.org/endangers
195 http://www.worldbeyondwar.org/2trillion

aid program sufficient to make the United States beloved rather than hated would cost a lot less money than the missiles and bombs for which price seems to be no concern at all.

What's needed is diplomacy. The U.S. government is happy to talk with Syria or Iran or Russia when the object is war. Why can it not talk to them when the object is peace?

Our Constitutional scholar Nobel peace laureate no-dumb-wars end-the-mindset president will be protested today at the White House and at his appearance in New York, and should be protested everywhere he goes.

Congress members should not know a moment's peace, but should be taught that cowardice is not a campaign strategy. None who voted for weapons[196] to Syria should be returned to Washington next year.

War as a first resort, as our biggest public program, as the be all and end all of U.S. foreign policy is a form of insanity that has no redeeming feature. War is our top destroyer of the natural environment[197], of the economy[198], of civil liberties[199], of self-governance, and of morality[200]. This is a case of a doctor trying to cure the world while suffering from a deadly and highly infectious disease that in his own mind is the epitome of health.

---

196        http://act.rootsaction.org/p/dia/action3/common/public/?action_KEY=10398
197 http://www.worldbeyondwar.org/environment
198 http://www.worldbeyondwar.org/impoverishes
199 http://www.worldbeyondwar.org/liberties
200 http://www.worldbeyondwar.org/immoral

You can't cure war fever with more war. You can only get to peace through peace.

Stop the bombing.

## *Parliament and Congress Have No Power to Legalize War*

Congress has fled town to avoid voting for or against a new war. Many of the big donors to Congressional campaigns would want Yes votes. Many voters would want No votes, if not immediately, then as soon as the panic induced by the beheading videos wears off, which could be within the next month. Better to just avoid displeasing anyone—other than people who notice you running away.

The standard for legal-ish cosmopolitan respectability in the U.S. now has become getting five kings and dictators to say ~~their~~ they're on your side as you start bombing a new country.

But the British Parliament is still at the level of believing an actual vote by a legislature is appropriate. Do Americans remember that their beloved founding fathers put war powers in the hands of the legislature because of the ugly history of royal wars in Britain? Times have changed.

But if we want to actually comply with the law, we have to admit that neither Parliament nor Congress has the power to legalize attacking Syria. This is because both the U.S. and the U.K. are parties to the United Nations Charter, which bans war with very narrow exceptions—exceptions that have not been in any way met.

And if you want to get really serious about laws, the Kellogg-Briand Pact has never been repealed, the U.S. and U.K. are parties to it, and it bans all war without exception.

Now, you can interpret the Kellogg-Briand Pact to allow self-defense because the right to military self-defense, even when it's unlikely to actually work, is just so obvious to your way of thinking. And the U.N. Charter explicitly allows military self-defense. But here's the problem: There's nothing defensive about attacking Syria, and President Obama himself described it as "offense" in an interview with Chuck Todd on NBC.

Another word for "offense" is aggression, which the Nuremberg tribunal called "essentially an evil thing . . . the supreme international crime, differing only from other war crimes in that it contains within itself the accumulated evil of the whole."

Asked about Congress's responsibilities on Tuesday, Senator Tim Kaine (D., Va.) claimed that presidents could fight defensive wars without Congress but needed Congressional authorizations for offensive ones. In fact, offensive wars are not legal by any common understanding. Asked, then, about international law, at an event at the Center for American Progress, Kaine reportedly said that bombing Syria, as distinct from Iraq, was "complicated" and that he was not sure "how they would do that, perhaps using principles of self-defense or defending Iraq against other threats. I think we'll find out more about what the administration says about that after the UN General Assembly," he said.

Only in America. Only the White House gets to invent legal rationale for blatant crimes, with the law makers and enforcers prepared to accept the rationale before they hear it.

Prior to the U.N. meeting, U.S. Ambassador Samantha Power wrote to the U.N. arguing that it is legal for the United States to attack Syria because it is legal for Iraq to defend itself. By this logic, if Canada experienced a violent rebellion, it would be legal for China to attack the United States.

It's fun to pretend that the rule of law doesn't matter to you because you have all the weapons. It's fun to take two-month vacations from Washington. Just don't count on everyone voting you back next year.

## A Good End Date for the New War Is Today

What I've seen[201] of public events, demonstrations, and protests of the latest U.S. war—just like the larger and more immediately effective public resistance 12 months ago—has been aimed, remarkably enough, at ending the war and opposing the policies of those engaging in it, and first among them the U.S. President.

201 http://stpeteforpeace.org/syria2014.html

What I've seen[202] of inside-the-Beltway-style peace lobby groups' strategy has been aimed, predictably enough, at setting a good end date for the new war and barring the use of U.S. ground troops.

Both approaches are represented by voluminous discussions on listserves, so I feel like I know a good sample of each far more intimately than I might ideally wish. They parallel rejection and support of lesser-evil voting, and are largely made by those who reject and accept the importance of lesser-evil voting. However, many who accept lesser-evilism in the polling booth do not accept it here. And I think they have a point.

If you vote for a decent candidate and he or she loses, an argument can be made that you've "wasted" your vote. But if you advocate for an immediate end to a war, and a Congress that is hearing from the President that the war should last three years, bans continuation of the war beyond a year-and-a-half, then an argument can be made that you helped frame the compromise. In any case, it would be difficult to make a persuasive case that your activism was wasted. If, on the other hand, you found out that some Congress members were interested in a 1-year limit, and you lobbied for just that, and then Congress enacted a 2-year limit, what could you be said to have accomplished?

Here's my basic contention: Congress knows how to compromise. We don't have to pre-compromise for them. (How'd that work out on healthcare?) (How'd that ever work out?) And when we do pre-compromise for them (such as the time AFSCME banned "single-payer" signs from "public option" rallies, so as to simulate

202 http://www.justforeignpolicy.org/node/1564

public demand for what "progressive" Congress members were pretending to already want) we give significant support and respectability to some serious outrages (such as privatized for-profit health insurance, but also such as bombing Iraq yet again and bombing the opposite side in Syria that was to be bombed a year ago and while arming that same side, which—if we're honest about it—is madness[203].

How many years of madness will be best, is an insane question. It's not a question around which to organize protests, demonstrations, nonviolent actions, lobbying, education, communication, or any other sort of movement building.

But isn't 2 years of war better than 3? And how are you going to get Congress members to limit it to 2 years if you've called them lunatics?

Of course 2 years is better than 3. But less than 2 is even better, and Congress is going to compromise as far as it dares, and knows perfectly well how to do so without help from us. Is there really evidence to imagine that Senators and Congress members shape their policies around who's most polite to them? Certainly they determine who's invited to meetings on Capitol Hill on that basis, but is being in those meetings our top priority? Does it do the most for us? And can't we still get some people into those meetings by calling mass murder "mass murder" while keeping open every opportunity for the funders and sanctioners of mass murder to oppose and stop it?

203 http://warisacrime.org/content/futility-asking-congress-block-next-gate

We need sit-ins in Congressional offices and protests on Capitol Hill. To a much lesser extent, we need discussions with Congress members and staffers. To the extent that different people must pursue those two tactics, the question will always remain whether mass public organizing should be guided by people who think like the former group or like the latter.

My position comes from the expectation that "support the troops" propaganda and the inevitably worsened situation after a year or two will make the struggle to then end a previously time-limited war harder, rather than easier—easier only if the public has come to its sense in the meantime. My position comes from the fact that there are already U.S. troops in Iraq and the belief that we're going to get them home sooner if we don't play along with the pretense that they aren't there or aren't there for combat. My concern is for human life, and when you prioritize an air war over a ground war—and when the "anti-war" movement does that—you risk creating a great, rather than a smaller, number of deaths, albeit non-U.S. deaths.

Now, the lobbyists' need to be polite to Congress can be a helpful guide to all protesters. While moral condemnation and humorous mockery can be useful tools, so can Gandhian respect for those who must be won over. But the demand of a peace movement must be for peace and alternatives to war. When the missile strikes were stopped a year ago, the arming of ISIS-and-friends proceeded anyway, and no useful policy was pursued instead of the missiles. The U.S. had decided to do nothing, as if that were the only other option. Effectively we'd put an end date on the U.S. staying out, as doing nothing was guaranteed not to resolve the problem.

A good end-date for this war is today. A good date to begin useful aid and diplomacy and arms embargoes and reparations is tomorrow. We have to change the conversation to those topics, instead of focusing on the question of how much mass-murdering madness is the appropriate amount. Not because we want it to continue for eternity if it can't be ended now, but because it will end sooner and be less likely to be repeated if we confront it for what it is.

We've been so strategic over the past decade that everybody in the United States knows the war on Iraq cost U.S. lives and money, but most have only the vaguest idea of how it destroyed Iraq[204] and how many people it killed. As a direct result, nobody knows where ISIS came from, and not enough people are fully aware of the high probability that the bombing will strengthen ISIS—which may be why ISIS openly asks for it in its 1-hour film.

How much insanity should we demand on our posters and signs and online petitions and letters to editors: not another drop[205].

## Operation Odysseus' Butcher Shop

The phrase "war myths" these days is generally taken to mean such nonsense as that war will make us safe, or civilians won't be killed, or surgical strikes will kill more enemies than they produce, or prosperity and freedom will follow war-making, etc. But I wonder whether "war myths" shouldn't be taken more literally,

204 http://waricacrime.org/iraq
205 http://worldbeyondwar.org

whether we don't in fact have a bunch of warmakers believing that they are Odysseus.

Remember Odysseus, the great Greek hero who went on lots of thrilling adventures on his way home from Troy and kicked a bunch of interloping suitors of his lonely wife out of his house in Ithaca when he got home?

Well, Odysseus didn't actually kick them out, did he? Do you remember what actually happened? Odysseus could have ordered them out upon his return. He could have announced his approach and had them gone before he arrived. Instead, he disguised himself and entered his house unannounced. He secretly hid all the weapons except those for himself and his son and loyal servants. He secretly blocked every door. The suitors were unarmed and trapped when Odysseus revealed who he was and started murdering them.

The suitors offered to more than repay him for what they had stolen from his house, to apologize, to try to make things right. Odysseus, who had a goddess making sure he succeeded in every detail, declined all offers and murdered every man but those his son said were loyal. He beheaded. He tortured. He dismembered. He cut off faces and cut out organs and fed bits of people to dogs. And then, seeing as how he was on such a glorious killing spree, he asked his wife's head servant whether any of the servant women had been disrespectful or misbehaved in any way. Those who had were quickly identified, and Odysseus murdered them immediately.

And there was a cute reunion scene with his wife, and everyone lived happily ever after, right?

Well, actually, there's a bit of the story we tend to overlook. Odysseus realized that the giant pile of corpses in his house had friends and relatives who would seek revenge exactly as barbarically as he had. So his goddess friend cast a spell of forgiveness on all of them, and by that means there was peace.

Now, in the world of the myth one might well wonder why Athena didn't just cast that spell on Odysseus the day before, let the suitors repay him, and skip the blood bath. But in the world of reality, one must ask whether our masters of war believe Athena is going to help them too.

They revenge themselves with righteous brutality on various dictators who have lapsed in their loyalty or death squads that have lost their utility, and the blowback is predictable, predicted, and tragic. No goddess ever shows up to cast a spell of forgiveness on victims' friends and family.

War supporters know there's no goddess in their fight, but often they begin to imagine that the other side will find forgiveness by seeing the justness of the war against them—although I don't believe there are any examples of this actually happening.

War propaganda maintains that the other side only speaks the language of violence, so violence will communicate to that other side our grievances, our suffering, our justifiable outrage, and our desire for peace. But of course, violence is not a language, not even when dressed up in Homer's art. A language is a substance that can be thought in. Violence cannot embody thought, only fantasy.

The happy little war that turned Libya into hell three years ago was called Operation Odyssey Dawn.

There have been many admirable suggestions[206] put forward to name Obama's latest war:

Operation Enduring Confusion

Operation Rolling Blunder

Operation Iraqi Liberation

Operation We're Indispensable - Guess What That Makes You

Operation Unchanging Hopelessness

But I think the appropriate tag for a mission based on the idea of special holy goodness and power, the idea that mass killing of civilians is justified by outrage at killing of civilians, and the notion that everyone will forgive it afterwards so it won't just make matters worse, is Operation Odysseus' Butcher Shop.

## Thoughts of a Beheaded Head

Dostoievski once had a character imagine what a head would think if for some seconds it were aware of having been cut off by an executioner's guillotine, or if somehow it were aware for a full minute, or even for five minutes.

206 https://twitter.com/hashtag/nameobamaisisoperation

I should think such a head would think thoughts entirely dependent on the circumstances and that the type of blade that committed the murder wouldn't affect the thoughts too greatly.

I loved you, it might think, thinking of its loved ones. I did well there, if might think, thinking of its accomplishments. I'm sorry, it might think, dwelling momentarily on its deepest regrets—as likely as not relatively trivial incidents in which the head together with its body had hurt someone's feelings.

I've died in a war, the head might think, despite opposing wars. I took the risk and enjoyed the thrill, yet the injustice remains. I didn't launch the war. I didn't make millions off it. I didn't win votes from it. I tried to tell people what it was, and here I am no better than a soccer ball about to cease existing as a consciousness.

As the beheaded head's remaining seconds stretched into what seemed to it a long period of time, it might be struck by the absurdity of the situation, and it might be horrified by the barbarism. I was supposed to not be the news, the head might think, and now I am the news. After pretending not to be human, my humanity—once ended—will now be used as a reason to escalate the war. No one will ask me. How could they?

But no one ever asked me, did they, even when I was connected to a neck and arms and legs? I reported on this battle or that atrocity. But did anyone ever ask whether the entire enterprise made me ashamed of my species? Did anyone ever ask whether the justifications used were any better than lunacy? My country decided 100 years ago that it would dominate the Middle East for oil—oil that will destroy the world itself if the wars don't.

In recent years my country destroyed Iraq, killing a half-million to a million-and-a-half people, leaving behind a hell on earth, including a government that both beheads people and bombs them, as well as handing over weaponry to this gang that beheaded my body—a gang that could only have arisen in the hell on earth that Washington created and which will never match Washington's scale of killing if it keeps beheading and crucifying for decades.

So what does the government of the people who read my reports do? It sends in more weapons to the close allies of ISIS and simultaneously starts bombing ISIS just one year after screaming that it must bomb the Syrian government that ISIS is fighting. And ISIS makes a movie demanding heavier U.S. attacks, and the U.S. obliges and launches heavier attacks. And ISIS recruitment soars, the weapons companies stocks soar, and I get my body cut off.

And because my body is gone from me, and because the war is begun, and because it is guaranteed to get worse rather than better, brave drone pilots will be told that they must continue the war so as not to offend themselves, and as they commit suicide after murdering people with joysticks, still more pilots will be called on so that the first ones will not have killed themselves in vain.

Why when we're alive do we act as if the whole thing isn't insane? Is it a function of our habit of acting as if our existence isn't insane? We puff ourselves up, don't we? We talk solemnly of strategy, energetically ignoring the intentional absurdity of the whole doomed project, just as we eat and eat and eat without ever once wondering what the junk we are eating will do to the worms who will dine on our flesh.

What if the world comes to its senses next week, the head might think as the world grows blurry around it. How will I feel to have missed it by so little? Well, I'll feel nothing of course, and so I do hope that it will happen. I really do. This man who's cut off my body has a loud laugh. He was sad yesterday morning and I could not ask him why. I wonder if people back home know that he thinks Americans can only understand the language of violence, so there's no sense talking to them.

## U.S. Sends Planes Armed with Depleted Uranium to Middle East

The U.S. Air Force says it is not halting its use of Depleted Uranium weapons, has recently sent them to the Middle East, and is prepared to use them.

A type of airplane, the A-10, deployed this month to the Middle East by the U.S. Air National Guard's 122nd Fighter Wing, is responsible for more Depleted Uranium (DU) contamination than any other platform, according to the International Coalition to Ban Uranium Weapons (ICBUW). "Weight for weight and by number of rounds more 30mm PGU-14B ammo has been used than any other round," said ICBUW coordinator Doug Weir, referring to ammunition used by A-10s, as compared to DU ammunition used by tanks.

Public affairs superintendent Master Sgt. Darin L. Hubble of the 122nd Fighter Wing told me that the A-10s now in the Middle East along with "300 of our finest airmen" have been sent there on a deployment planned for the past two years and have not been assigned to take part in the current fighting in Iraq or Syria, but "that could change at any moment." The crews will load PGU-14 depleted uranium rounds into their 30mm Gatling cannons and use them as needed, said Hubble. "If the need is to explode something—for example a tank—they will be used."

Pentagon spokesman Mark Wright told me, "There is no prohibition against the use of Depleted Uranium rounds, and the [U.S. military] does make use of them. The use of DU in armor-piercing munitions allows enemy tanks to be more easily destroyed."

On Thursday, several nations, including Iraq, spoke[207] to the United Nations First Committee, against the use of Depleted Uranium and in support of studying and mitigating the damage in already contaminated areas. A non-binding resolution[208] is expected to be voted on by the Committee this week, urging nations that have used DU to provide information on locations targeted. A number of organizations are delivering a petition[209] to U.S. officials this week urging them not to oppose the resolution.

207 http://reachingcriticalwill.org/disarmament-fora/unga/2014/statements
208      http://www.bandepleteduranium.org/en/new-un-depleted-uranium-resolution-calls-for-clean
209      http://act.rootsaction.org/p/dia/action3/common/public/?action_KEY=10503

In 2012 a resolution on DU was supported by 155 nations and opposed by just the UK, U.S., France, and Israel. Several nations have banned DU, and in June Iraq proposed a global treaty banning it—a step also supported by the European and Latin American Parliaments.

Wright said that the U.S. military is "addressing concerns on the use of DU by investigating other types of materials for possible use in munitions, but with some mixed results. Tungsten has some limitations in its functionality in armor-piercing munitions, as well as some health concerns based on the results of animal research on some tungsten-containing alloys. Research is continuing in this area to find an alternative to DU that is more readily accepted by the public, and also performs satisfactorily in munitions."

"I fear DU is this generation's Agent Orange," U.S. Congressman Jim McDermott told me. "There has been a sizable increase in childhood leukemia and birth defects in Iraq since the Gulf War and our subsequent invasion in 2003. DU munitions were used in both those conflicts. There are also grave suggestions that DU weapons have caused serious health issues for our Iraq War veterans. I seriously question the use of these weapons until the U.S. military conducts a full investigation into the effect of DU weapon residue on human beings."

Doug Weir of ICBUW said renewed use of DU in Iraq would be "a propaganda coup for ISIS." His and other organizations opposed to DU are guardedly watching a possible U.S. shift away from DU, which the U.S. military said it did not use in Libya in 2011. Master

Sgt. Hubble of the 122nd Fighter Wing believes that was simply a tactical decision. But public pressure had been brought to bear by activists and allied nations' parliaments, and by a UK commitment not to use DU.

DU is classed as a Group 1 Carcinogen by the World Health Organization, and evidence[210] of health damage produced by its use is extensive. The damage is compounded, Jeena Shah at the Center for Constitutional Rights (CCR) told me, when the nation that uses DU refuses to identify locations targeted. Contamination enters soil and water. Contaminated scrap metal is used in factories or made into cooking pots or played with by children.

CCR and Iraq Veterans Against the War have filed a Freedom of Information Act Request[211] in an attempt to learn the locations targeted in Iraq during and after the 1991 and 2003 assaults. The UK and the Netherlands have revealed targeted locations, Shah pointed out, as did NATO following DU use in the Balkans. And the United States has revealed locations it targeted with cluster munitions. So why not now?

"For years," Shah said, "the U.S. has denied a relationship between DU and health problems in civilians and veterans. Studies of UK veterans are highly suggestive of a connection. The U.S. doesn't want studies done." In addition, the United States has used DU in civilian areas[212] and identifying those locations could suggest violations of Geneva Conventions.

---

210 http://www.paxforpeace.nl/our-work/programmes/depleted-uranium
211 http://ccrjustice.org/files/Defense FOIA Request.pdf
212    http://www.paxvoorvrede.nl/media/files/pax-rapport-iraq-final-lowres-spread.pdf

Iraqi doctors will be testifying on the damage done by DU before the Tom Lantos Human Rights Commission[213] in Washington, D.C., in December. Meanwhile, the Obama Administration said on Thursday that it will be spending $1.6 million to try to identify atrocities committed in Iraq . . . by ISIS.

## Urgent: Right-Left Alliance Needed to Stop This War!

*Originally published by Ron Paul Institute for Peace and Prosperity[214]*

Last year, public pressure played a big role in stopping US missile strikes on Syria. The biggest difference between then and now was that televisions weren't telling people that ISIS might be coming to their neighborhood to behead them. There were other, smaller differences as well: Britain's opposition, Russia's opposition, and the difficulty of explaining to Americans that it now made sense to join a war on the same side as al Qaeda.

But there's another big difference between last year and this year. Last year was not a Congressional election year. With elections coming this November, Congress declared an early vacation in September and fled town in order to avoid voting a new war up or down. It did this while fully aware that the President would proceed with the war illegally. Most Congress members, including House Speaker John Boehner and Senate Leader Harry Reid,

213 http://tlhrc.house.gov/
214          http://ronpaulinstitute.org/archives/featured-articles/2014/october/08/urgent-right-left-alliance-needed-to-stop-this-war%21

believe that by allowing a war to happen without explicitly voting for or against it they can best win our votes for re-election without offending their funders.

Congress members have good reason to think that way. Numerous organizations and individuals are dumping endless energy and resources into trying to elect either Democrats or Republicans, regardless of their policies. Big groups on the left have told me that they will not have any time for opposing war until the elections are over, at which point they'll be happy to "hold accountable" any of the Democrats they've just reelected. There are organizations who do the same thing for Republicans.

When war was made the top election issue in exit polls in 2006, Democrats took power and their leader in the House, Rahm Emanuel, openly told the Washington Post that they would keep the war in Iraq going in order to campaign against it again in 2008. And so they did. Republicans elected opposing war in 2010 have been more rhetorical than substantive in their "opposition."

The current war, and the endless war it is part of, must be opposed by people across the political spectrum who put peace ahead of party. ISIS has a one-hour video asking for this war. Giving it to them, and boosting their recruitment, is insanity. Ending insane policies is not a left or right position. This is a war that involves bombing the opposite side in Syria from the side we were told we had to bomb a year ago, and simultaneously arming the same side that the U.S. government is bombing. This is madness. To allow this to continue while mumbling the obvious truth that "there is no military solution" is too great an evil to fit into any lesser-evil electoral calculation.

This war is killing civilians in such large numbers that the White House has announced that restrictions on killing civilians will not be followed. This war is being used to strip away our rights at home. It's draining our economy. It's impoverishing us—primarily by justifying the routine annual spending of roughly $1 trillion on war preparations. It's endangering us by generating further hatred. And all of this destruction, with no up-side to be found, is driven by irrational fear that has people telling pollsters they believe this war will endanger them and they're in favor of it.

According to the Congressional Research Service 79% of weapons shipments to Middle Eastern countries are from the United States, not counting arms given to allies of ISIS or used by the US military. Rather than arming this region to the teeth and joining in wars with US weapons on both sides, the United States could arrange for and lead an arms embargo. It could also provide restitution for what it has done in recent years, including the destruction of Iraq that allowed the creation of ISIS. Making restitution in the form of actual aid (as opposed to "military aid") would cost a lot less than lobbing $2 million missiles at people who view them as recruitment posters and tickets to martyrdom. That shift would also begin to make the United States liked rather than hated.

We won't get there unless people whose souls are un-owned by political parties take over town hall meetings and let Congress members know that they must work to end this war if they want to earn our votes.

# War Culture

## Operation Nazification

Annie Jacobsen's new book is called *Operation Paperclip: The Secret Intelligence Program That Brought Nazi Scientists to America*. It isn't terribly secret anymore, of course, and it was never very intelligent. Jacobsen has added some details, and the U.S. government is still hiding many more. But the basic facts have been available; they're just left out of most U.S. history books, movies, and television programs.

After World War II, the U.S. military hired sixteen hundred former Nazi scientists and doctors, including some of Adolf Hitler's closest collaborators, including men responsible for murder, slavery, and human experimentation, including men convicted of war crimes, men acquitted of war crimes, and men who never stood trial. Some of the Nazis tried at Nuremberg had already been working for the U.S. in either Germany or the U.S. prior to the trials. Some were protected from their past by the U.S. government for years, as they lived and worked in Boston Harbor, Long Island, Maryland, Ohio, Texas, Alabama, and elsewhere, or were flown by the U.S. government to Argentina to protect them from prosecution. Some trial transcripts were classified in their entirety to avoid exposing the pasts of important U.S. scientists. Some of the Nazis brought over were frauds who had passed themselves off as scientists, some of whom subsequently learned their fields while working for the U.S. military.

The U.S. occupiers of Germany after World War II declared that all military research in Germany was to cease, as part of the process of denazification. Yet that research went on and expanded in secret, under U.S. authority, both in Germany and in the United States, as part of a process that it's possible to view as nazification. Not only scientists were hired. Former Nazi spies, most of them former S.S., were hired by the U.S. in post-war Germany to spy on—and torture—Soviets.

The U.S. military shifted in numerous ways when former Nazis were put into prominent positions. It was Nazi rocket scientists who proposed placing nuclear bombs on rockets and began developing the intercontinental ballistic missile. It was Nazi engineers who had designed Hitler's bunker beneath Berlin, who now designed underground fortresses for the U.S. government in the Catoctin and Blue Ridge Mountains. Known Nazi liars were employed by the U.S. military to draft classified intelligence briefs falsely hyping the Soviet menace. Nazi scientists developed U.S. chemical and biological weapons programs, bringing over their knowledge of tabun and sarin, not to mention thalidomide—and their eagerness for human experimentation, which the U.S. military and the newly created CIA readily engaged in on a major scale. Every bizarre and gruesome notion of how a person might be assassinated or an army immobilized was of interest to their research. New weapons were developed, including VX and Agent Orange. A new drive to visit and weaponize outerspace was created, and former Nazis were put in charge of a new agency called NASA.

Permanent war thinking, limitless war thinking, and creative war thinking in which science and technology overshadowed death and suffering, all went mainstream. When a former Nazi spoke to a women's luncheon at the Rochester Junior Chamber of Commerce in 1953, the event's headline was "Buzz Bomb Mastermind to Address Jaycees Today." That doesn't sound terribly odd to us, but might have shocked anyone living in the United States anytime prior to World War II. Watch this Walt Disney television program[215] featuring a former Nazi who worked slaves to death in a cave building rockets. Before long, President Dwight Eisenhower would be lamenting that "the total influence—economic, political, even spiritual—is felt in every city, every State house, every office of the Federal government." Eisenhower was not referring to Nazism but to the power of the military-industrial complex. Yet, when asked whom he had in mind in remarking in the same speech that "public policy could itself become the captive of a scientific-technological elite," Eisenhower named two scientists, one of them the former Nazi in the Disney video linked above.

The decision to inject 1,600 of Hitler's scientific-technological elite into the U.S. military was driven by fears of the USSR, both reasonable and the result of fraudulent fear mongering. The decision evolved over time and was the product of many misguided minds. But the buck stopped with President Harry S Truman. Henry Wallace, Truman's predecessor as vice-president who we like to imagine would have guided the world in a better direction than Truman did as president, actually pushed Truman to hire the Nazis as a jobs program. It would be good for American industry, said our progressive hero. Truman's subordinates debated, but Truman decided. As bits of Operation Paperclip became known, the American Federation of Scientists, Albert Einstein, and others

215 http://www.youtube.com/watch?v=Zjs3nBfyIwM

urged Truman to end it. Nuclear physicist Hans Bethe and his colleague Henri Sack asked Truman:

> "Did the fact that the Germans might save the nation millions of dollars imply that permanent residence and citizenship could be bought? Could the United States count on [the German scientists] to work for peace when their indoctrinated hatred against the Russians might contribute to increase the divergence between the great powers? Had the war been fought to allow Nazi ideology to creep into our educational and scientific institutions by the back door? Do we want science at any price?"

In 1947 Operation Paperclip, still rather small, was in danger of being terminated. Instead, Truman transformed the U.S. military with the National Security Act, and created the best ally that Operation Paperclip could want: the CIA. Now the program took off, intentionally and willfully, with the full knowledge and understanding of the same U.S. President who had declared as a senator that if the Russians were winning the U.S. should help the Germans, and vice versa, to ensure that the most people possible died, the same president who viciously and pointlessly dropped two nuclear bombs on Japanese cities, the same president who brought us the war on Korea, the war without declaration, the secret wars, the permanent expanded empire of bases, the military secrecy in all matters, the imperial presidency, and the military-industrial complex. The U.S. Chemical Warfare Service took up the study of German chemical weapons at the end of the war as a means to continue in existence. George Merck both diagnosed biological weapons threats for the military and sold the military vaccines to handle them. War was business and business was going to be good for a long time to come.

But how big a change did the United States go through after World War II, and how much of it can be credited to Operation Paperclip? Isn't a government that would give immunity to both Nazi and Japanese war criminals in order to learn their criminal ways already in a bad place? As one of the defendants argued in trial at Nuremberg, the U.S. had already engaged in its own experiments on humans using almost identical justifications to those offered by the Nazis. If that defendant had been aware, he could have pointed out that the U.S. was in that very moment engaged in such experiments in Guatemala. The Nazis had learned some of their eugenics and other nasty inclinations from Americans. Some of the Paperclip scientists had worked in the U.S. before the war, as many Americans had worked in Germany. These were not isolated worlds.

Looking beyond the secondary, scandalous, and sadistic crimes of war, what about the crime of war itself? We picture the United States as less guilty because it maneuvered the Japanese into the first attack, and because it did prosecute some of the war's losers. But an impartial trial would have prosecuted Americans too. Bombs dropped on civilians killed and injured and destroyed more than any concentration camps—camps that in Germany had been modeled in part after U.S. camps for native Americans. Is it possible that Nazi scientists blended into the U.S. military so well because an institution that had already done what it had done to the Philippines was not in all that much need of nazification?

Yet, somehow, we think of the firebombing of Japanese cities and the complete leveling of German cities as less offensive that the hiring of Nazi scientists. But what is it that offends us about Nazi scientists? I don't think it should be that they engaged in mass-murder for the wrong side, an error balanced out in some minds but their later work for mass-murder by the right side. And I don't think it should be entirely that they engaged in sick human experimentation and forced labor. I do think those actions should offend us. But so should the construction of rockets that take thousands of lives. And it should offend us whomever it's done for.

It's curious to imagine a civilized society somewhere on earth some years from now. Would an immigrant with a past in the U.S. military be able to find a job? Would a review be needed? Had they tortured prisoners? Had they drone-struck children? Had they leveled houses or shot up civilians in any number of countries? Had they used cluster bombs? Depleted uranium? White phosphorous? Had they ever worked in the U.S. prison system? Immigrant detention system? Death row? How thorough a review would be needed? Would there be some level of just-following-orders behavior that would be deemed acceptable? Would it matter, not just what the person had done, but how they thought about the world?

## Thermonuclear Monarchy and Revolution

So now we (or at least the 0.03% of us who care to hunt for it) discover that U.S. military spending[216] is not actually being

216        http://www.tomdispatch.com/post/175815/tomgram%3A_mattea_kramer%2C_is_the_pentagon_doomed_--_to_be_flush_forever

cut at all, but increasing. Also going up: U.S. nuclear weapons spending[217]. Some of the new nukes will violate treaties[218], but the entire program violates the Nuclear Nonproliferation Treaty, which requires disarmament, not increased armament. The U.S. policy of first-strike and the U.S. practice of informing other nations that "all options are on the table" also violate the U.N. Charter's ban on threatening force.

But do nuclear weapons, by the nature of their technology, violate the U.S. Constitution? Do they violate the basic social contract and all possibility of self-governance? Thus argues a new book called *Thermonuclear Monarchy: Choosing Between Democracy and Doom* by Elaine Scarry. It's not unheard of for people to see out-of-control nuclear spending as a symptom of out-of-control military spending, itself a symptom of government corruption, legalized bribery, and a militaristic culture. Scarry's argument suggests a reversal: the root of all this evil is not the almighty dollar but the almighty bomb.

The argument runs something like this. The primary purpose of the social contract is to create peace and prevent war and other injury. The U.S. Constitution (Article I, Section 8, clause 11) bans the making of war without the approval of both houses of Congress. This approval was to be required not just for an existing military to attack another country, but for a military to be raised at all—standing armies not being anticipated. And it was understood that an army would not be raised and deployed into war unless

217     http://warisacrime.org/content/president-requests-unprecedented-spending-nuclear-weapons-maintenance-design-production
218     http://defensetech.org/2014/02/28/nuclear-bomb-upgrade-could-violate-key-treaty/

the citizen-soldiers went willingly, their ability to dissent by desertion not needing to be spelled out (or, let us say, their ability to dissent by *mass*-desertion, as desertion in the war that led to the Constitution was punished by death).

And yet, because this point was so crucial to the entire governmental project, Scarry argues, it was in fact spelled out—in the Second Amendment. Arms—that is 18th century muskets—were to be freely distributed among the people, not concentrated in the hands of a king. "Civilian" control over the military meant popular control, not presidential. The decision to go to war would have to pass through the people's representatives in Congress, and through the people as a whole in the form of soldiers who might refuse to fight. By this thinking, had the Ludlow Amendment, to create a public referendum before any war, passed in the 1930s, it would have been redundant.

Before the 1940s were over, in Scarry's view, a Ludlow Amendment wouldn't have been worth the paper it was written on, as the existence of nuclear weapons erases Constitutional checks on war. With nuclear weapons, a tiny number of people in a government—be it 1 or 3 or 20 or 500—hold the power to very quickly and easily kill millions or billions of human beings, and other species, and very likely themselves in the process. "We may have democracy, or we may have wealth concentrated in the hands of a few, but we can't have both," said Louis Brandeis. We may have democracy, or we may have thermonuclear bombs, but we can't have both, says Elaine Scarry.

Each of the series of presidents beginning with Truman and running up through Nixon is known to have repeatedly come close to choosing to use nuclear bombs, something the public has learned of, each time, only decades after the fact. No more recent president has said he *didn't* come close; we may very well learn their secrets on the usual schedule. When you add to that insanity, the long string of accidents, mistakes, and misunderstandings, the damage of the testing and the waste, and the repeated ability of ploughshares activists (and therefore anybody else) to walk right up to U.S. nuclear weapons to protest them, it's amazing that life exists on earth. But Scarry's focus is on what the new ability to kill off a continent at the push of a button has done to presidential power.

While wars since World War II have been non-nuclear, apart from depleted uranium weapons, they have also been endless and undeclared. Because presidents can nuke nations, they and Congress and the public have assumed that a president on his or her own authority can attack nations with non-nuclear weapons too. Now, I suspect that the military industrial complex, corrupt elections, and nuclear thinking all feed off each other. I don't want a single person who's trying to clean up election spending or halt fighter-jet production to stop what they're doing. But the possible influence of nuclear thinking on U.S. foreign policy is intriguing. Once a president has been given more power than any king has ever had, one might expect some people to do exactly what they've done and treat him like a king in all but name.

Scarry believes that we're suffering from the false idea that we're in a permanent emergency, and that in an emergency there's no time to think. In fact, the Constitutional constraints on war were intended precisely for emergencies, Scarry argues, and are needed precisely then. But an emergency that can be dealt with by raising an army is perhaps different from an emergency that will leave everyone on earth dead by tomorrow either with or without the U.S. government having the opportunity to contribute its measure of mass-killing to the general apocalypse. The latter is, of course, not an emergency at all, but an insistence on glorified ignorance to the bitter end. An emergency that allows time to raise an army is also different from an emergency involving 21st century "conventional" weapons, but not nearly as different as we suppose. Remember the desperate urgency to hit Syria with missiles last September that vanished the moment Congress refused to do it? The mad rush to start a war before anyone can look too closely at its justifications does, I think, benefit from nuclear thinking—from the idea that there is not time to stop and think.

So, what can we do? Scarry believes that if nukes were eliminated, Congress could take charge of debates over wars again. Perhaps it could. But would it approve wars? Would it approve public financing, free air time, and open elections? Would it ban its members from profiting from war? Would people killed in a Congressionally declared war be any less dead?

What if the Second Amendment as Scarry understands it were fulfilled to some slight degree, that is if weapons were slightly more equitably distributed as a result of the elimination of nukes? The government would still have all the aircraft carriers and missiles and bombs and predator drones, but it would have the same number of nukes as the rest of us. Wouldn't compliance with the Second Amendment require either the madness of giving everybody a missile launcher or the sanity of eliminating non-nuclear weapons of modern war-making along with the nuclear ones?

I think the historical argument that Scarry lays out against the concentration of military power in the hands of a monarch is equally a case either for distributing that power or for eliminating it. If large standing armies are the greatest danger to liberty, as James Madison supposed on his slave plantation, isn't that an argument against permanently stationing troops in 175 nations with or without nukes, as well as against militarizing local police forces at home? If unjustified war and imprisonment are the greatest violations of the social contract, must we not end for-profit mass incarceration by plea bargain along with for-profit mass-murder?

I think Scarry's argument carries us further in a good direction than she spells out in the book. It's a thick book full of extremely lengthy background information, not to say tangents. There's a wonderful account of the history of military desertion. There's a beautiful account of Thomas Hobbes as peace advocate. Much of this is valuable for its own sake. My favorite tangent is a comparison between Switzerland and the United States. Switzerland decided that air-raid shelters would help people survive in a nuclear war. While opposing and not possessing nuclear weapons, Switzerland has created shelters for more than the total number of people in the country. The United States claimed to have concluded that shelters would not work, and then spent more on building them exclusively for the government than it spent on all variety of needs and services for the rest of us. The nuclear nation has behaved as a monarchy, while the non-nuclear nation may preserve a remnant of humanity to tell the tale.

Scarry ends her book by stating that Article I and the Second Amendment are the best tools she's found for dismantling nuclear weapons, but that she'd like to hear of any others. Of course, mass nonviolent action, education, and organizing are tools that will carry any campaign beyond the confines of legal argumentation, but as long as we're within those confines, I'll throw out a proposal: Comply with the Kellogg-Briand Pact. It is far newer, clearer, and less ambiguous than the Constitution. It is, under the Constitution, unambiguously the Supreme Law of the Land as a treaty of the U.S. government. It applies in other nations as well, including a number of other nuclear weapons nations. It clarifies our thinking on the worst practice our species has developed, one that will destroy us all, directly or indirectly, if not ended, with or without nuclear: the practice of war.

The treaty that I recommend remembering bans war. When we begin to think in those terms, we won't see torture as the worst war crime, as Scarry suggests, but war itself as the worst crime of war. We won't suggest that killing is wrong because it's "nonbattlefield," as Scarry does at one point. We might question, as Scarry seems not to, that Hawaii was really part of the United States in 1941, or that U.S. torture really ended when Obama was elected. I'm quibbling with tiny bits in a large book, but only because I want to suggest that the arguments that best reject nuclear weaponry reject all modern war weaponry, its possession, and its use.

# The Genius of Erasmus

Desiderius Erasmus Roterodamus, who lived from October 27, 1466, to July 12, 1536, faced censorship in his day, and has never been as popular among the rich and powerful as has his contemporary Niccolò di Bernardo dei Machiavelli. But at a distance of half a millennium, we ought to be able to judge work on its merit—and we ought to have regular celebrations of Erasmus around the world. Some of his ideas are catching on. His name is familiar in Europe as that of the EU's student exchange program, named in his honor. We ought perhaps to wonder what oddball ideas these days might catch on in the 2500s—if humanity is around then.

In 1517, Erasmus wrote *The Complaint of Peace*, in which Peace, speaking in the first-person, complains about how humanity treats her. She claims to offer "the source of all human blessings" and to be scorned by people who "go in quest of evils infinite in number."

The *Complaint* is not a contemporary twenty-first century piece of thinking; its outdatedness in any number of areas is immediately obvious. But that's to be expected in an essay written 500 years ago in Latin for a readership made up of what we would call creationists, astrologers, monarchists, and Eurocentric bigots.

What ought to amaze us is the extent to which the *Complaint* does address the same troubles we face today and the same bad arguments used today in defense of wars. The *Complaint* offers rebuttals to such arguments that have never been surpassed. Its text could serve as the basis for dozens of important sermons were some preacher inclined to favor peace on earth.

Peace, in her complaint to us, begins by imagining that humans must be insane to pursue war instead of her. She does not complain out of indignation, but weeps over people who actively bring so much harm on themselves and are incapable of even realizing it. The first step, Erasmus/Peace says, is recognizing that you have a problem. Or rather, "It is one great step to convalescence to know the extent and inveteracy of a disease."

War was deemed to be the supreme international crime at Nuremberg following World War II, because it includes all other evils within it. Erasmus defined war in that manner a good four-and-a-half centuries earlier, calling war an ocean "of all the united plagues and pestilences in nature."

Erasmus (in the voice of Peace) notes that many other types of animals do not wage war on their own species. And he notes the universal presence of love and cooperation among humans, animals born unarmed and obliged to find safety in numbers.

Erasmus proposes that we think of ourselves as humans, and thereby become unwilling to make war on any of our brother and sister humans anywhere. Admittedly, 500 years may be a little rushed for some people to catch on to that idea.

On a search for peacefulness, Peace hunts in vain among seemingly polite and amicable princes, among academics whom she finds as corrupted by war as we find ours today, among religious leaders whom she denounces as the hypocrites we've come to know so well, and even among secluded monks. Peace looks into family life and into the internal mental life of an individual and finds no devotion to peace.

Erasmus points Christian readers toward the words supporting peace in the New Testament. One might accuse him of hand-picking his quotes and avoiding those that don't support his goal, except that Erasmus quite openly says that that's what he's doing and advises others to do the same. The vengeful God of the Old Testament should be ignored in favor of the peaceful God of Jesus, Erasmus writes. And those who can't so ignore Him, writes Erasmus, should re-interpret him as peaceful. Let "God of vengeance" mean vengeance "on those sins which rob us of repose."

Solomon the peace-maker was more worthy than David the war-maker, Peace says, despite David's war-making being at the bidding of God. So, imagine, Peace argues, if David's divinely commanded wars rendered him unholy, "what will be the effect of wars of ambition, wars of revenge, and wars of furious anger"—i.e. the wars of Erasmus' day and our own.

The cause of wars, Erasmus finds, is kings and their war-hungry chickenhawk advisors. The term in Latin is not exactly "chickenhawk" but the meaning comes through. Erasmus advises addressing the causes of war in greed and the pursuit of power, glory, and revenge. And he credits Jesus with having done the same, with having taught love and forgiveness as the basis for peace.

Kings, writes Erasmus, start wars to seize territory when they would be better off improving the territory they have now. Or they start wars out of a personal grudge. Or they start wars to disrupt popular opposition to themselves at home. Such kings, Erasmus writes, should be exiled for life to the remotest islands. And not just the kings but their privileged advisors. Ordinary people don't create wars, says Peace, those in power impose wars on them.

Powerful people calling themselves Christian have created such a climate, says Peace, that speaking up for Christian forgiveness is taken to be treasonous and evil, while promoting war is understood to be good and loyal and directed at a nation's happiness. Erasmus has little tolerance for Orwellian propaganda about "supporting the troops" and proposes that clergy refuse to bury in consecrated ground anyone slain in battle:

> "The unfeeling mercenary soldier, hired by a few pieces of paltry coin, to do the work of man-butcher, carries before him the standard of the cross; and that very figure becomes the symbol of war, which alone ought to teach every one that looks at it, that war ought to be utterly abolished. What hast thou to do with the cross of Christ on thy banners, thou blood-stained soldier? With such a disposition as thine; with deeds like thine, of robbery and murder, thy proper standard would be a dragon, a tiger, or wolf!"

> " . . . If you detest robbery and pillage, remember these are among the duties of war; and that, to learn how to commit them adroitly, is a part of military discipline. Do you shudder

*at the idea of murder? You cannot require to be told, that to*
*commit it with dispatch, and by wholesale, constitutes the*
*celebrated art of war."*

Peace proposes in her complaint that kings submit their grievances to wise and impartial arbiters, and points out that even if the arbiters are unjust neither side will suffer to remotely the extent that they would from war. Perhaps peace must be purchased—but compare the price to the cost of a war! For the price of destroying a town you could have built one, Peace says.

For arbitration to replace war, Peace says, we will need better kings and better courtiers. You can't get any more timely and relevant than that.

## *From Helen to Hillary: Women in War*

Accepted wisdom in U.S. culture, despite overwhelming evidence, holds that the two nuclear bombs dropped on Japan shortened World War II and saved more lives than the some 200,000 lives they took away.

And yet, weeks before the first bomb was dropped, on July 13, 1945, Japan sent a telegram to the Soviet Union expressing its desire to surrender and end the war. The United States had broken Japan's codes and read the telegram. U.S. President Harry Truman referred in his diary to "the telegram from Jap Emperor asking for peace."

Truman had been informed through Swiss and Portuguese channels of Japanese peace overtures as early as three months before Hiroshima. Japan objected only to surrendering unconditionally and giving up its emperor, but the United States insisted on those terms until after the bombs fell, at which point it allowed Japan to keep its emperor.

Presidential advisor James Byrnes had told Truman that dropping the bombs would allow the United States to "dictate the terms of ending the war." Secretary of the Navy James Forrestal wrote in his diary that Byrnes was "most anxious to get the Japanese affair over with before the Russians got in." Truman wrote in his diary that the Soviets were preparing to march against Japan and "Fini Japs when that comes about." Truman ordered the bomb dropped on Hiroshima on August 6th and another type of bomb, a plutonium bomb, which the military also wanted to test and demonstrate, on Nagasaki on August 9th.

Also on August 9th, the Soviets attacked the Japanese. During the next two weeks, the Soviets killed 84,000 Japanese while losing 12,000 of their own soldiers, and the United States continued bombing Japan with non-nuclear weapons. Then the Japanese surrendered.

The United States Strategic Bombing Survey concluded that,"… certainly prior to 31 December, 1945, and in all probability prior to 1 November, 1945, Japan would have surrendered even if the atomic bombs had not been dropped, even if Russia had not entered the war, and even if no invasion had been planned or contemplated." One dissenter who had expressed this same view to the Secretary of War prior to the bombings was General Dwight Eisenhower.

The Chairman of the Joint Chiefs of Staff Admiral William D. Leahy agreed: "The use of this barbarous weapon at Hiroshima and Nagasaki was of no material assistance in our war against Japan. The Japanese were already defeated and ready to surrender."

It was with knowledge of these undisputed but collectively ignored facts that I recently read a review[219] of a book called *The Girls of Atomic City: The Untold Story of the Women Who Helped Win World War II*. The women or girls involved did not in any way help win World War II, and the author and publisher surely know that. These women worked in Oak Ridge, Tennessee, producing the bombs that would kill, injure, traumatize, and destroy on a scale never before imagined—leaving us decades later in serious danger of accidental or intentional apocalypse. But the idea that they helped win or end a war is a lie.

That the atomic girls didn't know exactly what they were building is no excuse any more than the Nazi's "I was just following orders" was an excuse. But these women's ignorance of what they were making would, I think, diminish their heroism had they done something at all heroic. In reality, they blindly participated in mass-murder by knowingly assisting a war effort, and were willing to do so without being given any of the details. In other words,

___

219        http://www.dailyprogress.com/lifestyles/virginia-festival-of-the-book-kiernan-shares-the-seldom-heard/article_df7291e6-abb8-11e3-a287-001a4bcf6878.html

they proved capable of doing just what millions of men have done. Should we be proud?

The point of the book and the article seems to be that young women did something. The author describes them as "brave" and compares their bravery to that of U.S. soldiers off obediently killing and dying in the war. The review describes the U.S. government's eviction of 1,000 families from their homes in Tennessee to make room for the nuclear bomb making. "Only something of the magnitude of saving the nation could possibly justify causing such heartbreak," writes the reviewer. Really? What could justify the mass-slaughter of some 200,000 people? And what exactly was the nation saved from? Shouldn't such language ("saving the nation") be made to mean something rather than being tossed around carelessly? And hadn't the U.S. government just 10 years earlier evicted 500 families to build Shenandoah National Park, neither to save the nation nor to kill lots of foreigners, but just because?

The relationship of women to war has changed dramatically in recent decades, even while remaining the same. Attractive women recruiting young men into the army can trace their lineage to Helen of Troy. Women raped[220] and killed in war have a history as old as war. Women resisters to war are as old as war as well. But there are at least four big changes. First, women now participate in war, as well as in weapons production, in a major way. (Why the great ineluctable forces of genetics and destiny that always justify evil in weak minds will allow women to join in war but not allow men to abandon war is not clear to me.) Second, women—to a

---

220 http://davidswanson.org/node/3952

limited extent—participate in making the decision to wage wars. Third, women are not just secondary victims of war anymore; rather, female babies, toddlers, girls, women, and grandmothers make up about half of wars' casualties, 90% of whom are civilians. And fourth, with wars no longer solely advertised as ways to seize territory or develop manhood or bring glory to a flag, it has become common to advertise them as a way to bring women their rights and freedoms.

Not the right not to be bombed, of course. But the right, if they survive the war, to work and drive and vote and endure invasive ultrasounds, or whatever the West believes a woman's rights should be. In 2001, the United States was told that Afghanistan would be bombed for revenge. But since revenge is barbaric and vile, and since the criminals being punished were already dead, and since most of the people in Afghanistan had nothing to do with 9-11 and wished no part in any war, it was helpful to add another motivation. Afghanistan would also be bombed, we were told, for women's rights—rights that had indeed been devastated following U.S. efforts to provoke the Soviet Union and then arm religious fanatics against it. Five weeks into the bombing, Laura Bush, the U.S. "first lady," proclaimed: "Because of our recent military gains in much of Afghanistan, women are no longer imprisoned in their homes. The fight against terrorism is also a fight for the rights and dignity of women."

Of course, when U.S. special forces burst into a home and shot pregnant women, and then dug the bullets out with their knives in order to blame the murders on the women's husbands, the goal was not the advancement of women's rights. But the war had nothing to do with that in reality. The U.S. empowered the warlords of the Northern Alliance, whom the Revolutionary Association of Women of Afghanistan (RAWA) denounced as "brethren-in-creed of the Taliban and Al-Qaida." RAWA reported: "The war in Afghanistan has removed the Taliban, which so far does appear to be an improvement for women in certain limited parts of the country. In other areas, the incidence of rape and forced marriage is on the rise again, and most women continue to wear the burqa out of fear for their safety." After over a decade of U.S./NATO liberation, Afghanistan remains one of the worst places to be a woman or to become a mother. Child marriage, rape in marriage, and prosecution of rape victims for adultery remain legal and accepted. It was in this context that Amnesty International put up big posters on bus stops in Chicago during a NATO meeting, reading—without intended irony: "Human rights for women and girls in Afghanistan. NATO keep the progress going!"

"Progress" is rolling ahead in liberated Iraq as well, where the legal age of marriage is being lowered[221] from 18 to 9. Similarly in liberated Libya, women are worse off. Similarly in monarchies and dictatorships that the U.S. government chooses to arm rather than overthrow because of their cooperative behavior: women are not enjoying the blessings of freedom unimpeded in Saudi Arabia, Bahrain, Egypt, et cetera—although many women are struggling admirably to advance their rights by nonviolent and effective means.

Another place women's rights are suffering is in the U.S. military, where studies have found that a third[222] of women are sexually

221      http://www.globalresearch.ca/war-and-the-rights-of-children-americas-proxy-government-legalizes-pedophilia-in-occupied-iraq/5373303
222 http://davidswanson.org/node/4334

assaulted or raped by their fellow soldiers and commanders. One expert believes[223] that the frequency of such attacks on male recruits is just as high but less often reported. Of course, if that's true, it does nothing to mitigate the horror, but simply adds to it. So young women reading about the glories of "saving the nation" by building nukes should think hard before joining the military—hard enough, perhaps, to oppose it on the grounds that it's mass murder.

There's another story from Oak Ridge that ought to be read more widely, the story[224] of one woman and two men just sentenced to prison for nonviolently protesting the nuclear weapons facility still found there. Here's a story of heroism and inspiration with no falsehoods, a story of wisdom and thoughtful action requiring incredible bravery and selflessness. Why we strain so hard to find such stories outside of nonviolent activism would be a mystery to me, were the reasons not readily to be found in the massive investment that war profiteers make in selling the idea of war.

There's a broader story, as well, of heroic women advancing a movement against war and toward a culture of peace. Here's proof aplenty of that: http://codepink4peace.org ----- http://nobelwomensinitiative.org ----- http://wilpfus.org http://worldwidewamm.org ----- http://wand.org

And here's what we're up against: the coming promotion of a woman warmonger[225] as a token carrier of progressive liberalism. Don't fall for it.

223 http://davidswanson.org/node/4334
224 http://transformnowplowshares.wordpress.com/
225 http://warisacrime.org/hillary

# The War Activists

War activists, like peace activists, push for an agenda. We don't think of them as activists because they rotate in and out of government positions, receive huge amounts of funding, have access to big media, and get meetings with top officials just by asking—without having to generate a protest first.

They also display great contempt for the public and openly discuss ways to manipulate people through fear and nationalism—further shifting their image away from that of popular organizers. But war activists are not journalists, not researchers, not academics. They don't inform or educate. They advocate. They just advocate for something that most of the time, and increasingly, nobody wants.

William Kristol and Robert Kagan and their organization, the Foreign Policy Initiative, stand out as exemplary war activists. They've modified their tone slightly since the days of the Project for the New American Century, an earlier war activist organization. They talk less about oil and more about human rights. But they insist on U.S. domination of the world. They find any success by anyone else in the world a threat to the United States. And they demand an ever larger and more frequently used military, even if world domination can be achieved without it. War, for these war activists, is an end in itself. As was much more common in the 19th century, these agitators believe war brings strength and glory, builds character, and makes a nation a Super Power.

Kristol recently lamented U.S. public opposition to war. He does have cause for concern. The U.S. public is sick of wars, outraged by those in Iraq and Afghanistan, and insistent that new ones not be begun. In September, missile strikes into Syria were successfully opposed by public resistance. In February, a new bill to impose sanctions on Iran and commit the United States to joining in any Israeli-Iranian war was blocked by public pressure. The country and the world are turning against the drone wars.

The next logical step after ending wars and preventing wars would be to begin dismantling the infrastructure that generates pressure for wars. This hasn't happened yet. During every NCAA basketball game the announcers thank U.S. troops for watching from 175 nations. Weapons sales are soaring. New nukes are being developed. NATO has expanded to the edge of Russia. But the possibility of change is in the air. A new peace activist group at WorldBeyondWar.org has begun pushing for war's abolition.

Here's Kristol panicking:

> "A war-weary public can be awakened and rallied. Indeed, events are right now doing the awakening. All that's needed is the rallying. And the turnaround can be fast. Only 5 years after the end of the Vietnam war, and 15 years after our involvement there began in a big way, Ronald Reagan ran against both Democratic dovishness and Republican détente. He proposed confronting the Soviet Union and rebuilding our military. It was said that the country was too war-weary, that it was too soon after Vietnam, for Reagan's stern and challenging message. Yet Reagan won the election in 1980. And by 1990 an awakened America had won the Cold War."

Here's Kagan, who has worked for Hillary Clinton and whose wife Victoria Nuland has just been stirring up trouble in Ukraine as Assistant Secretary of State. This is from an article by Kagan much admired by President Barack Obama:

> *"As Yan Xuetong recently noted, 'military strength underpins hegemony.' Here the United States remains unmatched. It is far and away the most powerful nation the world has ever known, and there has been no decline in America's relative military capacity—at least not yet."*

This pair is something of a good-cop/bad-cop team. Kristol bashes Obama for being a wimp and not fighting enough wars. Kagan reassures Obama that he can be master of the universe if he'll only build up the military a bit more and maybe fight a couple more wars here and there.

The response[226] from some Obama supporters has been to point out that their hero has been fighting lots of wars and killing lots of people, thank you very much. The response from some peace activists is to play to people's selfishness with cries to bring the war dollars home. But humanitarian warriors are right to care about the world, even if they're only pretending or badly misguided about how to help. It's OK to oppose wars both because they kill huge numbers of poor people far from our shores and because we could have used the money for schools and trains. But it's important to add that for a small fraction of U.S. military spending we could ensure that the whole world had food and clean water

226  http://www.dailykos.com/story/2014/03/18/1285774/-Bill-Kristol-confuses-fiasco-fatigue-with-war-weariness?detail=email

and medicine. We could be the most beloved nation. I know that's not the status the war activists are after. In fact, when people begin to grasp that possibility, war activism will be finished for good.

# *War for Dummies*

Sorry for the headline if it got you hoping for a quick 1-step guide on how to bomb a country without breaking a sweat. I didn't actually mean that I could teach a dummy to wage a war. I meant that only dummies want to wage wars.

Need proof? Check out a recent Washington Post report[227].

Now there I go misleading you again. While it's true that the editors of the *Washington Post* are often dummies and often want wars to be waged, that's not what I mean right now. I think members of the U.S. government and its obedient media constitute an important but tiny exception to the rule this report points to.

The facts as reported on April 7th are these:

13% of us in the United States want our government to use force in Ukraine;

16% of us can accurately identify Ukraine's location on a map;

the median error by Americans placing Ukraine on a map is 1,800 miles;

some Americans, based on where they identified Ukraine on

---

227      http://www.washingtonpost.com/blogs/monkey-cage/wp/2014/04/07/the-less-americans-know-about-ukraines-location-the-more-they-want-u-s-to-intervene/

a map, believe that Ukraine is in the United States, some say it's in Canada, some Africa, some Australia, some Greenland, some Argentina, Brazil, China, or India;

only a small number believe Ukraine is in an ocean.

And here's the interesting bit:

> "[T]he further our respondents thought that Ukraine was from its actual location, the more they wanted the U.S. to intervene militarily. Even controlling for a series of demographic characteristics and participants' general foreign policy attitudes, we found that the less accurate our participants were, the more they wanted the U.S. to use force, the greater the threat they saw Russia as posing to U.S. interests, and the more they thought that using force would advance U.S. national security interests."

I take this to mean that some people believe that attacking Alaska or the continental United States (where they believe Ukraine to be located) will advance "U.S. national security interests." This suggests one of two things: either they believe the United States would be better off bombed (and perhaps suicidal tendencies account for some of the staggering stupidity reported by the *Washington Post*) or they believe the United States is located in Asia or Africa or somewhere other than where they've indicated that Ukraine is on the map.

I also take this report to mean the following: ignorant jackasses are the only statistically significant group that wants more wars.

Virtually nobody in the United States wants a U.S. war in Iran or Syria or Ukraine. Nobody. Except for serious hardcore idiots. We're talking about people who can't place Ukraine in the correct landmass, but who believe the United States should go to war there.

People informed enough to find Ukraine on a map are also informed enough to oppose wars. People who can't find Ukraine on a map but possess an ounce of humility or a drop of decency also oppose war. You don't have to be smart to oppose wars. But you have to be an unfathomably ignorant jackass to favor them. Or—back to that exception—you could work for the government.

Why, I wonder, don't pollsters always poll and report sufficiently to tell us whether an opinion correlates with being informed on an issue? I recall a poll[228] (by Rasmussen), tragic or humorous depending on your mood, that found 25% of Americans wanting their government to always spend at least three times as much on its military as any other nation spends, while 64% said their government spends the right amount on the military now or should spend more. This only gets tragic or humorous if you are aware that the United States already spends much more than three times what any other nation spends on its military. In other words, large numbers of people want military spending increased only because they don't know how high it is already.

But what I want to know is: Do the individuals who have the facts most wrong want the biggest spending increases? And I wonder: do pollsters want us to know how much opinions follow facts? If

---

228 http://warisacrime.org/content/poll-americans-dramatically-underestimate-what-their-government-spends-its-military

opinions follow factual beliefs, after all, it might make sense to replace some of the bickering of pundits on our televisions with educational information, and to stop thinking of ourselves as divided by ideology or temperament when what we're divided by is largely the possession of facts and the lack thereof.

## *War Is Good for Us, Dumb New Book Claims*

Ian Morris has stuck his dog's ear in his mouth, snapped a selfie, and proclaimed "Man Bites Dog." His new book *War: What Is It Good For? Conflict and Progress of Civilization from Primates to Robots* is intended to prove that war is good for children and other living things. It actually proves that defenders of war are growing desperate for arguments.

Morris maintains that the only way to make peace is to make large societies, and the only way to make large societies is through war. Ultimately, he believes, the only way to protect peace is through a single global policeman. Once you've made peace, he believes, prosperity follows. And from that prosperity flows happiness. Therefore, war creates happiness. But the one thing you must never stop engaging in if you hope to have peace, prosperity, and joy is—you guessed it—war.

This thesis becomes an excuse for hundreds of pages of a sort of Monty Python history of the technologies of war, not to mention the evolution of chimpanzees, and various even less relevant excursions. These pages are packed with bad history and guesswork, and I'm greatly tempted to get caught up in the details. But none of it has much impact on the book's conclusions. All of Morris's history, accurate and otherwise, is put to mythological use. He's telling a simplistic story about where safety and happiness originated, and advocating highly destructive misery-inducing behavior as a result.

When small, medium, and large societies have been and are peaceful, Morris ignores them. There are lots of ways to define peaceful[229], but none of them put the leading war maker at the top, and none of them place at the top only nations that could be imagined to fall under a Pax Americana.

When societies have been enlarged peacefully, as in the formation of the European Union, Morris applauds (he thinks the E.U. earned its peace prize, and no doubt all the more so for its extensive war making as deputy globocop) but he just skips over the fact that war wasn't used in the E.U.'s formation. (He avoids the United Nations entirely.)

When the globocop brings death and destruction and disorder to Afghanistan, Iraq, Libya, or Yemen, Morris sticks his fingers in his ears and hums. "Interstate wars" he informs us (like most of his other claims, without any footnotes) have "almost disappeared." Well isn't *that* great news?! (Morris grotesquely minimizes Iraqi deaths from the recent [nonexistent?] war[230], and of course supplies no footnote.)

---

229 http://www.visionofhumanity.org
230 http://warisacrime.org/iraq

In a culture that has long waged wars, it has been possible to say that wars bring courage, wars bring heroism, wars bring slaves, wars bring cultural exchange. One could have asserted at various points that wars were the only way to a great many ends, not just large societies that reduce small-scale murders. Barely a century ago William James was worried there was no way to build character without war, and defenders of war were advertising it as good for its participants in a much more direct way than Morris has been reduced to. Has war been the means of building empires and nations? Sure, but that neither means that empires are the only way to peace, nor that war was the only nation-building tool available, nor that we must keep waging wars in an age in which we aren't forming empires or nations any longer. That ancient pyramids may have been built by slaves hardly makes slavery the best or only way to preserve the pyramids.

Tying something good, such as ending slavery in the United States, to a war, such as the U.S. Civil War, doesn't make war the only way to end slavery. In fact, most nations that ended slavery did so without a war. Much less is continuing to wage wars the only possible way (or even a useful way at all) to hold off the restoration of slavery or to complete its eradication. And, by the way, a great many societies that Morris credits with making progress through war also had slavery, monarchy, women-as-property, environmental destruction, and worship of religions now defunct. Were those institutions also necessary for peace and prosperity, or are they irrelevant to it, or did we overcome some of them through peaceful means? Morris, at one point, acknowledges that slavery (not just war) generated European wealth, later crediting the industrial revolution as well—the godfather of which, in his mind, was no doubt peace created by war. (What did you expect, the Spanish Inquisition?)

The tools of nonviolence that have achieved so much in the past century are never encountered in Morris' book, so no comparison with war is offered. Nonviolent revolutions have tended to dismember empires or alter the leadership of a nation that remains the same size, so Morris must not view them as useful tools, even when they produce more free and prosperous societies. But it's not clear Morris can recognize those when he sees them. Morris claims that in the past 30 years "we" (he seems to mean in the United States, but could mean the world, it's not totally clear) have become "safer and richer than ever."

Morris brags about U.S. murder rates falling, and yet dozens of nations from every continent have lower murder rates than the U.S. Nor do larger nations tend to have lower murder rates than smaller nations. Morris holds up Denmark as a model, but never looks at Denmark's society, its distribution of wealth, its social supports. Morris claims the whole world is growing more equal in wealth.

Back here in reality, historians of the Middle Ages say that our age has the greater disparities—disparities that are growing within the United States in particular, but globally as well. Oxfam reports that the richest 85 people in the world have more money than the poorest 3.5 billion. That is the peace that Morris swears is not a wasteland. The United States ranks[231] third in average wealth but

---

231      http://www.washingtonpost.com/blogs/wonkblog/wp/2014/01/22/10-startling-facts-about-global-wealth-inequality/

27th in median wealth. Yet, somehow Morris believes the United States can lead the way to "Denmark" and that Denmark itself can only be Denmark because of how many people the United States kills in "productive wars" (even though they have "almost disappeared"). Morris writes these scraps of wisdom from Silicon Valley, where he says he sees nothing but wealth, yet where people with nowhere to sleep but in a car may soon be banned[232] from doing so.

We're also safer, Morris thinks, because he sees no climate emergency worth worrying about. He's quite openly in favor of wars for oil, yet never notices oil's effects until the end of the book when he takes a moment to brush such concerns aside.

We're also safer, Morris tells us, because there are no longer enough nukes in the world to kill us all. Has he never heard of nuclear famine[233]? Does he not understand the growing risks of proliferating nuclear weapons and energy? Two nations have thousands of nukes ready to launch in an instant, every one of them many times more powerful than the two nuclear bombs dropped thus far; and one of those nations is prodding the other one with a stick in Ukraine, resulting in more, not less, violence in the beneficiary of such expansionism. Meanwhile the officials overseeing U.S. nukes keep getting caught cheating on tests or shipping nukes across the country unguarded, and generally view nuclear weapons oversight as the lowest most dead-end career track. This makes us safer?

---

232   http://www.theguardian.com/commentisfree/2014/apr/15/ban-sleeping-in-cars-homeless-silicon-valley

233 http://www.wagingpeace.org/issues/nuclear-weapons/nuclear-famine/

Morris hypes lies[234] about Iran pursuing nuclear weapons. He opens the book with a tale of a near nuclear holocaust (one of many he could have chosen). And yet, somehow disarmament isn't on the agenda, at least not with the priority given to maintaining or increasing war spending. Not to worry, he assures us, "missile defense" actually works, or might someday, so that'll protect us—although he parenthetically admits it won't. The point is it's warlike, and war is good, because war spreads peace. That's the role the U.S. must play for the good of all: policeman of the world. Morris, while clearly a huge fan of Barack Obama, believes that all recent U.S. presidents should have a Nobel Peace Prize. Never does Morris comment on the fact that the rest of the world sees[235] the United States as the greatest threat to world peace.

Morris admits that the United States is encircling China with weapons, but he describes in sinister tones China's response of building weaponry that will only serve a function near China's own shores, not as defensive or unimperialistic, but at "asymmetrical"— and we all know what that means: unfair! China might make it hard for the globocop to wage war on and around China. This Morris sees as the looming danger. The solution, he thinks, is for the United States to keep its militaristic edge (never mind that its military makes China's look like a child's toy). More drone killing is not only good but also (and this sort of nonsense always makes you wonder why its advocate bothers advocating) inevitable. Of course, the United States won't start a war against China, says Morris, because launching wars hurts a nation's reputation so

234 http://justworldbooks.com/manufactured-crisis/
235    http://www.huffingtonpost.com/2014/01/02/greatest-threat-world-peace-country_n_4531824.html

severely. (You can see how badly the U.S. reputation has suffered in Morris' eyes following its latest string of wars.)

And yet, what lies on the horizon, almost inevitably, Morris contends, is World War III. There's nothing you can do about it. Don't bother working for peace[236], Morris says. But a solution may arrive nonetheless. If we can go on dumping our money into wars for just one more century, or maybe more, proliferating weapons, destroying the environment, losing our liberties in the model land of the free, then—if we're really lucky—the computer programmers of Silicon Valley will save us, or some of us, or something, by . . . wait for it . . . hooking us up to computers so that our minds all meld together.

Morris may be more confident than I that the result of this computerized rapture will be worldwide empathy rather than revulsion. But then, he's had longer to get used to living with the way he thinks.

## Honestly, War Is Over

*Remarks in Los Angeles, May 10, 2014.*

Thank you to Pat Alviso and all the individuals and groups involved in setting this event up. Thank you to Lila Garrett for doing twice what I do at twice my age, including hosting the best radio show around. And thank you to our friend, recently lost, Tim Carpenter, for whom there is a memorial event today in

---

236 http://worldbeyondwar.org

Massachusetts. We will not forget you, Tim, and we will carry on.
Now, about ending war.

When we start talking about ending war, one common reaction—
not as common as "You're a lunatic," but fairly common—is to
propose that if we want to get rid of war we'll have to get rid of
something else first, or sometimes it's a series of something elses.
We'll have to get rid of bankers or bribery or the current structure
of our government, or the corporate media monopoly. We'll have
to get rid of racism or bigotry or extreme materialism. We'll have
to abolish capitalism or environmental exploitation or religion or
greed or resource shortages or sociopaths, and then we'll be able
to move on to abolishing war.

Now, I think there's truth and falsehood in a lot of such two-
step proposals. War is made easier by many evil things. Ending
war would be easier if we ended those things. Ending war and
some other things together might be an easier job because of
the broader coalition that would work on it. And I'm in favor of
ending lots of bad things—racism, bribery, predatory capitalism,
mass incarceration, the White House Correspondents Dinner,
etc.—and I would be even if doing so didn't help end war.

But war is not made necessary by anything else. The United States
has roughly 5% of the world's population and 50% of the world's
military spending. Many nations spend 10% or 5% or less what
the United States spends on war, but they don't have only 5% of
the racism or 5% as many sociopaths (how ever those are defined).
Nations with plenty of bigotry and serious resource shortages

manage to nonetheless avoid U.S. levels of war investment (whether measured absolutely or as a proportion of wealth). The U.S. media at the moment seems to care about burned Nigerians more than burned Ukrainians; racism can serve imperialism but can also be trumped by it.

In addition, if you look at particular wars launched and possible wars not launched, it becomes clear that the decisions are entirely contingent on human choices. When a particular war is stopped, the lesson we ought to take away is not that the forces of consumerism and capitalism and exploitation will build up greater pressure, making it more likely than before that another war will soon be launched. The lesson we ought to take away, on the contrary, is that because one war has been stopped, the next war can be stopped as well, and the one after it, and the next 100 after that one.

I'm a big fan of the journalist Seymour Hersh, including of the help he's been in exposing the fraudulent case that was built up to support a White House proposal last summer for missile strikes into Syria—and the help he's been in exposing the massive scale of the attack that was being contemplated. Some of us had figured out all on our own that when Secretary of State John Kerry said the missile strikes would shift the balance in the war AND be so small as to have no effect on the war, at least one of those two assertions had to be false. It turns out that the plan was for a major assault, not a tiny one. What the result would have been nobody can be sure—beyond widespread death, injury, trauma, and suffering. Two wings of B-52 bombers carrying 2,000-pound bombs were to take out "electric power grids, oil and gas depots, all known logistic and weapons depots, all known command and control facilities, and all known military and intelligence buildings." This was not a few missiles. This was shock and awe, targeting numerous facilities in densely populated urban areas. If you need an example of the Obama White House immediately expanding a war like this one once begun, the obvious example is Libya.

But when Hersh writes and talks about what went on back in August and September, he doesn't seem to even consider the possibility that public pressure might have played even the slightest role in preventing the missile strikes. Democracy Now! interviewed Hersh and didn't raise the topic. I don't mean to pick on Seymour Hersh or Democracy Now! Nobody else has done any different. A friend of mine, a former CIA officer, Ray McGovern, has been doing some great writing about Syria. He, like Hersh, considers the steps taken by the Chairman of the Joint Chiefs of Staff, the Congress, the Russians, the President. Nowhere is the public mentioned.

Now, even if the public played no role whatsoever, that fact in itself would be worthy of serious consideration. Members of both houses of Congress from both parties said they had heard more from their constituents on the missiles-into-Syria proposal than they had heard ever before on anything else, and that what they heard was more one-sided than anything they'd experienced before. If the public had no impact, or if Congress had no impact, the scale of the pretense otherwise—and the possible futility of ever lobbying Congress on anything—would make for a remarkable story.

Virtually this entire country was opposed to the missile strikes. Add to that the fact that Congress members were on break and being directly confronted at district townhall meetings, accused of joining a war on the side of al Qaeda, accused of falling for propaganda again. It didn't hurt that Jewish holidays left AIPAC missing in action. It was an advantage that many people in the halls of power were themselves reluctant to launch a war. But why were they? Why were members of Congress stating that they didn't want to be the guy who voted for another Iraq war? Why did the House of Commons oppose a prime minister on war for the first time since Yorktown? Why did the conversation swing away from the missile strikes?

President Obama and his Secretary of State were telling us to watch Youtubes of suffering children and support that suffering or support missile strikes. That's not a half-hearted sales pitch. Wall Street was completely sold: Raytheon, the company that made the missiles, saw its stock hit an all-time high. The leaders of both big political parties were on board. The corporate news outlets were gung ho. John Kerry was calling Bashar al Assad a new Hitler. The illegality of the proposed action was hardly a blip in the conversation, the way it might have been before Afghanistan and Iraq and Libya and the drone wars. Illegality had become the new normal.

Russia and Syria came up with a solution, but they'd been willing to do that for some time. President Obama allowed Congress to have a say as he had not on Libya and does not on most drone strikes (we all, including Congress, pretend it's up to the president to allow Congress to act). But why did he? I think it can help to contrast the war-and-peace climate in the U.S. in 2013 with a different, imaginary one. I proposed this to Ray McGovern, and he completely agreed.

Imagine that the wars on Afghanistan and Iraq were considered the peak of U.S. glory, were routinely celebrated, were what everyone had come to hope for as the ideal outcomes for all future wars. Imagine that those who voted against the war on Iraq were shamed and shunned and forced to defend their mistake. Imagine 90% of the country rather than 5 or 10% favored every new war proposal. Imagine that doubt of new assertions about chemical weapons use or other supposed reasons for wars was unheard of. Imagine crowds chanting their demands for more wars, bigger wars, more costly wars, greater destruction, more extravagant atrocities. Imagine the phones in Washington ringing off the hook and the online petitions flooding in with a demand for war rather than a demand to avoid it. In such a climate, would the balance have tipped the little bit that it tipped, bumping war—which is never a last resort—into the position of second resort, from the first-resort action that it had been the day before?

Now, to claim that public pressure, both over the past decade or longer and immediately, may have had some impact is not to reject other factors. This was a horribly timed, horribly marketed war that any self-respecting member of the world's second-oldest profession, war propaganda, should be ashamed of. Another war might have been harder to stop. Nor would it be right to claim a complete victory, with the U.S. government continuing to arm and train and support fighters in the war, and with no investment in humanitarian aid or diplomacy or nonviolent peace workers to match the public demand. The crisis in Syria rolls on, reinforcing the ridiculous notion that if you aren't going to bomb a country, there's nothing else you can do for it. But the resolution of the Syrian Missile Crisis, like the blocking of a sanctions-and-possible-war-on-Iran bill earlier this year, suggests possible victories to come, as well as suggesting that no underlying force makes any war inevitable.

If I had to pick a factor to eliminate, in hopes that war would be eliminated as well, and if I had the magical ability to effectively eliminate any factor I chose, I think I would pick, rather than bigotry or greed, the factor of dishonesty. While you can have dishonesty without war, you cannot have war without dishonesty. You can have lies about other, much smaller public programs: police, schools, parks, courts, housing, agriculture, research, environmental protection, diplomacy, etc., but you can also create and fund such programs *without* lying about them. In contrast, there's no example of an honest war, and there's reason to believe that there cannot be one.

This isn't new, and it extends as far back as historical records, probably farther. Enemies are dehumanized, threats and abuses are invented or exaggerated, victims in need of rescue or protection or vengeance are airbrushed or pulled out of thin air. Victory is always right around the corner. And if nothing is accomplished, the war is glorified as an end in itself. This country began with these lies about Native Americans. In 1812, among other occasions,

Canada was depicted as eager to be liberated. Then Mexico was falsely said to have invaded the United States. Spain was said to have blown up the *Maine*. President Wilson pretended the troops and arms on the *Lusitania* had not been public knowledge. The Gulf of Tonkin incident launched war on Vietnam despite never happening. The Gulf War began two-decades of devastation for Iraq after a completely fictional skit created by a public relations company pretended babies had been taken out of incubators.

These are not exceptions. Every war requires such lies about fake motives and omission of real motives, as well as lies about how the war is proceeding. One-sided slaughters of civilians on a scale that ancient and medieval wars couldn't approach are depicted as sporting contests on battlefields in which the aggressor suffers. Polls find a majority in the United States believing Iraqis benefitted from the war that destroyed Iraq. That lie is more dangerous than the WMD lies ever were. Lies about the glory of WWI after 100 years of war failing to end all war, lies about victory in Korea and nobility in Vietnam: these are major undertakings for governments like ours for a reason.

A central lie for war-makers is the pretense of working for peace. The United States worked for the breakup of Yugoslavia, intentionally prevented negotiated agreements among the parties, and engaged in a massive bombing campaign, 15 years ago, that killed large numbers of people, injured many more, destroyed civilian infrastructure and hospitals and media outlets, and created a refugee crisis that did not exist until after the bombing had begun. This was accomplished through lies, fabrications, and exaggerations about atrocities, and then justified anachronistically as a response to violence that it generated.

The United States backed an invasion of Rwanda on October 1, 1990, by a Ugandan army led by U.S.-trained killers, and supported their attack on Rwanda for three-and-a-half years. People fled the invaders, creating a huge refugee crisis, ruined agriculture, wrecked economy, and shattered society. The United States and the West armed the warmakers and applied additional pressure through the World Bank, IMF, and USAID. And among the results of the war was increased hostility between Hutus and Tutsis. Eventually the government would topple. First would come the mass slaughter known as the Rwandan Genocide. And before that would come the murder of two presidents. At that point, in April 1994, Rwanda was in chaos almost on the level of post-liberation Iraq or Libya. The U.S.-backed government post-slaughter took war into the Congo, where 6 million people have since been killed. And we're taught that Rwanda is a case where more violence was needed, but where the so-called international community, consisting of representatives of 1 percent of nations containing 8 percent of humanity, supposedly failed to act.

*Never again!* is a shout we hear about Rwanda and about World War II, understood as a war that should have been and a war that righteously was. It's stunning how many people go back 73 years to find an example they support of what has been our top public investment ever since. But was the good war actually good? It is widely accepted that World War I was unnecessary, yet without World War I its sequel is unimaginable. Ending World War I with punishment of an entire nation rather than of the war makers was understood by wise observers at the time to make World War II very likely. The arms race between the two world wars was widely and correctly understood to be making the second war more likely. U.S. and other Western corporations profited by enriching and arming dangerous governments in Germany and Japan, which also had the support of Western governments between the wars. The United States had tutored Japan in imperialism and then provoked it through territorial expansion, economic sanctions, and assistance to the Chinese military. Winston Churchill obtained a secret commitment from U.S. President Franklin Roosevelt to bring the United States into the war. The U.S. government expected the Japanese attack, took numerous actions it knew were likely to provoke it, and prior to the attack: ordered its Navy to war with Japan, instituted a draft, collected the names of Japanese Americans, and ignored peace activists marching in the streets for years against the long build-up to a war with Japan. Japanese Prime Minister Fumimaro Konoye proposed talks with the United States in July 1941, which Roosevelt rejected. President Roosevelt lied to the U.S. public about Nazi attacks on ships and plans to take over the Americas in an effort to win support for entering the war. President Roosevelt and the U.S. government blocked efforts to allow Jewish refugees into the United States or elsewhere. Facts about Nazi crimes in concentration camps were available but played no part in war propaganda until after the war was over. Wise voices predicted accurately that continuing the war would mean the escalation of those crimes. After gaining air superiority, the Allies declined to raid the camps or bomb the railway lines to them. No crimes apart from the war, by any nation, remotely matched in scale the death and destruction of the war itself. The U.S. military and government knew that Japan would surrender without the dropping of nuclear bombs on Japanese cities, but dropped them anyway. The U.S. military put numerous Japanese and German war criminals on its staff following the war. U.S. doctors, engaging in human experimentation during and after World War II, widely viewed the Nuremberg Code as applicable only to Germans. Nonviolent resistance to Nazism in Denmark, Sweden, the Netherlands, and even in Berlin — poorly planned and developed though it was in that day and age — showed remarkable potential. World War II gave the world: wars in which civilians are the primary victims, as well as a permanent massive U.S. military aggressively present around the globe.

It takes two sides to wage a war between wealthy nations. The crimes of one side don't excuse the crimes of the other. The point of recognizing them is to avoid their repetition. Japan's president, with U.S. support, hopes to remove peace from Japan's Constitution. The U.S. government is backing a coup in Ukraine that includes Nazis among its leaders. We are handicapped if we don't know we've been here before. If we only ever say "Never again!" after horrors rather than before them, then the life expectancy of our species is severely limited.

World War II became the good war in contrast to Vietnam, or what the Vietnamese call the American War. Afghanistan became a good war in contrast to Iraq. But we don't view cases of slavery or child abuse or rape as good because other cases are worse. Afghanistan was and is as illegal and immoral and counterproductive on its own despicable terms as Iraq. Decades of horrible policies preceded the latest assault, just as with Iraq. Allies were made enemies and demonized, just as in Iraq. The bulk of the population that just wants to live in peace was deemed essentially valueless, just as in Iraq. There was no U.N. authorization, just as in Iraq. And every effort was made to avoid any peaceful resolution, just as with Iraq. A group of mostly Saudi hijackers had spent time in a number of nations and U.S. states. The Taliban government was willing to turn Osama bin Laden over to a neutral country to be put on trial. The Taliban was not itself al Qaeda, and the vast majority of the people of Afghanistan not only did not support the attacks of 911 but had never heard about them. Over a dozen years into this war, the idea to keep 5,000 troops there for another 10 years and beyond is being reported, not as a decision to keep troops there but as a decision to keep fewer than 10,000, as if keeping 10,000 troops in a country were just the norm. In fact, the U.S. has some million troops in 175 nations; that's an average of 5,714.

Three years ago, the White House claimed that Libyan president Muammar Gaddafi—conveniently, as the head of a government on a Pentagon list of governments to be overthrown—had threated to massacre the people of Benghazi with "no mercy," but the *New York Times* reported that Gaddafi's threat was directed at rebel fighters, not civilians, and that Gaddafi promised amnesty for those "who throw their weapons away." Gaddafi also offered to allow rebel fighters to escape to Egypt if they preferred not to fight to the death. Yet President Obama warned of imminent genocide. The result of NATO joining the war was probably more killing, not less. It certainly extended a war that looked likely to end soon with a victory for Gaddafi.

Last year, the White House claimed with Bush-like certainty that the government of Syria had used chemical weapons. Piece by piece the evidence for that claim has fallen apart. It now looks quite unlikely that the government used chemical weapons, and altogether certain that President Obama possessed no solid evidence that it had. It's also certain that the use of chemical weapons, just like the so-called harboring of bin Laden, and just like the supposed stockpiling of weapons in Iraq, would not have been a legal or moral or practical reason for a war even if true. The same goes for Iran possessing a nuclear weapons program, which we've been told for 30 years, but which has never been true. Read Gareth Porter's new book if you haven't.

And how are the drone wars dependent on lies? Let me count the ways. There's the lie that murder is legal if it's part of a war, the lie that the warmaker gets to make that determination, the lie that a war can be limitless in time and space, the lie that killing people is more humane than arresting and prosecuting them, the lie that the people killed are small in number, the lie that the people killed pose an imminent threat to the United States, the lie that Obama's claimed justification for killing one U.S. citizen actually justified it despite conflicting with all known facts of the case and despite being presented in a speech rather than a court of law, the lie that the killing of other U.S. citizens is therefore justified too, the lie that killing non-U.S. citizens requires less justification, the lie that the killings are discriminate and targeted unlike the killing done by bad weapons like poison gas, the lie that whole communities aren't traumatized by the constant buzzing threat, the lie that we're being made safer rather than generating enemies, and the lie that a drone war is better than a ground war whereas the drone wars have actually created wars where there weren't any before.

The very word Ukraine at this point is so packaged in lies as to practically make a liar of anyone who utters it. First there's the lie that one must choose sides and declare anyone on one's chosen side angelic and beyond all reproach. This really shuts down conversation, and action. Many well-intended people sought to nonviolently reform or replace a deeply flawed Ukrainian government. That doesn't change the fact that the coup was violent, that the new government is of dubious legitimacy, that the new government contains neo-Nazi leaders, or that the new government immediately sought to deny acceptance to the Russian language. The story of a popular democratic uprising also misses the growing threat to Russia of U.S. and NATO military expansion eastward over the years, the current efforts to bring Ukraine into NATO, and the extensive efforts of the U.S. government to influence Ukrainian politics and activism, to the tune of $5 billion, with the outcome of the coup being the installation of the U.S. State Department's chosen man as president. Obama refers to the duly elected government of Ukraine as if a NATO member but it isn't and wasn't elected. We've seen the U.S. media push and then retract claims about Russian troops in Ukraine (while largely avoiding the massing of U.S. troops and weaponry nearby), and about anti-Semitic actions by Eastern Ukrainians that turned out to be fictional. Federalists are called separatists (and terrorists) and are said to be taking orders from Moscow, although reporters who actually meet them report that they are independent of Russia. Meanwhile, the neo-Nazis of the U.S.-backed coup wave flags of the U.S. Confederacy as well as of

Nazism, and burn people to death by the dozens. Their opponents have burned Nazis in effigy, with no sense of irony, and violently attacked them. No major group of ideal saints seems to be involved in this crisis at all. But imagine the relentless barrage of images of burned bodies we would be subjected to if those bodies were in a different country—well, I guess, not in Bahrain or Saudi Arabia or Egypt or Jordan or . . .—but I mean in a country on the list to be overthrown, like Syria or Iran.

And imagine the news it would be if the government of Syria sent tanks to attack Syrians, but unarmed crowds (perhaps a bit saintly after all) persuaded the drivers of the tanks to abandon that mission. This happened in Ukraine just after CIA director John Brennan visited. He's used to drones. Drones don't stop to have a beer with the enemy. This Prague Spring-like moment of militarism collapsing in the face of humanity is hardly a U.S. news story in the way that speculation about evil intentions by Russia has become. According to Hillary Clinton, Vladimir Putin is a new Hitler. According to Obama, the U.S. destruction of Iraq (and murder of a half-million to a million-and-a-half people) was nowhere near as bad as Russia accepting Crimea's vote to rejoin Russia. There should not have been Russian troops on the streets. Crimea's departure from Ukraine should be agreed to by the government of Ukraine, if it comes up with one. But the vote by Crimea has no parallel in the U.S. war on Iraq, or in Nazi invasions. Iraqis did not choose to have their home destroyed. Poland did not vote to be invaded. And if Quebec voted to leave Canada and join the U.S. it's hard to imagine Putin screaming about Nazis or declaring it worse than the Soviet occupation of Afghanistan.

The U.S. public, to its credit, is not longing for a U.S. war in Ukraine. Seven percent want military options considered (poll by McClatchy-Marist, April 7-10), up from six percent a bit earlier (Pew, March 20-23), or 12 percent for U.S. ground troops and 17 percent for air strikes (CNN, March 7-9). The *Washington Post* says 13% want U.S. military action, and 16% can find Ukraine on a map. Americans place Ukraine in Africa, Asia, Alaska, or the Americas. And the further people place Ukraine on the map from where it actually is, the more they want it attacked—including people who place Ukraine in the United States. So, either they're suicidal, or they think the United States is itself in Africa or somewhere else. There's a Canadian comedy show called "Talking to Americans" in which the host asks people on the street in the United States whether they believe it's reached the point where there's no choice but to bomb _____ (and he makes up the name of a fictional country). People who hear the country's name for the first time declare that in fact it must be bombed. They're sorry that it must be bombed, but the world is full of bad people and there just isn't any other choice. Sometimes I think de-funding war to fund education presents a chicken and egg problem.

Congress members including the House so-called "Defense" Appropriations subcommittee chair are using Ukraine as a reason to keep a war slush fund going for another year, as well as a reason to halt any reduction in nuclear weapons. Some profiteers would no doubt be happy to make billions from weapons even if the weapons are never used. Sadly, it doesn't tend to work out that way. And their playing around with a conflict between two nuclear nations is as suicidal as any fossil fuel lobbying.

If we're going to stop not just one war, but the machinery that drives us toward more wars, we're going to have to come to an understanding that war can be eliminated from the world. That's the mission of a new project I'm working on called WorldBeyondWar. org. As long as it is believed that there must be wars, the United States is going to want to sell the weaponry, get involved, and be guaranteed overwhelmingly superior force. Some people believe we're trapped in a hopelessly pro-war culture. See if you know who this quote is from:

> *"We don't evaluate what's right and wrong. We live in a society.
> We live in a culture. We have to live within that culture."*

If you said the owner of the Los Angeles Clippers, you were right. He sounds like a jerk because overt racism is not an unquestionable part of our culture anymore. In fact, it can get you banned from the NBA. But when a professor from Stanford named Ian Morris publishes a nonsensical book claiming that war is good for us, his career carries on just fine. When a weapons CEO jokes on NPR, as I heard him do prior to the attack on Libya, that if the occupation of Afghanistan has to end he hopes there can be an occupation of Libya, nobody demands his resignation.

But if you step outside of our culture for a moment, in your mind, and think Why is it OK to joke about mass murder for profit? Why is it acceptable for Congress Members to talk about militarism as a jobs program? Why did a Congressman publicly say he was voting against Iraq war funding because his brother died in Vietnam, and not because 4 million died in Vietnam and 1 million in Iraq and mass murder is the responsibility of each and every one of us because no man is an island? When you ask those questions, then the Donald-Sterling everybody's doing it defense looks shameful, even about something that everyone really is doing.

Not everyone's buying the lies. The lies aren't working well enough to sell any war, but they are working well enough to keep alive the idea that there might be a good war some day. Ridding ourselves of that idea is a matter of survival at this point. Or in the words of George W. Bush, "Fool me once shame on *you*, fool me—umm—err --- uh --- *can't get fooled again.*"

Polling for war support is not just low on Ukraine. It's very similar on U.S. desire for a war with Iran, or for U.S. military involvement in Syria. Many more Americans believe in ghosts and UFOs, according to the polls, than believe that these would be good wars. The U.S. public never got behind the war on Libya, and for years a majority has said that the wars on Iraq and Afghanistan never should have been launched. The search for a good war is beginning to look as futile as the search for the mythical city of El Dorado. And yet that search remains our top public project.

The U.S. military swallows 55.2 percent of federal discretionary spending, according to the National Priorities Project. Televised U.S. sporting events thank members of the military for watching from 175 nations. U.S. aircraft carriers patrol the world's seas. U.S. drones buzz the skies of nations thousands of miles from our shores.

No other nation spends remotely comparable funds on

militarism, and much of what the United States buys has no defensive purpose—unless "defense" is understood as deterrence or preemption or, indeed, aggression. As the world's number one supplier of weapons to other nations, ours may be said to extend its search for a good war beyond its own affairs as well.

A 2006 National Intelligence Estimate found that U.S. wars were generating anti-U.S. sentiment. Former military officials, including Stanley McChrystal, say drone strikes are producing more enemies than they are killing. A WIN/Gallup poll of 65 nations at the end of 2013 found the U.S. far ahead of any other as the nation people believed was the greatest threat to peace in the world. When I lived near Vicenza, Italy, pre-911, people tended to like Americans despite the Army base. Now that they've built an enormous new base despite overwhelming local opposition, feelings are not quite as friendly. People who tried to stop the base just posted a video online of themselves cutting a fence, going in, and planting marijuana seeds everywhere—set to music; you should watch it.

Tim Carpenter always used to talk about healthcare, not warfare. He had his priorities right. But we spend twice per capita what any other nation spends on healthcare, and we get worse healthcare as a result of how we spend it. We spend SEVERAL TIMES what any other nation spends on war and war preparation. And we get a lower level of safety because of how we spend it. Canadians don't go without healthcare, and there are no anti-Canadian terrorist networks. It's the country that routinely bombs people in the name of fighting terrorism that is generating all the terrorism.

It is the ethics of a coward to believe that safety justifies all, but of a fool to commit immoral acts that actually endanger oneself. And what is more immoral than modern wars, with deaths and injuries so massive, so one-sided, and so heavily civilian?

Military spending produces fewer jobs than spending on education or infrastructure, or even on tax cuts for working people, according to studies by the Political Economy Research Institute. It is the ethics of a sociopath to justify killing for economic gain, but of a fool to do so for economic loss.

The military is our top consumer of petroleum and creator of superfund sites, in addition to being the hole into which we sink the funds that could address the real danger of climate change.

War justifies secrecy and the erosion of liberties: warrantless surveillance, lawless imprisonment, torture, and assassination, even as wars are marketed as defending "freedom." Did you see the report last week that Haji Gulalai, Afghanistan's "torturer-in-chief," over a period of several years of the U.S. occupation is now living in a two-story pink house in a suburb of Los Angeles, having brought a dozen relatives with him, not bothered to learn English, and remaining unemployed? He sounds a lot like George W. Bush. Both should be prosecuted, as should Condoleezza Rice who has just been stopped from speaking at Rutgers' graduation by student protests.

Another thing the keeping war around does is keep weapons around that could destroy the planet. Maintenance of nuclear and other weapons for war risks intentional or accidental catastrophe.

The downsides to war, even for an aggressor nation with overwhelming fire power, are voluminous. The upside would seem to be that if we keep fighting wars, one of them might turn out to be a good one. But, here's the thing: We don't need a good one. We have the knowledge and the resources to avoid conflicts, to resolve conflicts nonviolently, and to resist violence nonviolently more effectively than it can be resisted using violence.

It would cost about $30 billion per year to end starvation and hunger around the world. It would cost about $11 billion per year to provide the world with clean water. Round up to $50 billion per year to provide the world with both food and water. That's 5 percent of the roughly $1 trillion the U.S. wastes every year on militarism. Foreign aid is $23 billion now. It would cost very little to make the U.S. the most beloved rather than most feared nation on earth. Refraining from war-making would cost nothing and on the contrary save a fortune that could be spent at home and abroad. Spending a bit of it on useful projects would save many times the number of lives that would be spared by avoiding the warmaking.

What if we invested in peace education, nonviolent activist training, conflict negotiation, human-shields and nonviolent peace teams, aid, diplomacy, the rule of law, and sustainable energy? To hear President Obama talk you'd think we were already headed that way and the world was outraged about it. "Typically," Obama said last week, "criticism of our foreign policy has been directed at the failure to use military force." Really? That's why people rank the U.S. as the greatest threat to peace in the world? Of course, by critics Obama means corporate television and rightwing warmongers and Republicans. Perhaps he even means his own Republican Secretary of so-called Defense Chuck Hagel who just made this comment in support of incredible levels of military spending: *"We want our soldiers, sailors, airmen and Marines active around the world, deploying with greater frequency and agility, with the skills and expertise needed to build security capacity in each region." Really? Who's we?*

I want to close with a few things you can do, before taking questions. There are sign-up cards for WorldBeyondWar.org around in the room. They have a survey question at the top that it would be very helpful if everyone could answer Yes or No. Then there's a short statement to sign if you agree with it. Thousands of people have signed from 57 nations thus far. This is how we're going to build an international pivot to peace instead of a pivot to war in Asia. Then there are places to check if you'd like to join in in any way.

You can also start planning, and maybe some of you are already, for the International Day of Peace on September 21st. Join an existing event and enlarge it, or start a new one and we'll help promote it. There are resources you can use at WorldBeyondWar. org. Also start planning for an October 4th global day of actions against drones.

Connecticut has established a commission to work on converting from war to peace industries. Los Angeles and/or California could use one of those. Other things to tell Congress (and come to RootsAction.org where I work on online activism and where you can create your own online petitions):

1. Repeal the authorizations for the use of military force from Afghanistan and Iraq

2. End the occupation of Afghanistan

3. End drone murders

4. Disband NATO

And I would add, out of the millions of other things you might tell Congress, do not put troops back into the Philippines, do not build a Navy base on Jeju Island South Korea, and do not build a new Marine base on Okinawa, Japan. Ten days from today I'll be speaking at an event in Washington with a mayor from Okinawa who was elected to stop the construction of a base that the people of Okinawa overwhelmingly oppose. Congress should hear his message from you while he's in town. And I hope he has as good a crowd as this one today. Thank you for being here.

# Celebrating Independence from America in England

*Remarks at Independence from America event outside Menwith Hill "RFA" (NSA) base in Yorkshire.*

First of all, thank you to Lindis Percy and everyone else involved in bringing me here, and letting me bring my son Wesley along. And thank you to the Campaign for the Accountability of American Bases. I know you share my view that accountability of American bases would lead to *elimination* of American bases.

And thank you to Lindis for sending me her accounts of refusing to be arrested unless the police disarmed themselves. In the United States, refusing any sort of direction from a police officer will get you charged with the crime of refusing a lawful order, even when the order is unlawful. In fact, that's often the only charge levied against people ordered to cease protests and demonstrations that in theory are completely legal. And, of course, telling a U.S. police officer to disarm could quite easily get you locked up for insanity if it didn't get you shot.

Can I just say how wonderful it is to be outside of the United States on the Fourth of July? There are many wonderful and beautiful things in the United States, including my family and friends, including thousands of truly dedicated peace activists, including people bravely going to prison to protest the murders by drone of others they've never met in distant lands whose loved ones will probably never hear about the sacrifices protesters are making. (Did you know the commander of a military base in New York State has court orders of protection to keep specific nonviolent peace activists away from his base to ensure his physical safety—or is it his peace of mind?) And, of course, millions of Americans who tolerate or celebrate wars or climate destruction are wonderful and even heroic in their families and neighborhoods and towns—and that's valuable too.

I've been cheering during U.S. World Cup games. But I cheer for neighborhood, city, and regional teams too. And I don't talk about the teams as if I'm them. I don't say "We scored!" as I sit in a chair opening a beer. And I don't say "We won!" when the U.S. military destroys a nation, kills huge numbers of people, poisons the earth, water, and air, creates new enemies, wastes trillions of dollars, and passes its old weapons to the local police who restrict our rights in the name of wars fought in the name of freedom. I don't say "We lost!" either. We who resist have a responsibility to resist harder, but not to identify with the killers, and certainly not to imagine that the men, women, children, and infants being murdered by the hundreds of thousands constitute an opposing team wearing a different uniform, a team whose defeat by hellfire missile I should cheer for.

Identifying with my street or my town or my continent doesn't lead the same places that identifying with the military-plus-some-minor-side-services that calls itself my national government leads. And it's very hard to identify with my street; I have such little control over what my neighbors do. And I can't manage to identify with my state because I've never even seen most of it. So, once I start identifying abstractly with people I don't know, I see no sensible argument for stopping anywhere short of identifying with everybody, rather than leaving out 95% and identifying with the United States, or leaving out 90% and identifying with the so-called "International Community" that cooperates with U.S. wars. Why not just identify with all humans everywhere? On those rare occasions when we learn the personal stories of distant or disparaged people, we're supposed to remark, "Wow, that really humanizes them!" Well, I'd like to know, what were they before those details made them humanized?

In the U.S. there are U.S. flags everywhere all the time now, and there's a military holiday for every day of the year. But the Fourth of July is the highest holiday of holy nationalism. More than any other day, you're likely to see children being taught to pledge allegiance to a flag, regurgitating a psalm to obedience like little fascist robots. You're more likely to hear the U.S. national anthem, the Star Spangled Banner. Who knows which war the words of that song come from?

That's right, the War of Canadian Liberation, in which the United States tried to liberate Canadians (not for the first or last time) who welcomed them much as the Iraqis would later do, and the British burned Washington. Also known as the War of 1812, the bicentennial was celebrated in the U.S. two years ago. During that war, which killed thousands of Americans and Brits, mostly through disease, during one pointless bloody battle among others, plenty of people died, but a flag survived. And so we celebrate the survival of that flag by singing about the land of the free that imprisons more people than anywhere else on earth and the home of the brave that strip-searches airplane passengers and launches wars if three Muslims shout "boo!"

Did you know the U.S. flag was recalled? You know how a car will be recalled by the manufacturer if the brakes don't work? A satirical paper called the Onion reported that the U.S. flag had been recalled after resulting in 143 million deaths. Better late than never.

There are many wonderful and rapidly improving elements in U.S. culture. It has become widely and increasingly unacceptable to be bigoted or prejudiced against people, at least nearby people, because of their race, sex, sexual orientation, and other factors. It still goes on, of course, but it's frowned upon. I had a conversation last year with a man sitting in the shadow of a carving of confederate generals on a spot that used to be sacred to the Ku Klux Klan, and I realized that he would never, even if he thought it, say something racist about blacks in the United States to a stranger he'd just met. And then he told me he'd like to see the entire Middle East wiped out with nuclear bombs.

We've had comedians' and columnists' careers ended over racist or sexist remarks, but weapons CEOs joke on the radio about wanting big new occupations of certain countries, and nobody blinks. We have antiwar groups that push for celebration of the military on Memorial Day and other days like this one. We have so-called progressive politicians who describe the military as a jobs program, even though it actually produces fewer jobs per dollar than education or energy or infrastructure or never taxing those dollars at all. We have peace groups that argue against wars on the grounds that the military needs to be kept ready for other, possibly more important wars. We have peace groups that oppose military waste, when the alternative of military efficiency is not what's needed. We have libertarians who oppose wars because they cost money, exactly as they oppose schools or parks. We have humanitarian warriors who argue for wars because of their compassion for the people they want bombed. We have peace groups that side with the libertarians and urge selfishness, arguing for schools at home instead of bombs for Syrians, without explaining that we could give actual aid to Syrians and ourselves for a fraction of the cost of the bombs.

We have liberal lawyers who say they can't tell whether blowing children up with drones is legal or not, because President Obama has a secret memo (now only partially secret) in which he legalizes it by making it part of a war, and they haven't seen the memo, and as a matter of principle they, like Amnesty International and Human Rights Watch, ignore the U.N. Charter, the Kellogg Briand Pact, and the illegality of war. We have people arguing that bombing Iraq is now a good thing because it finally gets the U.S. and Iran talking to each other. We have steadfast refusals to mention a half-million to a million-and-a-half Iraqis based on the belief that Americans can only possibly care about 4,000 Americans killed in Iraq. We have earnest crusades to turn the U.S. military into a force for good, and the inevitable demand of those who begin to turn against war, that the United States must *lead* the way to peace—when of course the world would be thrilled if it just brought up the rear.

And yet, we also have tremendous progress. A hundred years ago Americans were listening to snappy tunes about how hunting Huns was a fun game to play, and professors were teaching that war builds national character. Now war has to be sold as necessary and humanitarian because nobody believes it's fun or good for you anymore. Polls in the United States put support for possible new wars below 20 percent and sometimes below 10 percent. After the House of Commons over here said No to missile strikes on Syria, Congress listened to an enormous public uproar in the U.S. and said No as well. In February, public pressure led to Congress backing off a new sanctions bill on Iran that became widely understood as a step toward war rather than away from it. A new war on Iraq is having to be sold and developed slowly in the face of huge public resistance that has even resulted in some prominent advocates of war in 2003 recently recanting.

This shift in attitude toward wars is largely the result of the wars on Afghanistan and Iraq and the exposure of the lies and horrors involved. We shouldn't underestimate this trend or imagine that it's unique to the question of Syria or Ukraine. People are turning against war. For some it may be all about the money. For others it may be a question of which political party owns the White House. The Washington Post has a poll showing that almost nobody in the U.S. can find Ukraine on a map, and those who place it furthest from where it really lies are most likely to want a U.S. war there, including those who place it in the United States. One doesn't know whether to laugh or cry. Yet the larger trend is this: from geniuses right down to morons, we are, most of us, turning against war. The Americans who want Ukraine attacked are fewer than those believing in ghosts, U.F.O.s, or the benefits of climate change.

Now, the question is whether we can shake off the idea that after hundreds of bad wars there just might be a good one around the corner. To do that we have to recognize that wars and militaries make us less safe, not safer. We have to understand that Iraqis aren't ungrateful because they're stupid but because the U.S. and allies destroyed their home.

We can pile even more weight on the argument for ending the institution of war. These U.S. spy bases are used for targeting missiles but also for spying on governments and companies and activists. And what justifies the secrecy? What allows treating everyone as an enemy? Well, one necessary component is the concept of an enemy. Without wars nations lose enemies. Without enemies, nations lose excuses to abuse people. Britain was the first enemy manufactured by the would-be rulers of the United States on July 4, 1776. And yet King George's abuses don't measure up to the abuses our governments now engage in, justified by their traditions of war making and enabled by the sort of technologies housed here.

War is our worst destroyer of the natural environment, the worst generator of human rights abuses, a leading cause of death and creator of refugee crises. It swallows some $2 trillion a year globally, while tens of billions could alleviate incredible suffering, and hundreds of billions could pay for a massive shift to renewable energies that might help protect us from an actual danger.

What we need now is a movement of education and lobbying and nonviolent resistance that doesn't try to civilize war but to take steps in the direction of abolishing it—which begins by realizing that we can abolish it. If we can stop missiles into Syria, there's no magical force that prevents our stopping missiles into every other country. War is not a primal urge of nations that must burst out a little later if once suppressed. Nations aren't real like that. War is a decision made by people, and one that we can make utterly unacceptable.

People in dozens of countries are now working on a campaign for the elimination of all war called World Beyond War. Please check out WorldBeyondWar.org or talk to me about getting involved.

Our goal is to bring many more people and organizations into a movement not aimed at a specific war proposal from a specific government, but at the entire institution of war everywhere. We'll have to work globally to do this. We'll have to throw our support behind the work being done by groups like the Campaign for Accountability of American Bases and the Movement for the Abolition of War and the Campaign for Nuclear Disarmament and Veterans For Peace and so many more.

Some friends of ours in Afghanistan, the Afghan Peace Volunteers, have proposed that everyone living under the same blue sky who wants to move the world beyond war wear a sky blue scarf. You can make your own or find them at TheBlueScarf.org. I hope by wearing this to communicate my sense of connection to those back in the United States working for actual freedom and bravery, and my same sense of connection to those in the rest of the world who have had enough of war. Happy Fourth of July!

## U.S. Out of Germany

If Germany hasn't had enough, we in the United States sure have. Despite the supposed ending of World War II, the U.S. still keeps[237] over 40,000 armed soldiers permanently in Germany. Despite the ending of the Cold War, the U.S. still spies on the German government with relentless malevolence and incompetence[238],

---

237 http://warisacrime.org/Applications/Microsoft Office 2011/Microsoft Word. app/Contents/bit.ly/mappingmilitarism
238        http://www.thedailybeast.com/articles/2014/07/08/the-cia-s-bumbling-german-spy-was-more-austin-powers-and-less-james-bond.html

building on the fine tradition in which the CIA was created[239]. Germany has kicked out[240] the latest CIA "station chief"—a job title that seems to give one's career the longevity and utility of a Defense Against the Dark Arts professor at Hogwarts. Does Germany need a better CIA station chief? A reformed NSA? A properly reviewed and vetted U.S. occupation? What does Germany get out of this deal?

Protection from Russia? If the Russian government weren't demonstrating a level of restraint that dwarfs even that of the Brazilian soccer team's defense there would be full-scale war in Ukraine right now. Russia is no more threatening Germany than Iran is preparing to nuke Washington or the U.N. is confiscating guns in Montana.

Germany must gain something, surely? Perhaps protection from evil Muslims dehumanized in the manner that U.S. war marketers first developed for the dehumanization of Germans 100 years ago? Surely Germans are smart enough to have noticed that violent resistance to foreign aggression targets the nations responsible, not those declining to take part. Hosting bases of the military that gives Israel the weapons with which it slaughters the people of Gaza, whatever else it may be, is decidedly not a security strategy.

So what does Germany gain? The warm feeling that comes with knowing that all those acres and facilities with which so much good could be accomplished are being donated to the wealthiest

239    http://www.amazon.com/The-Secret-History-Joseph-Trento/dp/B002GJU3O6
240    http://www.washingtonpost.com/world/europe/germany-expels-us-intelligence-station-chief-over-spying-allegations/2014/07/10/dc60b1f0-083c-11e4-8a6a-19355c7e870a_story.html

nation on earth which refuses to care for its own people, chip in its share for the poor of the world, or slow its push for the destruction of the globe's climate even as Germany leads in the other direction?

Come on. Germany is a battered wife, a victim of Stockholm syndrome, a schizophrenic accomplice unwilling to relinquish its gang membership. Germany should know better. Germany should throw out the rest of the CIA and 40,000 members of the U.S. military and their families. What does the United States get out of this codependent criminality?

A launching area closer to numerous nations it wishes to attack? That's a desire of the Pentagon, and of Chuck Hagel who claims that ISIS is a threat to the United States because he no doubt conceives of the United States as existing wherever it maintains troops (which is just about everywhere[241]). That is not a desire of the U.S. public.

An unaccountable recklessly funded institution that makes enemies of allies, prevents cooperation across borders, destroys the rule of law and diplomatic initiatives, and erodes the rights of people at home and abroad in order to spy on governments, corporations, and those first to beginning murmuring their displeasure (and for all we know, soccer coaches as well)? Many of us are willing to forego this benefit.

The U.S. war machine does not, in fact, benefit the nations it occupies or the nation in whose name it occupies. It endangers both, strips away the rights of both, damages the natural environment

241        http://bit.ly/mappingmilitarism

of both, impoverishes both, and devotes the energies of both to destructive enterprises or mutual disagreements that distract from the necessary work of actual defense from actual dangers, such as the industrial destruction of our air, land, and oceans.

Pulling U.S. troops out of Germany would be the clearest signal that the United States, which has engaged in 200 military actions during the "post-war period," is ready at long last to actually end the war.

## A Finger in My Soup

I'd heard of such horror stories and assumed they were mostly fictional or concocted as the bases for lawsuits, and then I was actually served a bowl of soup that had a finger in it.

I'm not going to name the well-known chain restaurant where I was dining, but I am going to tell you how its staff reacted when I complained. I mean, once I'd determined that there really was a fucking finger in my bowl of soup, and once I'd fished it out with a fork and a spoon, and splattered it on the table so that Joseph, my dining companion, could see it, and once the people at the surrounding tables were staring and remarking rather loudly, and in one case I think beginning to vomit, well, it wasn't hard to get the waiter's attention.

He came rushing over when I waived. "There's a finger in my soup," I said.

"There's one on your table, too," he pointed out.

"That's the one," I said.

"And it's not your finger?"

"No, it's not my fucking finger. Let me talk to your manager."

He smiled. He actually smiled and pointed to a little tag on his uniform that read "Manager." Joseph spoke up: "How did the finger get in his soup?"

"The cooks must have put it there," said the manager.

"And are you going to do anything about it?" I yelled.

"Well," he replied, calmly, but a bit as if I were the one who'd done something wrong, "if the cooks put it there, they had a reason. I support the cooks, don't you?"

"Support the cooks?" I gasped. "I'll tell you what I will do is I'll take down your name and each of their names, and the names of each of the witnesses in this room, and you'll be hearing from me."

From the waiter's reaction to that statement, I at first imagined I was beginning to get through to him. He looked shocked. But he turned from side to side and addressed the whole room. "He's against the cooks!" he said with great outrage. "He doesn't support the cooks!"

And I swear to god the people in this place seemed to be with him. The rather menacing reaction of several people led Joseph to grab my arm and pull me out of my seat and toward the door.

Thirty seconds later we were sitting in Joseph's cheap used car, which he was trying in vain to start, turning the key, pumping the gas, and cursing.

"Where did you get this piece of junk?" I asked.

"I bought it," he said, as he punched the dashboard and tried again. "I bought it yesterday at Victory Vehicles."

"I wonder who's declaring victory," I remarked.

"What's that supposed to mean? Ugh! Damn this thing!"

"Did you give them more than $10?" I asked.

Joseph gave me a look eerily similar to the look the waiter had just given me in the restaurant. "Are you doubting the salesmen?" he asked.

"Doubting them?" I said. "I'm not fucking doubting them. I'm doubting you. They ripped you off, and . . . "

"Don't you SUPPORT the salesmen?" Joseph screamed at me. He seemed possessed.

I opened my door and got out of the car. It wasn't going anywhere anyway. People were inching their way cautiously out of the restaurant, but they weren't looking at me. They were looking past me.

I turned and saw the flashing lights of countless police cars, plus all kinds of vans, trucks, ambulances, and other emergency vehicles. They appeared to be surrounding the restaurant and its parking lot and to be erecting almost permanent looking barriers. In fact there was an effort underway to construct a wall around the area.

I looked back, and Joseph had gotten out of the car as well and was staring, horror-struck at a pair of people in something resembling astronaut suits walking swiftly and directly toward us.

They halted a few feet away, and one of them spoke, her voice amplified by something in her space suit. "This area is quarantined," she said. "Some or all of you have been infected by a curable but highly contagious and highly destructive virus. We'll need to determine the state of the infection and administer a remedy. Please speak with one of our emergency personnel."

Tables were being set up in neat rows through the parking lot, with pairs of chairs at each table, and a person in an astronaut suit in one of each pair of chairs.

"Where have you been during the last 48 hours?" asked a quite polite and friendly gentleman across a metal table from me, as we both sat in folding chairs in the parking lot of a restaurant that I will still leave unnamed. I was not feeling as friendly as he.

"Why?" I demanded, rather aggressively.

"Hmm." He studied me. "Have you been near any military bases?"

"No."

"Hmm."

"I mean, not that I know of."

"What about a television? Have you been near a television?"

"Definitely not."

"Hmm." He thought for a while, and then asked, "Have you noticed anyone demanding that you support people?"

That question just about knocked my chair over backwards. When I recovered, I told him everything I've just told you.

"Come with me," he said, getting up.

A half-hour later, my interviewer had persuaded his colleagues that I was not infected, and had set me up with a chair and some actually edible food, in a position to watch what he called the administering of remedies.

One of the astronaut-suited workers was seated at a table across from a young woman wearing an American flag dress. The astronaut was asking questions:

"If someone's dog bit you, would you be upset?"

"Of course."

"And what if I questioned your loyalty and willingness to support the dog trainers?"

The woman's reaction was so swift and violent that I suspect it even surprised her questioner: "How dare you?" she hissed. "I support the dog trainers and would never question a dog killing and devouring me. Maybe you don't support the dog trainers! Eh? How could you suggest such a thing to me?"

The questioner moved on. "And what if someone proposed that the government of your nation destroy a poor nation, kill a million people, create millions of refugees, poison the natural environment, waste several trillion dollars, leave behind a violent hell of traumatized resentment, and take away a lot of your rights and liberties in the name of prosecuting this horrendous war that will endanger you by making your nation hated?"

The woman seemed unsure what to say.

"Would you favor that policy?"

She snorted in indignation. "Of course, not! Why would anyone . . . "

"Don't you support the troops?"

"How dare you . . . " And she was off on a rant about her love for the troops and her absolute support for anything they might be ordered to do.

"Drink this."

"Why?"

"The troops want you to."

"Give it to me."

The woman took the large bottle of greenish liquid and downed it in about 10 seconds.

Her questioner tried some of the same questions again, making notes all the time.

"Would you support slaughtering hundreds of thousands of men, women, and children, to enrich a few corporations and give some politicians a thrill of power?"

"Of course, not."

"Do you favor ending current wars?"

"Yes, of course."

"But don't you support the troops?"

She paused and stared, and then blurted out: "Support the. . . . what? What does that even mean? If I oppose a policy I oppose people enacting that policy. That says nothing about whether I like those people or not, most of whom I've never met of course. What the hell?"

Moments later, the questioner was leading the woman in the American flag dress over to join me in the viewing section. "Wait," she said, addressing the space-suited emergency worker, "why am I wearing this dress?"

"He'll explain," the worker said, gesturing toward me.

## Worth Fighting For?

I was not sure I would like a book called *Worth Fighting For* by a former soldier who walked across the United States to raise money for the Pat Tillman Foundation. The website of that foundation celebrates military "service" and the "higher calling" for which Tillman left professional football, namely participation in the U.S. war on the people of Afghanistan and Iraq. Rather than funding efforts to put an end to war, as Tillman actually might have wished by the end of his life, the foundation hypes war participation, funds veterans, and to this day presents Tillman's death[242] thusly:

> *"On the evening of April 22, 2004, Pat's unit was ambushed as it traveled through the rugged, canyon terrain of eastern Afghanistan. His heroic efforts to provide cover for fellow soldiers as they escaped from the canyon led to his untimely and tragic death via fratricide."*

Those heroic efforts happened, if they happened, in the context of an illegal and immoral operation that had Tillman defending foreign invaders from Afghans defending their homes. And the last two words above ("via fratricide") tell a different story from the rest of the paragraph, page, and entire website of the Pat Tillman Foundation. Tillman was shot by U.S. troops[243]. And he may not have died a thorough-going supporter of what he was engaged in. On September 25, 2005, the *San Francisco Chronicle* reported that Tillman had become critical of the Iraq war and had scheduled a meeting with the prominent war critic Noam Chomsky to take place when he returned from Afghanistan, all information that Tillman's mother and Chomsky later confirmed. Tillman couldn't confirm it because he had died in Afghanistan in 2004 from three bullets to the forehead.

Rory Fanning's book—*Worth Fighting For*—relates, however, that Tillman looked forward to getting out of the military and sympathized with the actions of Fanning, a member of his

---

242 http://pattillmanfoundation.org/about-us/#military-career
243    http://www.latimes.com/nation/nationnow/la-na-nn-pat-tillman-soldier-10-years-remorse-20140420-story.html

battalion who became a conscientious objector and refused to fight. According to Fanning, Tillman "knew his very public circumstances forced him to stick it out."

That's obviously a different use of the word "forced" from "gravity forced the weight to drop" or "the missile striking the house forced the people inside to split apart into fragments of flesh and gore." Imagine the benefits to the cause of peace if the one troop who had a name, face, and voice had shattered the bullshit choruses of "Support the Troops!" by doing what Fanning did, and thus living to tell the tale? Instead Tillman stuck it out and left many believing that military propagandists had either become quite fortunate or something worse, when Tillman did not live to quite possibly oppose—better late than never—what he had been doing.

When I worked with a number of talented people to draft articles of impeachment for George W. Bush that were introduced by Congressman Dennis Kucinich, they included this[244]:

*"The White House and the Department of Defense (DOD) in 2004 promoted a false account of the death of Specialist Pat Tillman, reporting that he had died in a hostile exchange, delaying release of the information that he had died from friendly fire, shot in the forehead three times in a manner that led investigating doctors to believe he had been shot at close range.*

*"A 2005 report by Brig. Gen. Gary M. Jones reported that in the days immediately following Specialist Tillman's death,*

244 http://warisacrime.org/busharticleX

*U.S. Army investigators were aware that Specialist Tillman was killed by friendly fire, shot three times to the head, and that senior Army commanders, including Gen. John Abizaid, knew of this fact within days of the shooting but nevertheless approved the awarding of the Silver Star, Purple Heart, and a posthumous promotion.*

*"On April 24, 2007, Spc. Bryan O'Neal, the last soldier to see Specialist Pat Tillman alive, testified before the House Oversight and Government Reform Committee that he was warned by superiors not to divulge information that a fellow soldier killed Specialist Tillman, especially to the Tillman family. The White House refused to provide requested documents to the committee, citing 'executive branch confidentiality interests.'"*

What made Pat Tillman a particular hero to many in the United States was that he had given up huge amounts of money to go to war. That he had passed up the evil of hoarding wealth in order to engage in something even more evil does not register with supporters of war. And had the U.S. Army not killed him, and had he not subsequently killed himself (the leading cause of U.S. military deaths now being suicide), Tillman might have lengthened his life by leaving the NFL, which abandons its players to an average lifespan in their 50s and in some cases dementia in their 40s—an issue that arises in Fanning's book as he meets with former NFL greats to raise money for the Pat Tillman Foundation.

Tillman was, by all accounts, kind, humble, intelligent, courageous, and well-intentioned. He clearly inspired many, many people whom he met, and whom he never met, to be better people. Fanning would, I think, include himself in that list. But when Fanning decided to walk across the country raising funds, and finding support and shelter for himself along the way, in the name of Pat Tillman, he was playing on the beliefs of a propagandized public, beliefs that he himself had ceased to fully share. A sheriff, in a typical example, takes Fanning's empty water bottles, drives 12 miles to refill them, and hands them back to Fanning with tears in his eyes, saying, "What Pat did for our country is one of the bravest, most admirable things I can remember anyone doing. Take this for your cause." And he handed Fanning $100.

Was generating hatred and resentment in Afghanistan by killing helpless people a service to the United States? Was the environmental destruction and economic cost and eroded civil liberties a benefit to us all? In the minds of the people whom the Pat Tillman Foundation is still trying to milk for funding, perhaps so. Such a foundation not only saves the government from providing for veterans (or anyone else) while investing more in weaponry, but it also generates public support for and identification with supposed military heroism. It's a double-victory for the makers of war in Washington, most of whom are far more misguided than Pat Tillman ever was, but most of whom are more remarkable for cowardice than bravery.

As I say, I wasn't 100% sure I would like Fanning's book. I believe things are worth working for, struggling for, suffering for, and dying for, but not fighting for. What could he mean? I was very pleasantly surprised, and recommend the book enthusiastically. It recounts an adventure worth having that contained no fighting at all. It's a tale told with wisdom, erudition, kindness, humor, humility, and generosity of which I think Tillman might have been proud.

Like the guy in that Craig's List movie, Fanning finds people going out of their way to help him as he very publicly walks across the country, doing interviews along the way, speaking at events, and chronicling his progress on a website (now gone). This does not, of course, prove that anyone without a public cause or celebrity label, or anyone of any race or sex or appearance, could safely and successfully find the same sort of selfless support from so many Americans. It is heartening and encouraging, nonetheless, to read. And these accounts come interspersed with descriptions and historical background on the places Fanning walks through that suggest he has a future as a travel writer if he wants it. Intermingled as well quite seamlessly is an account of how Fanning himself moved from being "a devout Christian to an atheist and from a conservative Republican to a socialist." He later adds that he ceased opposing environmentalists and became one. As this world needs such transformations on a large scale, a smart account by someone who's been through one has great value.

One aspect of Fanning's own drama that sheds light on the notion that Tillman was "forced" to "support the troops" even while being one (that is, support a war he may have disagreed with), is the description of how hard it was for Fanning to turn against the military (a process that may perhaps remain incomplete for him even now). Fanning had joined after 9-11 for similar reasons to Tillman, believing it his duty. He then found he "did not have it in him" to kill. And he saw the injustice and absurdity of capturing people falsely ratted out by rivals to an ignorant foreign occupier eager to punish (and torture) anyone it could. He came to see himself as an imperialist pawn rather than a rescuer on a mission for humanity. When he refused to go along to get along, he was ostracized and abused by everyone around him except Pat Tillman and his brother Kevin Tillman. Despite his refusal to fight, Fanning was sent to Afghanistan again, made to do chores, labeled "bitch" by his commander, and forced to sleep outside alone in the snow. And Fanning supported his own abuse, attempting to make himself ill, afraid of the shame of his own behavior rather than wishing to expose the shame of the evil behavior of those around him.

Fanning recounts a conversation with a military chaplain. Fanning made the case that the whole war was unjust. The chaplain made the case that God wanted him to do it anyway. The loser in that contest was apparently Fanning's use for the concept of "God."

But Fanning's struggle continued within himself even after getting home and getting out. "After I left the military," he writes, "the hardest thing I had to do was look someone in the eyes. I was afraid I would be exposed for breaking my oath." Not for having been part of an operation of mass-murder, but for having abandoned it. That's how Fanning thought even after getting out, so one can imagine how Tillman thought while still in—and while in with a world telling him he was a god himself for being there. Fanning sees the contradiction. "I knew U.S. imperialism was destroying the planet," he writes, "but I still felt guilty for leaving."

Through Fanning's walk he gives talks that avoid mentioning what he (and perhaps Tillman) actually thought, until—three-quarters of the way along—a boy asks him which branch of the military to join, and he answers "I don't think you should join any of them." He then gives the $100 from the sheriff to a homeless man under an overpass.

# War in Our Collective Imagination
*Remarks at Veterans For Peace Convention, Asheville, NC, July 27, 2014.*

I started seeing graphics pop up on social media sites this past week that said about Gaza: "It's not war. It's murder." So I started asking people what exactly they think war is if it's distinct from murder. Well, war, some of them told me, takes place between armies. So I asked for anyone to name a war during the past century (that is, after World War I) where all or even most or even a majority of the dying was done by members of armies. There may have been such a war. There are enough scholars here today that somebody probably knows of one. But if so, it isn't the norm, and these people I was chatting with through social media couldn't think of any such war and yet insisted that that's just what war is. So, is war then over and nobody told us?

For whatever reasons, I then very soon began seeing a graphic sent around that said about Gaza: "It's not war. It's genocide." And the typical explanation I got when I questioned this one was that the wagers of war and the wagers of genocide have different attitudes. Are we sure about that? I've spoken to advocates for recent U.S. wars who wanted all or part of a population wiped out. Plenty of supporters of the latest attacks on Gaza see them as counter-terrorism. In wars between advanced militaries and poor peoples most of the death and injury is on one side and most of it—by anyone's definition—civilian. This is as true in Afghanistan, where war rolls on largely unchallenged, as in Gaza, about which we are newly outraged.

Well, what's wrong with outrage? Who cares what people call it? Why not criticize the war advocates rather than nitpicking the war opponents' choice of words? When people are outraged they will reach for whatever word their culture tells them is most powerful, be it murder or genocide or whatever. Why not encourage that and worry a little more about the lunatics who are calling it *defense* or *policing* or *terrorist removal*? (Eight-year-old terrorists!)

Yes, of course. I've been going after CNN news readers for claiming Palestinians want to die and NBC for yanking its best reporter and ABC for claiming scenes of destruction in Gaza that just don't exist in Israel are in fact in Israel—and the U.S. government for providing the weapons and the criminal immunity. I've been promoting rallies and events aimed at swaying public opinion against what Israel has been doing, and against the sadistic bloodthirsty culture of those standing on hills cheering for the death and destruction below, quite regardless of what they call it. But, as you're probably aware, only the very most open-minded war advocates attend conventions of Veterans For Peace. So, I'm speaking here backstage, as it were, at the peace movement.

Among those of us who want to stop the killing, are there better and worse ways to talk about it? And is anything revealed by the ways in which we tend to talk about it when we aren't hyper-focused on our language?

I think so. I think it's telling that the worst word anyone can think of isn't war. I think it's even more telling that we condemn things by contrasting them with war, framing war as relatively acceptable. I think this fact ought to be unsettling because a very good case can be made that war, in fact, is the worst thing we do, and that the distinctions between war and such evils as murder or genocide can require squinting very hard to discern.

We've all heard that guns don't kill people, people kill people. There is a parallel belief that wars don't kill people, people who misuse wars, who fight bad wars, who fight wars improperly, kill people. This is a big contrast with many other evil institutions. We don't oppose child abuse selectively, holding out the possibility of just and good incidents of child abuse while opposing the bad or dumb or non-strategic or excessive cases of child abuse. We don't have Geneva Conventions for proper conduct while abusing children. We don't have human rights groups writing reports on atrocities and possible law violations committed in the course of abusing children. We don't distinguish UN-sanctioned child abuse. The same goes for numerous behaviors generally understood as always evil: slavery or rape or blood feuds or duelling or dog fighting or sexual harassment or bullying or human experimentation or—I don't know—producing piles of I'm-Ready-for-Hillary posters. We don't imagine there are good, just, and defensible cases of such actions.

And this is the core problem: not support for bombing Gaza or Afghanistan or Pakistan or Iraq or anywhere else that actually gets bombed, but support for an imaginary war in the near future between two armies with different colored jerseys and sponsors, competing on an isolated battlefield apart from any villages or towns, and suffering bravely and heroically for their non-murderous non-genocidal cause while complying with the whistles blown by the referees in the human rights organizations whenever any of the proper killing drifts into lawless imprisonment or torture or the use of improper weaponry. Support for specific possible wars in the United States right now is generally under 10 percent. More people believe in ghosts, angels, and the integrity of our electoral system than want a new U.S. war in Ukraine, Syria, Iran, or Iraq. The *Washington Post* found a little over 10 percent want a war in Ukraine but that the people who held that view were the people who placed Ukraine on the world map the furthest from its actual location, including people who placed it in the United States. These are the idiots who favor specific wars. Even Congress, speaking of idiots, on Friday told Obama no new war on Iraq.

The problem is the people, ranging across the population from morons right up to geniuses, who favor imaginary wars. Millions of people will tell you we need to be prepared for more wars in case there's another Adolf Hitler, failing to understand that the wars and militarism and weapons sales and weapons gifts—the whole U.S. role as the arsenal of democracies and dictatorships alike—increase rather than decrease dangers, that other wealthy countries spend less than 10 percent what the U.S. does on their militaries, and that 10 percent of what the U.S. spends on its military could end global starvation, provide the globe with clean water, and fund sustainable energy and agriculture programs that would go further toward preventing mass violence than any stockpiles of weaponry. Millions will tell you that the world needs a global policeman, even though polls of the world find the widespread belief that the United States is currently the greatest threat to peace on earth. In fact if you start asking people who have opposed every war in our lifetimes or in the past decade to work on opposing the entire institution of war, you'll be surprised by many of the people who say no.

I'm a big fan of a book called *Addicted to War*. I think it will probably be a powerful tool for war abolition right up until war is abolished. But its author told me this week that he can't work to oppose all wars because he favors some of them. Specifically, he said, he doesn't want to ask Palestinians to not defend themselves. Now, there's a really vicious cycle. If we can't shut down the institution of war because Palestinians need to use it, then it's harder to go after U.S. military spending, which is of course what funds much of the weaponry being used against Palestinians. I think we should get a little clarity about what a war abolition movement does and does not do. It does not tell people what they must do when attacked. It is not focused on advising, much less instructing, the victims of war, but on preventing their victimization. It does not advise the individual victim of a mugging to turn the other cheek. But it also does not accept the disproven notion that violence is a defensive strategy for a population. Nonviolence has proven far more effective and its victories longer lasting. If people in Gaza have done anything at all to assist in their own destruction, it is not the supposed offenses of staying in their homes or visiting hospitals or playing on beaches; it is the ridiculously counterproductive firing of rockets that only encourages and provides political cover for war/ genocide/ mass murder.

I'm a huge fan of Chris Hedges and find him one of the most useful and inspiring writers we have. But he thought attacking Libya was a good idea up until it quite predictably and obviously turned out not to be. He still thinks Bosnia was a just war. I could go on through dozens of names of people who contribute mightily to an anti-war movement who oppose abolishing war. The point is not that anyone who believes in 1 good war out of 100 is to blame for the trillion dollar U.S. military budget and all the destruction it brings. The point is that they are wrong about that 1 war out of 100, and that even if they were right, the side-effects of maintaining a culture accepting of war preparations would outweigh the benefits of getting 1 war right. The lives lost by not spending $1 trillion a year in the U.S. and another $1 trillion in the rest of the world on useful projects like environmental protection, sustainable agriculture, medicine and hygiene absolutely dwarf the number of lives that would be saved by halting our routine level of war making.

If you talk about abolishing war entirely, as many of us have begun focusing on through a new project called World Beyond War[245], you'll also find people who want to abolish war but believe it's impossible. War is natural, they say, inevitable, in our genes, decreed by our economy, the unavoidable result of racism or consumerism or capitalism or exceptionalism or carnivorism or

---

245 http://worldbeyondwar.org

nationalism. And of course many cultural patterns interact with and facilitate war, but the idea that it's in our genes is absurd, given how many cultures in our species have done and do without it. I don't know what—if anything—people usually mean when they call something "natural" but presumably it's not the provocation of suicide, which is such a common result of participating in war, while the first case of PTSD due to war deprivation has yet to be discovered. Most of our species' existence, as hunter-gatherers, did not know war, and only the last century—a split-second in evolutionary terms—has known war that at all resembles war today. War didn't used to kill like this. Soldiers weren't conditioned to kill. Most guns picked up at Gettysburg had been loaded more than once. The big killers were diseases, even in the U.S. Civil War, the war that the U.S. media calls the most deadly because Filipinos and Koreans and Vietnamese and Iraqis don't count. Now the big killer is a disease in our thinking, a combination of what Dr. King called self-guided missiles and misguided men.

Another hurdle for abolishing war is that the idea rose to popularity in the West in the 1920s and 1930s and then sank into a category of thought that is vaguely treasonous. War abolition was tried and failed, the thinking goes, like communism or labor unions and now we know better. While abolishing war is popular in much of the world, that fact is easily ignored by the 1% who misrepresent the 10% or 15% who live in the places that constitute the so-called International Community. Nothing is more powerful than an idea whose time has come or weaker than an idea whose time has come and gone. Or so we think. But the Renaissance was, as its name suggests, an idea whose time came again, new and improved and victorious. The 1920s and 1930s are a resource for us. We have stockpiles of wisdom to draw upon. We have example of where things were headed and how they went of track.

Andrew Carnegie took war profits and set up an endowment with the mandate to eliminate war and then to hold a board meeting, determine the second worst thing in the world, and begin eliminating that. This sounds unique or eccentric, but is I believe a basic understanding of ethics that ought to be understood and acted upon by all of us. When someone asks me why I'm a peace activist I ask them why in the hell anyone isn't. So, reminding the Carnegie Endowment for Peace what it's legally obligated to do, and dozens of other organizations along with it, may be part of the process of drawing inspiration from the past. And of course insisting that the Nobel Committee not bestow another peace prize on a war-thirsty presidential candidate or any other advocate of war is part of that.

The case against war that is laid out at WorldBeyondWar.org includes these topics:

War is immoral.[246]

War endangers us.[247]

War threatens our environment.[248]

War erodes our liberties.[249]

War impoverishes us.[250]

We need $2 trillion/year for other things.[251]

246 http://worldbeyondwar.org/immoral
247 http://worldbeyondwar.org/endangers
248 http://worldbeyondwar.org/environment
249 http://worldbeyondwar.org/liberties
250 http://worldbeyondwar.org/impoverishes
251 http://worldbeyondwar.org/2trillion

I find the case to be overwhelming and suspect many of you would agree. In fact Veterans For Peace and numerous chapters and members of Veterans For Peace have been among the first to sign on and participate. And we've begun finding that thousands of people and organizations from around the world agree as people and groups from 68 countries and rising have added their names on the website in support of ending all war. And many of these people and organizations are not peace groups. These are environmental and civic groups of all sorts and people never involved in a peace movement before. Our hope is of course to greatly enlarge the peace movement by making war abolition as mainstream as cancer abolition. But we think enlargement is not the only alteration that could benefit the peace movement. We think a focus on each antiwar project as part of a broader campaign to end the whole institution of war will significantly change how specific wars and weapons and tactics are opposed.

How many of you have heard appeals to oppose Pentagon waste? I'm in favor of Pentagon waste and opposed to Pentagon efficiency. How can we not be, when what the Pentagon does is evil? How many of you have heard of opposition to unnecessary wars that leave the military ill-prepared? I'm in favor of leaving the military ill-prepared, but not of distinguishing unnecessary from supposedly necessary wars. Which are the necessary ones? When sending missiles into Syria is stopped, in large part by public pressure, war as last resort is replaced by all sorts of other options that were always available. That would be the case anytime any war is stopped. War is never a last resort any more than rape or child abuse is a last resort. How many of you have seen opposition to U.S. wars that focuses almost exclusively on the financial cost and the suffering endured by Americans? Did you know polls find Americans believing that Iraq benefitted and the United States suffered from the war that destroyed Iraq? What if the financial costs and the costs to the aggressor nation were in addition to moral objections to mass-slaughter rather than instead of? How many of you have seen antiwar organizations trumpet their love for troops and veterans and war holidays, or groups like the AARP that advocate for benefits for the elderly by focusing on elderly veterans, as though veterans are the most deserving? Is that good activism?

I want to celebrate those who resist and oppose war, not those who engage in it. I love Veterans For Peace because it's for peace. It's for peace in a certain powerful way, but it's the being for peace that I value. And being for peace in the straightforward meaning of being against war. Most organizations are afraid of being for peace; it always has to be peace and justice or peace and something else. Or it's peace in our hearts and peace in our homes and the world will take care of itself. Well, as Veterans For Peace know, the world doesn't take care of itself. The world is driving itself off a cliff. As Woody Allen said, I don't want to live on in the hearts of my countrymen, I want to live on in my apartment. Well, I don't want to find peace in my heart or my garden, I want to find peace in the elimination of war. At WorldBeyondWar.org is a list of projects we think may help advance that, including, among others:

Creating an easily recognizable and joinable mainstream international movement to end all war.

Education about war, peace, and nonviolent action — including all that is to be gained by ending war.

Improving access to accurate information about wars. Exposing falsehoods.

Improving access to information about successful steps away from war in other parts of the world.

Increased understanding of partial steps as movement in the direction of eliminating, not reforming, war.

Partial and full disarmament.

Conversion or transition to peaceful industries.

Closing, converting or donating foreign military bases.

Democratizing militaries while they exist and making them truly volunteer.

Banning foreign weapons sales and gifts.

Outlawing profiteering from war.

Banning the use of mercenaries and private contractors.

Abolishing the CIA and other secret agencies.

Promoting diplomacy and international law[252], and consistent enforcement of laws against war, including prosecution of violators.

Reforming or replacing the U.N. and the ICC.

Expansion of peace teams and human shields.

Promotion of nonmilitary foreign aid and crisis prevention.

Placing restrictions on military recruitment and providing potential soldiers with alternatives.

Thanking resisters for their service.

Encouraging cultural exchange.

Discouraging racism and nationalism.

Developing less destructive and exploitative lifestyles.

Expanding the use of public demonstrations and nonviolent civil resistance to enact all of these changes.

---

252 http://www.worldbeyondwar.org/world-peace-law/

I would add learning from and working with organizations that have been, like Veterans For Peace, working toward war abolition for years now and inspiring others to do the same. And I would invite you all to work with WorldBeyondWar[253] toward our common goal.

# Causes of War Krugman Overlooked

While I'm working on a campaign to abolish war[254], it's helpful and appreciated that a columnist for one of the most effective war promoting institutions in the world, the *New York Times*[255], on Sunday mused aloud about why in the world wars are still waged.

Paul Krugman rightly pointed to the destructive nature of wars even for their victors. He admirably presented the insights of Norman Angell who figured out that war didn't pay economically over a century ago. But Krugman didn't get much further than that, his one proposal to explain wars fought by wealthy nations being political gain for the war makers.

Robert Parry has pointed out[256] the falsity of Krugman's pretense that Vladimir Putin is the cause of trouble in Ukraine. One might also question Krugman's claim that George W. Bush actually "won"

---

253 http://WorldBeyondWar.org
254 http://worldbeyondwar.org
255 http://www.nytimes.com/2014/08/18/opinion/paul-krugman-why-we-fight.html?hp&action=click&pgtype=Homepage&module=c-column-top-span-region&region=c-column-top-span-region&WT.nav=c-column-top-span-region
256     http://consortiumnews.com/2014/08/18/the-powerful-group-think-on-ukraine/

his reelection in 2004, considering what went on in Ohio's vote counting.

Yes, indeed, a great many fools will rally around any high official who wages war, and it's good for Krugman to point that out. But it's just plain bizarre for an economist to lament the cost (to the U.S.) of the U.S. war on Iraq as reaching possibly $1 trillion, and never notice that the United States spends roughly $1 trillion on preparations for war each and every year through basic routine military spending—itself economically destructive, as well as morally and physically destructive.

What drives the spending that Eisenhower warned would drive the wars? Profits, legalized bribery, and a culture that searches for the causes of war primarily among the 95 percent of humanity that invests dramatically less in war-making than the United States does.

Krugman dismisses economic gain as relevant only to poor nations' internal wars, but doesn't explain why U.S. wars concentrate in oil-rich areas. "I am saddened," wrote Alan Greenspan, "that it is politically inconvenient to acknowledge what everyone knows: the Iraq war is largely about oil." As Krugman is no doubt aware, rising oil prices are not lamented by *everyone,* and the high cost of weaponry is not a downside from the perspective of weapons makers. Wars don't economically benefit societies, but they do enrich individuals. That same principle is central to explaining the U.S. government's conduct on any area other than war; why should war be different?

No particular war, and certainly not the institution as a whole, has a single simple explanation. But it's certainly true that if Iraq's top export were broccoli there'd have been no 2003 war. It's also possible that if war profiteering were illegal and prevented there'd have been no war. It's also possible that if the U.S. culture didn't reward war-making politicians, and/or the *New York Times* reported on war honestly, and/or Congress had made a habit of impeaching war-makers, and/or campaigns were publicly financed, and/or U.S. culture celebrated nonviolence rather than violence there'd have been no war. It's also possible that if George W. Bush and/or Dick Cheney and a few others were healthier psychologically there'd have been no war.

We should be wary of creating the assumption that there are always rational calculations behind wars. The fact that we can never quite find them is almost certainly not a failure of imagination, but a reluctance to recognize the irrational and evil behavior of our political officials. Global domination, machismo, sadism, and lust for power contribute significantly to the discussions of war planners.

But what makes war common in certain societies and not others? Extensive research suggests that the answer has nothing to do with economic pressures or the natural environment or other impersonal forces. Rather the answer is cultural acceptance. A culture that accepts or celebrates war will have war. One that spurns war as absurd and barbaric will know peace.

If Krugman and his readers are beginning to think of war as a bit archaic, as something requiring an explanation, that can only be good news for the movement to abolish war making.

The next big leap might come sooner if we all try to see the world for a moment from the perspective of someone outside the United States. After all, the idea that the U.S. should not be bombing Iraq only sounds like a denial that there is a major crisis in Iraq requiring swift action, to people who suppose that crises require bombs to solve them—and most of those people, by some coincidence, seem to live in the United States.

## War in the Hundred Acre Woods

In the 1920s and 1930s, anybody who was anybody tried to figure out how to rid the world of war. Collectively, I'd say they got three-quarters of the way to an answer. But from 1945 to 2014, they've been ignored when possible (which is most of the time), laughed at when necessary, and on the very rare occasions that require it: attacked.

What a flock of idiots the leading thinkers of a generation all must have been. World War II happened. Therefore, war is eternal. Everyone knows that.

But slavery abolitionists pushed on despite slavery happening another year, and another year. Women sought the right to vote in the next election cycle following each one they were barred from. Undoubtedly war is trickier to get rid off, because governments claim that all the other governments (and any other war makers) must go first or do it simultaneously. The possibility of someone else launching a war, combined with the false notion that war is the best way to defend against war, creates a seemingly permanent maze from which the world cannot emerge.

But *difficult* is far too easily distorted into *impossible*. War will have to be abolished through a careful and gradual practice; it will require cleaning up the corruption of government by war profiteers; it will result in a very different world in just about every way: economically, culturally, morally. But war will not be abolished at all if the meditations of the abolitionists are buried and not read.

Imagine if children, when they'd just gotten a bit too old for Winnie the Pooh and we're becoming old enough to read serious arguments, were told that A.A. Milne also wrote a book in 1933-1934 called *Peace With Honour*. Who wouldn't want to know what the creator of Winnie the Pooh thought of war and peace? And who wouldn't be thrilled to discover his wit and humor applied in all seriousness to the case for ending the most horrific enterprise to remain perfectly acceptable in polite society?

Now, Milne had served as a war propagandist and soldier in World War I, his 1934 view of Germany as not really wanting war looks (at least at first glance) ludicrous in retrospect, and Milne himself abandoned his opposition to war in order to cheer for World War II. So we can reject his wisdom as hypocrisy, naiveté, and as having been rejected by the author. But we'd be depriving ourselves of insight because the author was imperfect, and we'd be prioritizing the ravings of a drunk over statements made during a period of sobriety. Even the ideal diagnostician of war fever can sound like a different man once he's contracted the disease himself.

In *Peace With Honour*, Milne shows that he has listened to the rhetoric of the war promoters and found that the "honor" they fight for is essentially prestige (or what is more recently called in the United States, "credibility"). As Milne puts it:

> *"When a nation talks of its honour, it means its prestige. National prestige is a reputation for the will to war. A nation's honour, then, is measured by a nation's willingness to use force to maintain its reputation as a user of force. If one could imagine the game of tiddleywinks assuming a supreme importance in the eyes of statesmen, and if some innocent savage were to ask why tiddleywinks was so important to Europeans, the answer would be that only by skill at tiddleywinks could a country preserve its reputation as a country skillful at tiddleywinks. Which answer might cause the savage some amusement."*

Milne debates popular arguments for war and comes back again and again to ridiculing it as a foolish cultural choice dressed up as necessary or inevitable. Why, he asks, do Christian churches sanction mass murder by bombing of men, women, and children? Would they sanction mass conversion to Islam if it were required to protect their country? No. Would they sanction widespread adultery if population growth were the only path to defense of their country? No. So why do they sanction mass murder?

Milne tries a thought experiment to demonstrate that wars are optional and chosen by individuals who could choose otherwise. Let us suppose, he says, that an outbreak of war would mean the certain and immediate death of Mussolini, Hitler, Goering, Goebbels, Ramsay MacDonald, Stanley Baldwin, Sir John Simon, one unnamed cabinet minister chosen by lot on the day war is declared, the ministers responsible for the military, Winston Churchill, two unnamed Generals, two unnamed Admirals, two unnamed directors of armaments firms chosen by lot, Lords Beaverbrook and Rothermere, the editors of *The Times* and *The Morning Post,* and corresponding representatives of France. Would there, in this situation, ever be a war? Milne says definitely not. And therefore war is not "natural" or "inevitable" at all.

Milne makes a similar case around wartime conventions and rules:

> *"As soon as we begin making rules for war, as soon as we say that this is legitimate warfare and that the other is not, we are admitting that war is merely an agreed way of settling an argument."*

But, Milne writes—accurately depicting the 1945 to 2014 history of a U.N. and NATO-run world—you cannot make a rule against aggressive war and keep defensive war. It won't work. It's self-defeating. War will roll on under such circumstances, Milne predicts—and we know he was right. "To renounce aggression is not enough," writes Milne. "We must also renounce defence."

What do we replace it with? Milne depicts a world of nonviolent dispute resolution, arbitration, and a changed conception of honor or prestige that finds war shameful rather than honorable. And not just shameful, but mad. He quotes a war supporter remarking, "At the present moment, which may prove to be the eve of another Armageddon, we are not ready." Asks Milne: "Which of these two facts [Armageddon or unpreparedness] is of the more importance to civilization?"

## *Losing Losers and the Pentagon That Hires Them*

At the 200th anniversary of the jackasses of 1812 getting the U.S. capital burned by the British in 1814, I found myself watching a new film by Rory Kennedy called Last Days in Vietnam[257]. This film covers the moment of loss, of defeat, of the U.S. military at long last receiving its final ass kicking by the Vietnamese, for whom these were not the last days of Vietnam but the last days of the American War and of Western military occupation.

As in the Middle East these days, where the United States has been busy losing wars in Afghanistan and Iraq, and wrecking Libya and Pakistan and Yemen and Palestine on the side, Vietnam was a disaster by the time the movie begins. As the U.S. news media blames ISIS for the state of Iraq, *Last Days in Vietnam* blames the North Vietnamese. This is the story of the loss in Vietnam, but it is told primarily by the losers.

257 http://www.lastdaysinvietnam.com

A Pentagon-funded online celebration[258] of the U.S. war on Vietnam describes the incidents shown in this film thus:

"The American evacuation ends. Saigon falls to the North Vietnamese troops, and organized South Vietnamese resistance to the communist forces ends. President Duong Van Minh announces the unconditional surrender of the Republic of Vietnam."

I recommend Veterans For Peace[259] for a counter to the Pentagon's current $65 million campaign to glorify the U.S. war on Vietnam. And I recommend watching Last Days in Vietnam[260] for an understanding of how wars end. In particular, this film should be watched by anyone who has managed to continue after all these decades to falsely associate war with victory or winning or success or accomplishment.

The final months of U.S. presence in Vietnam were a time of denial, by the U.S. ambassador and others, that the North Vietnamese were coming to kick them out. Every American and every one of their Vietnamese allies and collaborators, and all of the family members of both groups, could have been safely evacuated. Instead, there was a last-minute mad rush with helicopters dumped into the ocean after they unloaded passengers onto ships, and many left behind to be killed.

The film blames Congress for rejecting President Ford's request to fund an evacuation. But the Pentagon could quite easily have

258 http://www.vietnamwar50th.com
259 http://www.vietnamfulldisclosure.org
260 http://www.lastdaysinvietnam.com

simply done it, and President Ford apparently never instructed the ambassador to do so. So, the spooky music plays, and the color of blood flows down the map from North to South as the barbaric communist aggressors who go so far as to use *violence*, something Americans would never do, approach Saigon. And they only come because President Nixon was driven out by the peaceniks. Never mind that that was several months earlier, they never would have come had Nixon been in the White House.

Of course, the views of the losers tend to obscure as much as to reveal. The war had to end. The people fighting for their homes had to prevail, sooner or later, over the people fighting for the fact that they'd already been fighting and couldn't face the shame of stopping. But Last Days in Vietnam shows the Americans watching the rushed evacuation from home, the Americans who had earlier "served" in Vietnam. And they believed all their efforts had "come to nothing."

Nothing? Nothing? Four million men, women, and children slaughtered. The U.S. society calls that nothing. The Germans are expected to know how many millions their government killed. The Japanese are required to study the past sins of Japan. But the United States is supposed to gaze at its navel, glorify its sinners, and pretend that its defeats are neutral, indifferent, nothingness. Try telling that story about Afghanistan or Iraq or Gaza, I dare you.

# Monty Python State Department

Scene: A cafe. One table is occupied by a group of Vikings wearing horned helmets.

Whenever the word "war" is repeated, they begin singing and/or chanting.

A man and woman enter. The man is played by Eric Idle, the woman is played by Graham Chapman (in drag), and the Secretary of State is played by Terry Jones, also in drag.

Man: You sit here, dear.

Woman: All right.

Man: Morning!

Secretary of State: Morning!

Man: Well, what've you got?

Secretary of State: Well, there's sanctions and prosecutions; sanctions drone strikes and prosecutions; sanctions and war; sanctions prosecutions and war; sanctions prosecutions drone strikes and war; war prosecutions drone strikes and war; war sanctions war war prosecutions and war; war drone strikes war war prosecutions war cyber war and war;

Vikings: War war war war...

Secretary of State: ...war war war sanctions and war; war war war war war war targeted assassinations war war war...

Vikings: War! Lovely war! Lovely war!

Secretary of State: ...or a United Nations resolution combined with infiltration, a USAID fake Twitter application, a CIA overthrow, trained enhanced interrogators and with crippling sanctions on top and war.

Woman: Have you got anything without war?

Secretary of State: Well, there's war sanctions drone strikes and war, that's not got much war in it.

Woman: I don't want ANY war!

Man: Why can't she have sanctions prosecutions war and drone strikes?

Woman: THAT'S got war in it!

Man: Hasn't got as much war in it as war sanctions drone strikes and war, has it?

Vikings: War war war war... (Crescendo through next few lines...)

Woman: Could you do the sanctions prosecutions war and drone strikes without the war then?

Secretary of State: Urgghh!

Woman: What do you mean 'Urgghh'? I don't like war!

Vikings: Lovely war! Wonderful war!

Secretary of State: Shut up!

Vikings: Lovely war! Wonderful war!

Secretary of State: Shut up! (Vikings stop) Bloody Vikings! You can't have sanctions prosecutions war and drone strikes without the war.

Woman: I don't like war!

Man: Sshh, dear, don't cause a fuss. I'll have your war. I love it. I'm having war war war war war war war targeted assassinations war war war and war!

Vikings: War war war war. Lovely war! Wonderful war!

Secretary of State: Shut up!! Targeted assassinations are off.

Man: Well could I have her war instead of the targeted

assassinations then?

Secretary of State: You mean war war war war war war... (but it is too late and the Vikings drown her words)

Vikings: (Singing elaborately...) War war war war. Lovely war! Wonderful war! War w-a-a-a-a-a-a-a-r war w-a-a-a-a-a-a-a-r war. Lovely war! Lovely war! Lovely war! Lovely war! Lovely war! War war war war!

*No actual diplomats were harmed in the making of this production.*

# 43 Million People Kicked Out of Their Homes

War, our leaders tell us, is needed to make the world a better place. Well, maybe not so much for the 43 million people who've been driven out of their homes and remain in a precarious state as internally displaced persons (24 million), refugees (12 million), and those struggling to return to their homes.

The U.N.'s figures for the end of 2013 (found here[261]) list Syria as the origin of 9 million such exiles. The cost of escalating the war in Syria is often treated as a financial cost or—in rare cases—as a human cost in injury and death. There is also the human cost of ruining homes, neighborhoods, villages, and cities as places in which to live.

Just ask Colombia which comes in second place following years

---

261 http://www.unhcr.org/pages/49c3646c4d6.html

of war—a place where peace talks are underway and desperately needed with—among other catastrophes—nearly 6 million people deprived of their homes.

The war on drugs is rivaled by the war on Africa, with the Democratic Republic of the Congo coming in third after years of the U.S.-backed deadliest war[262] since World War II, but only because the war on "terror" has slipped. Afghanistan is in fourth place with 3.6 million desperate, suffering, dying, and in many cases understandably angry and resentful at losing a place to live. (Remember that over 90% of Afghans not only didn't participate in the events of 9-11 involving Saudis flying planes into buildings, but have never even heard[263] of those events.) Post-liberation Iraq is at 1.5 million displaced and refugees. Other nations graced by regular U.S. missile strikes that make the top of the list include Somalia, Pakistan, Yemen—and, of course, with Israeli help: Palestine.

Humanitarian wars have a homelessness problem. Part of that problem finds its way to Western borders where the people involved should be greeted with restitution rather than resentment. Honduran children aren't bringing Ebola-infected Korans. They're fleeing a U.S.-backed coup and Fort Benning-trained torturers. The "immigration problem" and "immigrants rights" debate should be replaced with a serious discussion of refugee rights, human rights, and the-right-to-peace.

Start here[264].

---

262 http://davidswanson.org/node/4299
263 http://www.rawstory.com/rs/2010/11/think-tank-afghans-dont-know-911/
264 http://worldbeyondwar.org/individual

# *Beyond 935 Lies*

Charles Lewis' book, *935 Lies*, would make a fine introduction to reality for anyone who believes the U.S. government usually means well or corporations tend to tell the truth in the free market. And it would make an excellent introduction to the decline and fall of the corporate media. Even if these topics aren't new to you, this book has something to add and retells the familiar quite well.

The familiar topics include the Gulf of Tonkin, the Pentagon Papers, Watergate, the civil rights movement, U.S. aggression and CIA overthrows, Pinochet, Iran-Contra, lying tobacco companies, and Edward R. Murrow. Lewis brings insight to these and other topics, and if he doesn't document that things were better before the 1960s, he does establish that horrible things have been getting worse since, and are now much more poorly reported on.

The *New York Times* and *Washington Post* were afraid not to print the Pentagon Papers. Nowadays a typical decision was that of the *New York Times* to bury its story on warrentless spying in 2004, with the explanation that printing it might have impacted an election. TV news today would not show you the civil rights movement or the war on Vietnam as it did at the time.

Lewis has hope for new media, including the Center for Public Integrity, which he founded in 1989, and which has produced numerous excellent reports, including on war profiteering, and which Lewis says is the largest nonprofit investigative reporting organization in the world.

Points I quibble with:

1. Human Rights Watch as a model media organization? Really[265]?

2. The New America Foundation as a model media organization? Really[266]?

3. Think tanks as a great hope for integrity in public life? Really[267]?

4. After making 935 of the George W. Bush gang's lies a book title, you aren't sure he "knowingly" lied? Seriously?

This is the guy who wanted an excuse to attack Iraq before he had one. He told Tony Blair they could perhaps paint a U.S. plane in U.N. colors, fly it low, and hope for it to get shot at—after which conversation the two men spoke to the media about how they were trying to avoid war. This was January 31, 2003, and is quite well documented, but I don't think a single reporter who was lied to that day has taken any offense or asked for an apology. This is the president who rushed the war to prevent completion of inspections. This is the president who made dozens of wild claims about weapons without evidence—in fact with evidence to the contrary.

Not only does overwhelming evidence show us that Bush knew his claims about WMDs to be false, but the former president has shown us that he considers the question of truth or falsehood to be laughably irrelevant. When Diane Sawyer asked Bush why he had claimed with such certainty that there were so many weapons in Iraq, he replied: "What's the difference? The possibility that [Saddam] could acquire weapons, If he were to acquire weapons, he would be the danger." What's the difference? It's the difference between lying

265 http://act.rootsaction.org/p/dia/action/public/?action_KEY=9860
266 http://www.sourcewatch.org/index.php?title=New_America_Foundation
267 http://www.projectcensored.org/11-wealthy-donors-corporations-set-think-tanks-agendas/

and meaning well. This interview is available on video.

5. Why not bring the trend of lying about wars up to date, I wonder. Since I wrote *War Is A Lie* we've had all the lies about drone wars, the lies about Gadaffi threatening to slaughter civilians, the lies about Iranian nukes and Iranian terrorism, the lies about Russian invasions and attacks in Ukraine, the lies about chemical weapons use in Syria, the lies about humanitarian and barbaric justifications for attacking Iraq yet again. It's hard to even keep up with the pace of the lies. But we ought to be able to properly identify the mother of all lies, and I don't think it was the Gulf of Tonkin.

6. Lewis's model of integrity is Edward R. Murrow. Among Murrow's independent and heroic credentials, according to Lewis, is that he met with President Roosevelt hours after the attack on Pearl Harbor. Now, I take nothing away from Murrow's reporting and the stand he later took for a free press. But why did Lewis bring up this meeting? And once he'd brought it up why did he not mention that Murrow told his wife that night that FDR had given him the "biggest story of my life, but I don't know if it's my duty to tell it or forget it." The Murrow depicted by Lewis would have known what his duty was. Murrow later told John Gunther that the story would put his kid through college if he told it. He never did.

That many people will not immediately know what the story was is testimony to a pattern that Lewis documents. Some lies take many, many years to fall apart. The biggest ones[268] sometimes take the longest.

---

268    http://warisacrime.org/content/pearl-harbor-day-day-cherish-13-trillion-we-blow-war-preparation-every-year

# *Again the Peace Prize Not for Peace*

The Nobel Peace Prize is required by Alfred Nobel's will, which created it, to go to "the person who shall have done the most or the best work for fraternity between nations, for the abolition or reduction of standing armies and for the holding and promotion of peace congresses." The Nobel Committee insists on awarding the prize to either a leading maker of war or a person who has done some good work in an area other than peace.

The 2014 prize has been awarded to Kailash Satyarthi and Malala Yousafzay, which is not a person but two people, and they have not worked for fraternity between nations or the abolition or reduction of standing armies but for the rights of children. If the peace prize is to be a prize for random good works, then there is no reason not to give it to leading advocates for the rights of children. This is a big step up from giving it to leading makers of war. But then what of the prize for peace and the mission of ending war that Nobel included in his will in fulfillment of a promise to Bertha von Suttner?

Malala Yousafzay became a celebrity in Western media because she was a victim of designated enemies of Western empire. Had she been a victim of the governments of Saudi Arabia or Israel or any other kingdom or dictatorship being used by Western governments, we would not have heard so much about her suffering and her noble work. Were she primarily an advocate for the children being traumatized by drone strikes in Yemen or Pakistan, she'd be virtually unknown to U.S. television audiences.

But Malala recounted her meeting with U.S. President Barack Obama a year ago and said, "I also expressed my concerns that drone attacks are fueling terrorism. Innocent victims are killed in these acts, and they lead to resentment among the Pakistani people. If we refocus efforts on education, it will make a big impact." So, she actually advocated pursuing education rather than war, and yet the Nobel Committee had not a word to say about that in announcing its selection, focusing on eliminating child labor rather than on eliminating war. The possibility exists then that either of this year's recipients might give an antiwar acceptance speech. There has, after all, only been one pro-war acceptance speech, and that was from President Obama. But many speeches have been unrelated to abolishing war.

Fredrik S. Heffermehl, who has led efforts to compel the Nobel Committee to give the peace prize for peace, said on Friday, "Malala Yousafzay is a courageous, bright and impressive person. Education for girls is important and child labor a horrible problem. Worthy causes, but the committee once again makes a false pretense of loyalty to Nobel and confuses and conceals the plan for world peace that Nobel intended to support.

"If they had wished to be loyal to Nobel they would have stressed that Malala often has spoken out against weapons and military with a fine understanding of how ordinary people suffer from militarism. Young people see this more clearly than the grown ups."

The leading contenders for this year's prize, as speculated in the media, included the Pope who has in fact spoken against all war, abandoning the "just war" idea; and some advocate or other for Japan's Article Nine which forbids war and ought to be a model for other nations but is being threatened in Japan instead. These recipients would at least have bordered on Nobel's ideal, as perhaps might be said for last year's recipient, the Organisation for the Prohibition of Chemical Weapons.

Also on the list was a Russian newspaper supportive of Western aggression, the President of Uruguay for legalizing marijuana, Edward Snowden for leaking evidence of U.S. spying, Denis Mukwege for helping victims of sexual violence, and Chelsea Manning for exposing U.S. war crimes. Manning would have made a certain amount of sense, and her work has probably gone some way toward discouraging war. The same might be said, to a lesser degree, of Snowden. But none of these fit the description in Nobel's will. If the peace prize were actually awarded to a leading peace activist, at this point the world would be rather scandalized and scratch its collective head in wonderment at what the significance could be in that person's work.

Look at this list of recent recipients of a prize meant for peace: The European Union; Ellen Johnson Sirleaf, Leymah Gbowee and Tawakkol Karman; Liu Xiaobo; Barack H. Obama; Martti Ahtisaari; Intergovernmental Panel on Climate Change (IPCC) and Albert Arnold (Al) Gore Jr.; Muhammad Yunus and Grameen Bank.

There you have the two leading makers of war in the world: Obama and the E.U. You have advocates for green energy and small loans and women's rights and human rights. Martti Ahtisaari's prize announcement actually quoted from Nobel's will, but he himself supported NATO and Western militarism.

While good work in other areas can in fact contribute to peace, it is unlikely to do so in the absence of recognition of the goal of peace and of work directly aimed at abolishing war.

The National Priorities Project, a U.S. organization that actually works against militarism, was nominated this year, as no doubt were others relevant to the purpose for which the peace prize was created.

## *Pranking the CIA: The New Get Rich Quick Story*

When *New York Times* reporter James Risen published his previous book, *State of War*, the *Times* ended its delay of over a year and published his article on warrantless spying rather than be scooped by the book. The *Times* claimed it hadn't wanted to influence the 2004 presidential election by informing the public of what the President was doing. But this week a *Times* editor said on *60 Minutes* that the White House had warned him that a terrorist attack on the United States would be blamed on the *Times* if one followed publication— so it may be that the *Times'* claim of contempt for democracy was a cover story for fear and patriotism. The *Times* never did report various other important stories in Risen's book.

One of those stories, found in the last chapter, was that of Operation Merlin—possibly named because only reliance on magic could have made it work—in which the CIA gave nuclear weapon plans to Iran with a few obvious changes in them. This was supposedly supposed to somehow slow down Iran's nonexistent efforts to build nuclear weapons. Risen explained Operation Merlin on *Democracy Now* this week and was interviewed about it by *60 Minutes* which managed to leave out any explanation of what it was. The U.S. government is prosecuting Jeffrey Sterling for allegedly being the whistleblower who served as a source for Risen, and subpoenaing Risen[269] to demand that he reveal his source(s).

The Risen media blitz this week accompanies the publication of his new book, *Pay Any Price*. Risen clearly will not back down. This time he's made his dumbest-thing-the-CIA-did-lately story the second chapter rather than the last, and even the *New York Times* has already mentioned it. We're talking about a "torture works," "Iraq has WMDs," "let's all stare at goats" level of dumbness here. We're talking about the sort of thing that would lead the Obama administration to try to put somebody in prison. But it's not clear there's a secret source to blame this time, and the Department of So-Called Justice is already after Sterling and Risen.

Sterling, by the way, is unheard of by comparison with Chelsea Manning or Edward Snowden or the other whistleblowers Risen reports on in his new book. The public, it seems, doesn't make a hero of a whistleblower until after the corporate media has made the person famous as an alleged traitor. Sterling, interestingly, is a whistleblower who could only be called a "traitor" if it were treason to expose treason, since people who think in those terms almost

---

269          http://act.rootsaction.org/p/dia/action3/common/public/?action_
KEY=9775

universally will view handing nuclear plans to Iran as treason. In other words, he's immune from the usual attack, but stuck at the first-they-ignore-you stage because there's no corporate interest in telling the Merlin story.

So what's the new dumbness from Langley? Only this: a gambling-addicted computer hack named Dennis Montgomery who couldn't sell Hollywood or Las Vegas on his software scams, such as his ability to see content in videotape not visible to the naked eye, sold the CIA on the completely fraudulent claim that he could spot secret al Qaeda messages in broadcasts of the Al Jazeera television network. To be fair, Montgomery says the CIA pushed the idea on him and he ran with it. And not only did the CIA swallow his hooey, but so did the principals committee, the membership of which was, at least for a time: Vice President Dick Cheney, former National Security Advisor Condoleezza Rice, So-Called Defense Secretary Donald Rumsfeld, Secretary of State Colin Powell, CIA Director George Tenet, and Attorney General John Ashcroft. Tenet plays his usual role as dumber-than-a-post bureaucrat in Risen's account, but John Brennan is noted as having been involved in the Dennis Montgomery lunacy as well. The Bush White House grounded international flights as a result of Montgomery's secret warnings of doom, and seriously considered shooting planes out of the sky.

When France demanded to see the basis for grounding planes, it quickly spotted a steaming pile of *crottin de cheval* and let the U.S. know. So, the CIA moved on from Montgomery. And Montgomery moved on to other contracts working on other horse droppings for the Pentagon. And nothing shocking there. "A 2011 study by the Pentagon," Risen points out, "found that during the ten years after 9/11, the Defense Department had given more than $400 billion to contractors who had previously been sanctioned in cases involving $1 million or more in fraud." And Montgomery was not sanctioned. And we the people who enriched him with millions weren't told he existed. Nothing unusual there either. Secrecy and fraud are the new normal in the story Risen tells, detailing the fraudulent nature of drone murder profiteers, torture profiteers, mercenary profiteers, and even fear profiteers—companies hired to generate hysteria. So forcefully has the dumping of money into militarism been divorced in public discourse from the financial burden it entails that Risen is able to quote Linden Blue, vice chairman of General Atomics, criticizing people who take money from the government. He means poor people who take tiny amounts of money for their basic needs, not drone makers who get filthy rich off the pretense that drones make the world safer.

The root of the problem, as Risen sees it, is that the military and the homeland security complex have been given more money than they can reasonably figure out what to do with. So, they unreasonably figure out what to do with it. This is compounded, Risen writes, by fear so extreme that people don't want to say no to anything that might possibly work even in their wildest dreams—or what Dick Cheney called the obligation to invest in anything with a 1% chance. Risen told *Democracy Now* that military spending reminded him of the Wall Street banks. In his book he argues that the big war profiteers have been deemed too big to fail.

Risen tells several stories in *Pay Any Price*, including the story of
the pallets of cash. Of $20 billion shipped to Iraq in $100 bills, he
writes, $11.7 billion is unaccounted for—lost, stolen, misused, or
dumped into a failed attempt to buy an election for Ayad Allawi.
Risen reports that some $2 billion of the missing money is actually
known to be sitting in a pile in Lebanon, but the U.S. government
has no interest in recovering it. After all, it's just $2 billion, and the
military industrial complex is sucking down $1 trillion a year from
the U.S. treasury.

When Risen, like everyone else, cites the cost of recent U.S. wars
($4 trillion over a decade, he says), I'm always surprised that nobody
notices that it is the wars that justify the "regular" "base" military
spending of another $10 trillion each decade at the current pace.
I also can't believe Risen actually writes that "to most of America,
war has become not only tolerable but profitable." What? Of course
it's extremely profitable for certain people who exert inordinate
influence on the government. But "most of America"? Many (not
most) people in the U.S. have jobs in the war industry, so it's
common to imagine that spending on war and preparations for
war benefits an economy. In reality[270], spending those same dollars
on peaceful industries, on education, on infrastructure, or even on
tax cuts for working people would produce more jobs and in most
cases better paying jobs—with enough savings to help everyone
make the transition from war work to peace work. Military
spending radically increases inequality and diverts funding from
services that people in many less-militarized nations have. I also
wish that Risen had managed to include a story or two from that

270  http://www.peri.umass.edu/236/hash/0b0ce6af7ff999b11745825d80aca0b8/
publication/489/

group making up 95% of U.S. war victims: the people of the places where the wars are waged.

But Risen does a great job on veterans of U.S. torture suffering moral injury, on the extensiveness of waterboarding's use, and on a sometimes comical tale of the U.S. government's infiltration of a lawsuit by 9/11 families against possible Saudi funders of 9/11—a story, part of which is given more context in terms of its impact in Afghanistan in Anand Gopal's recent book. There's even a story with some similarity to Merlin regarding the possible sale of U.S.-made drones to U.S. enemies abroad.

These SNAFU collection books have to be read with an eye on the complete forest, of course, to avoid the conclusion that what we need is war done right or—for that matter—Wall Street done right. We don't need a better CIA but a government free of the CIA[271]. That the problems described are not essentially new is brought to mind, for me, in reading Risen's book, by the repeated references to Dulles Airport. Still, it is beginning to look as if the Dulles brothers aren't just a secretive corner of the government anymore, but the patron saints of all Good Americans. And that's frightening. Secrecy is allowing insanity, and greater secrecy is being employed to keep the insanity secret. How can it be a "State Secret" that the CIA fell for a scam artist who pretended to see magical messages on Al Jazeera? If Obama's prosecution of whistleblowers doesn't alert people to the danger, at least it is helping sell Jim Risen's books, which in turn ought to wake people up better than a middle-of-the-night visit in the hospital from Alberto Gonzales and Andrew Card.

---

271 http://act.rootsaction.org/p/dia/action/public/?action_KEY=7880

There's still a thin facade of decency to be found in U.S. political culture. Corrupt Iraqi politicians, in Risen's book, excuse themselves by saying that the early days of the occupation in 2003 were difficult. A *New York Times* editor told *60 Minutes* that the first few years after 9/11 were just not a good time for U.S. journalism. These should not be treated as acceptable excuses for misconduct. As the earth's climate begins more and more to resemble a CIA operation, we're going to have nothing but difficult moments. Already the U.S. military is preparing to address climate change with the same thing it uses to address Ebola or terrorism or outbreaks of democracy. If we don't find people able to think on their feet, as Risen does while staring down the barrel of a U.S. prison sentence, we're going to be in for some real ugliness.

# *War Culture*

According to a book by George Williston called *This Tribe of Mine: A Story of Anglo Saxon Viking Culture in America*, the United States wages eternal war because of its cultural roots in the Germanic tribes that invaded, conquered, ethnically cleansed, or— if you prefer—*liberated* England before moving on to the slaughter of the Native Americans and then the Filipinos and Vietnamese and on down to the Iraqis. War advocate, former senator, and current presidential hopeful Jim Webb himself blames Scots-Irish American culture.

But most of medieval and ancient Europe engaged in war. How did Europe end up less violent than a place made violent by

Europe? Williston points out that England spends dramatically less per capita on war than the United States does, yet he blames U.S. warmaking on English roots. And, of course, Scotland and Ireland are even further from U.S. militarism despite being closer to England and presumably to Scots-Irishness.

"We view the world through Viking eyes," writes Williston, "viewing those cultures that do not hoard wealth in the same fashion or make fine iron weapons as child-like and ripe for exploitation." Williston describes the passage of this culture down to us through the pilgrims, who came to Massachusetts and began killing—and, quite frequently, beheading—those less violent, acquisitive, or competitive than they.

Germans and French demonstrated greater respect for native peoples, Williston claims. But is that true? Including in Africa? Including in Auschwitz? Williston goes on to describe the United States taking over Spanish colonialism in the Philippines and French colonialism in Vietnam, without worrying too much about how Spain and France got there.

I'm convinced that a culture that favors war is necessary but not sufficient to make a population as warlike as the United States is now. All sorts of circumstances and opportunities are also necessary. And the culture is constantly evolving. Perhaps Williston would agree with me. His book doesn't make a clear argument and could really have been reduced to an essay if he'd left out the religion, the biology metaphors, the experiments proving telepathy or prayer, the long quotes of others, etc. Regardless, I think it's important to be clear that we can't blame our culture in the way that some choose to blame our genes. We have to blame the U.S. government, identify ourselves with humanity rather than a tribe, and work to abolish warmaking[272].

In this regard, it can only help that people like Williston and Webb are asking what's wrong with U.S. culture. It can be shocking to an Israeli to learn that their day of independence is referred to by Palestinians as The Catastrophe (Nakba), and to learn why. Similarly, many U.S. school children might be startled to know that some native Americans referred to George Washington as The Destroyer of Villages (Caunotaucarius). It can be difficult to appreciate how peaceful native Americans were, how many tribes did not wage war, and how many waged war in a manner more properly thought of as "war games" considering the minimal level of killing. As Williston points out, there was nothing in the Americas to compare with the Hundred Years War or the Thirty Years War or any of the endless string of wars in Europe—which of course are themselves significantly removed in level of killing from wars of more recent years.

Williston describes various cooperative and peaceful cultures: the Hopi, the Kogi, the Amish, the Ladakh. Indeed, we should be looking for inspiration wherever we can find it. But we shouldn't imagine that changing our cultural practices in our homes will stop the Pentagon being the Pentagon. Telepathy and prayer are as likely to work out as levitating the Pentagon in protest. What we need is a culture dedicated to the vigorous nonviolent pursuit of the abolition of war.

272 http://worldbeyondwar.org/individual

# *No More Wars on Anything*

Searching new articles on ye olde internets the past couple of days for the word "war," I turned up roughly equal uses of "war" to refer to wars and to refer to other things entirely. Apparently there is a war on graft, a propaganda war, a number of price wars, a war of words, a Republican war on women, and a woman who has been breast-feeding and is now suffering from "war-torn nipples."

While a war on women or a war on the poor can involve as much cruelty and suffering as an actual war, it isn't an actual war. It's a different phenomenon, requiring a different set of solutions.

While a war on terror or a war on drugs can include actual war, it is not just actual war, and it is better understood if its components are split apart. While a cyber war can cause damage, it is a very different creature from a, you know, war war—different physically, visually, legally, morally, and in terms of measures of prevention. A war on poverty or racism or any bad thing that we want eliminated is quite different from a war on a nation or a population which, typically, only a certain section of a war's supporters actually wants *eliminated*.

I don't just mean that other wars fail to compare to war in terms of investment ("If the war on poverty were a real war we'd actually be putting money into it!"). I mean that war is entirely the wrong way, metaphorically or literally, to think about ending poverty. And I don't just mean that war always fails, although it does. ("The war on terror has brought more terror and the war on drugs has brought more drugs; maybe we should have a war on happiness!") I mean that war is a violent, reckless, irrational lashing out at a problem in order to very noisily make seen than one is "doing something." This is entirely different from trying to develop a world without poverty or without racism or—for that matter—without war. You cannot have a war upon the makers of war and expect to get peace out of it.

It is certainly important to recognize who is causing a problem. The 1% is hoarding wealth and imposing poverty. Promoters of sexism are driving sexism. Et cetera. But treating them as war enemies makes no more sense, and will work no better, than your local police treating your public demonstration as an act of terrorism. We don't have to kill the 1% or win them over. We have to win over and engage in strategic nonviolent action with enough people to control our world.

War language in non-war discourse in our culture is not limited to the word "war" but includes the full range of barbaric, counter-productive, advocacy of violence—serious, metaphorical, and joking. The "war on crime" includes state-sanctioned murder and worse. Wars on abortion doctors and sex offenders and political opponents include state-modeled murder. The state uses murder to relate to other states, as individuals use it to relate to other individuals.

Acceptance of war, of course, makes it easier to use war language in other settings. If war were thought of as something as evil as slavery or rape or child abuse, we wouldn't be so eager to launch a war on cancer (or send soldiers to kill Ebola). But acceptance of the war metaphor throughout our lives must also make it easier to accept actual war. If we have a war on cancer, why in the world not have a war on beheaders? If there's a war on women, why not launch a war to defend every right of women except the right not to be bombed?

I'm proposing that we try thinking differently as well as talking differently, that our foreign policy make use of diplomacy, aid, and the rule of law, rather than mass-murder—or what might in strategic terms be called terrorism generation; and that our domestic policies follow suit, that we don't just madly attack social ills, but transform the systems that generate them. A war on climate change doesn't sound like it includes a radical reduction in consumerism and capitalism, as it must. It sounds more like a big but token investment in solar panels and perhaps a very shiny train. And a war on climate change is already something the Pentagon is beginning to use to mean actual war on human beings.

So, how should we talk differently? Here's one idea for certain contexts: Instead of engaging in a war on poverty, lets work on the movement to abolish poverty, to end poverty, or to eliminate or overcome poverty, to make poverty a thing of the past. Instead of lamenting a war on women, let's work to expose and put a stop to cruelty, abuse, violence, unfairness, brutality, and discrimination against women. In doing so, we can be more specific about what the problems and solutions are. Instead of a war on graft, let's end political corruption. Instead of a propaganda war, let's expose propaganda and counter it with accurate information and calm, wise understanding. Instead of price wars, market competition. Instead of a war of words, rudeness. I imagine most people can rewrite "war-torn nipples" without much assistance.

A logical place to start, I think, is on a campaign to abolish (not wage war on) war[273].

## Valor, Remembrance, and Complicity

November 11th in the United States is marked and marred by a holiday that relatively recently had its name changed to "Veterans Day" and its purpose converted and perverted into celebrating war. This year a "Concert for Valor[274]" will be held on the National Mall in Washington, D.C.

> "Thank you for your service" is not a conversation, but it's a start. Keep it going. Ask him where he served. Ask her what she did in the military. Listen, learn and, most importantly, ask: "What's next?"

In the box above is a blurb from the concert website. "Thank you for your service" and "Support the troops" are phrases used to get people to support wars without thinking about whether they should be supporting wars. Notice that you're supposed to thank veterans first and ask them which war they were in and what they did in it afterwards. What if you oppose war? Or what if you oppose some wars and some tactics?

273 http://worldbeyondwar.org/individual
274 http://www.theconcertforvalor.com

Here's the disgusted response[275] to the Concert for Valor from a veteran who's sick of being thanked for his so-called service:

> "There is no question that we should honor people who fight for justice and liberty. Many veterans enlisted in the military thinking that they were indeed serving a noble cause, and it's no lie to say that they fought with valor for their brothers and sisters to their left and right. Unfortunately, good intentions at this stage are no substitute for good politics. The war on terror is going into its 14th year. If you really want to talk about "awareness raising," it's years past the time when anyone here should be able to pretend that our 18-year-olds are going off to kill and die for good reason. How about a couple of concerts to make that point?"

I'm going to repeat here something I said in *War Is A Lie*[276]:

Random House defines a hero as follows (and defines heroine the same way, substituting "woman" for "man"):

> "1. a man of distinguished courage or ability, admired for his brave deeds and noble qualities.
>
> "2. a person who, in the opinion of others, has heroic qualities or has performed a heroic act and is regarded as a model or ideal: He was a local hero when he saved the drowning child...
>
> "4. Classical Mythology.
>
> "a. a being of godlike prowess and beneficence who often came to be honored as a divinity."

275    http://www.tomdispatch.com/post/175912/tomgram%3A_rory_fanning,_why_do_we_keep_thanking_the_troops/
276 http://warisalie.org

Courage or ability. Brave deeds and noble qualities. There is something more here than merely courage and bravery, merely facing up to fear and danger. But what? A hero is regarded as a model or ideal. Clearly someone who bravely jumped out a 20-story window would not meet that definition, even if their bravery was as brave as brave could be. Clearly heroism must require bravery of a sort that people regard as a model for themselves and others. It must include prowess and beneficence. That is, the bravery can't just be bravery; it must also be good and kind. Jumping out a window does not qualify. The question, then, is whether killing and dying in wars should qualify as good and kind. Nobody doubts that it's courageous and brave. But is it as good a model as that of the man arrested this week for the crime of giving food to the hungry[277]?

If you look up "bravery" in the dictionary, by the way, you'll find "courage" and "valor." Ambrose Bierce's Devil's Dictionary defines "valor" as

> "a soldierly compound of vanity, duty, and the gambler's hope.
> 'Why have you halted?' roared the commander of a division
> at Chickamauga, who had ordered a charge: 'move forward,
> sir, at once.'
> 'General,' said the commander of the delinquent brigade, 'I
> am persuaded that any further display of valor by my troops
> will bring them into collision with the enemy.'"

But would such valor be good and kind or destructive and foolhardy? Bierce had himself been a Union soldier at Chickamauga

277          http://www.usatoday.com/story/news/nation-now/2014/11/05/fort-lauderdale-arrest-for-feeding-homeless/18525049/

and had come away disgusted. Many years later, when it had become possible to publish stories about the Civil War that didn't glow with the holy glory of militarism, Bierce published a story called "Chickamauga" in 1889 in the San Francisco Examiner that makes participating in such a battle appear the most grotesquely evil and horrifying deed one could ever do. Many soldiers have since told similar tales.

It's curious that war, something consistently recounted as ugly and horrible, should qualify its participants for glory. Of course, the glory doesn't last. Mentally disturbed veterans are kicked aside in our society. In fact, in dozens of cases documented between 2007 and 2010, soldiers who had been deemed physically and psychologically fit and welcomed into the military, performed "honorably," and had no recorded history of psychological problems. Then, upon being wounded, the same formerly healthy soldiers were diagnosed with a pre-existing personality disorder, discharged, and denied treatment for their wounds. One soldier was locked in a closet until he agreed to sign a statement that he had a pre-existing disorder — a procedure the Chairman of the House Veterans Affairs Committee called "torture."

Active duty troops, the real ones, are not treated by the military or society with particular reverence or respect. But the mythical, generic "troop" is a secular saint purely because of his or her willingness to rush off and die in the very same sort of mindless murderous orgy that ants regularly engage in. Yes, ants. Those teeny little pests with brains the size of . . . well, the size of something smaller than an ant: they wage war. And they're better at it than we are.

Ants wage long and complex wars with extensive organization and unmatched determination, or what we might call "valor." They are absolutely loyal to the cause in a way that no patriotic humans can match: "It'd be like having an American flag tattooed to you at birth," ecologist and photojournalist Mark Moffett told Wired magazine. Ants will kill other ants without flinching. Ants will make the "ultimate sacrifice" with no hesitation. Ants will proceed with their mission rather than stop to help a wounded warrior.

The ants who go to the front, where they kill and die first, are the smallest and weakest ones. They are sacrificed as part of a winning strategy. "In some ant armies, there can be millions of expendable troops sweeping forward in a dense swarm that's up to 100 feet wide." In one of Moffett's photos, which shows "the marauder ant in Malaysia, several of the weak ants are being sliced in half by a larger enemy termite with black, scissor-like jaws." What would Pericles say at their funeral?

"According to Moffett, we might actually learn a thing or two from how ants wage war. For one, ant armies operate with precise organization despite a lack of central command." And no wars would be complete without some lying: "Like humans, ants can try to outwit foes with cheats and lies." In another photo, "two ants face off in an effort to prove their superiority — which, in this ant species, is designated by physical height. But the wily ant on the right is standing on a pebble to gain a solid inch over his nemesis." Would honest Abe approve?

In fact, ants are such dedicated warriors that they can even fight civil wars that make that little skirmish between the North and South look like touch football. A parasitic wasp, Ichneumon eumerus, can dose an ant nest with a chemical secretion that causes the ants to fight a civil war, half the nest against the other half. Imagine if we had such a drug for humans, a sort of a prescription-strength Fox News. If we dosed the nation, would all the resulting warriors be heroes or just half of them? Are the ants heroes? And if they are not, is it because of what they are doing or purely because of what they are thinking about what they are doing? And what if the drug makes them think they are risking their lives for the benefit of future life on earth or to keep the anthill safe for democracy?

Here ends the War Is A Lie[278] excerpt. Are ants too hard to relate to? What about children. What if a teacher persuaded a bunch of 8 years olds, rather than 18 year olds to fight and kill and risk dying for a supposedly great and noble cause? Wouldn't the teacher be a criminal guilty of mass-murder? And what about everyone else complicit in a process of preparing the children for war—including perhaps uniformed and be-medalled officers coming into Kindergartens, as in fact happens in reality? Isn't the difference with 18 year olds that we have a tendency to hold them responsible, at least in part, as well as whoever instigates the killing spree? Whether we should or not need not be decided, for us to decide to treat veterans with humanity while utterly rejecting any celebration of what they've done.

Here's CODEPINK planning[279] a protest of the Concert for Valor. I urge you to join in. I also encourage you to keep in mind and spread understanding of the history of November 11th. Again,

---

278 http://warisalie.org
279 https://www.facebook.com/codepinkalert/posts/10152804112374695

I'm going to repeat, and modify, something I've said in a previous November:

Ninety-six years ago on the 11th hour of the 11th day of the 11th month of 1918, fighting ceased in the "war to end all wars." The war brought a new scale of death, the flu, prohibition, the Espionage Act, the foundations of World War II, the crushing of progressive political movements, the institution of flag worship, the beginning of pledges of allegiance in schools and the national anthem at sporting events. It brought everything but peace.

Thirty million soldiers had been killed or wounded and another seven million had been taken captive during World War I. Never before had people witnessed such industrialized slaughter, with tens of thousands falling in a day to machine guns and poison gas. After the war, more and more truth began to overtake the lies, but whether people still believed or now resented the pro-war propaganda, virtually every person in the United States wanted to see no more of war ever again. Posters of Jesus shooting at Germans were left behind as the churches along with everyone else now said that war was wrong. Al Jolson wrote in 1920 to President Harding:

> "*The weary world is waiting for*
> *Peace forevermore*
> *So take away the gun*
> *From every mother's son*
> *And put an end to war.*"

Congress passed an Armistice Day resolution calling for

"exercises designed to perpetuate peace through good will and mutual understanding ... inviting the people of the United States to observe the day in schools and churches with appropriate ceremonies of friendly relations with all other peoples." Later, Congress added that November 11th was to be "a day dedicated to the cause of world peace."

While the ending of warfare was celebrated every November 11th, veterans were treated no better than they are today. When 17,000 veterans plus their families and friends marched on Washington in 1932 to demand their bonuses, Douglas MacArthur, George Patton, Dwight Eisenhower, and other heroes of the next big war to come attacked the veterans, including by engaging in that greatest of evils with which Saddam Hussein would be endlessly charged: "using chemical weapons on their own people." The weapons they used, just like Hussein's, originated in the U.S. of A.

It was only after another war, an even worse war, a war that has in many ways never ended to this day, that Congress, following still another now forgotten war—this one on Korea—changed the name of Armistice Day to Veterans Day on June 1, 1954. And it was six-and-a-half years later that Eisenhower warned us that the military industrial complex would completely corrupt our society.

Veterans Day is no longer, for most people, a day to cheer the elimination of war or even to aspire to its abolition[280]. Veterans Day is not even a day on which to mourn or to question why suicide is the top killer of U.S. troops or why so many veterans

---

280 http://worldbeyondwar.org

have no houses at all in a nation in which one high-tech robber baron monopolist is hoarding $66 billion, and 400 of his closest friends have more money than half the country. It's not even a day to honestly, if sadistically, celebrate the fact that virtually all the victims of U.S. wars are non-Americans, that our so-called wars have become one-sided slaughters. Instead, it is a day on which to believe that war is beautiful and good. Towns and cities and corporations and sports leagues call it "military appreciation day" or "troop appreciation week" or "genocide glorification month." OK, I made up that last one. Just checking if you're paying attention.

Veterans For Peace has created a new tradition in recent years of returning to the celebration of Armistice Day. They even offer a tool kit so you can do the same[281].

In the UK, Veterans For Peace are marking what is still called Remembrance Day, and Remembrance Sunday[282] on November 9th, with white poppies and peace banners in opposition to the British government's pro-war slant on remembering World War I.

In North Carolina, a veteran has come up with his own way[283] of making every day Remembrance Day. But it's the celebrators of war that seem to be guiding the cultural trends. Here's the frequency of use of the word "valor" according to Google:[284]

---

281      http://www.veteransforpeace.org/our-work/reclaiming-armistice-day-november-11th/
282 http://veteransforpeace.org.uk/2014/the-cenotaph/
283      http://www.indyweek.com/indyweek/cary-artists-exhibit-reminds-us-of-the-cost-of-war/Content?oid=4282710
284 http://davidswanson.org/node/4577

Bruce Springsteen will be performing at the Concert for Valor. He once wrote this lyric: "Two faces have I." Here's one that I'm willing to bet won't be on display: "Blind faith in your leaders or in anything will get you killed," Springsteen warns in the video below before declaring war good for absolutely nothing.

http://www.youtube.com/watch?v=mn91L9goKfQ

You'll need lots of information, Springsteen advises potential draftees or recruits. If you don't find lots of information at the Concert for Valor, you might try this teach in[285] that evening at the Washington Peace Center.

## The World Gets the Wars Americans Deserve

Having been on the road, I have two brilliant insights to report.

1. No matter what sort of fascist state were ever established in this part of the world, Amtrak would never get the trains to run on time.

2. Respecting people and giving them credit for being smarter than the television depicts them is vastly easier when you stay home.

The well-known line is that people get the governments they deserve. Of course nobody should be abused the way the U.S. and many other governments abuse them, no matter what their intellectual deficiencies. If anything, stupid people should have

---

285 http://washingtonpeacecenter.org/node/13366

better, kinder governments. But my common response to that well-known line is to point out the bribery and gerrymandering and limited choices and relentless propaganda. Surely the clown show in Washington is not the people's fault. Some of my best friends are people and they often display signs of intelligence.

But the primary thing the U.S. government does is wage wars, and it wages them against other people who had no say in the matter. Of course I don't want wars waged against Americans either, but the general impression one gets from traveling around and speaking and answering questions at public events in the United States is not so much that people are indifferent to the destruction of the globe as long as they don't miss their favorite television show, as that people are unclear on what destruction means and can't identify a globe when it's placed in a lineup with six watermelons.

War and peace are concepts people have heard of, but ask them which they favor and you'll get blank stares. "Do you support all wars, some wars, or no wars?" I ask to get a sense of the crowd, but a fourth answer takes the majority: "Uhhh, I dunno."

A few people want to end war by having a bunch of anti-war wars, but they all work in the State Department and I haven't been invited to speak there.

A few elderly people believe we simply must have wars, and every last one of them has the identical reason: Pearl Harbor. You can explain to them the stupid vindictive conclusion of World War I, the decades of militarization, of antagonization of Japan (protested for many years by U.S. peace activists), of Wall Street funding the Nazis. You can point out the madness of a rogue nation waging hundreds of disastrous wars all over the world for 70 years and getting people to support this project by finding a single example of a supposedly justifiable war 70 years ago. You can challenge them to find any other major public project that has to go back that far to justify itself. You can quote them the wisdom of peace activists from the 1920s and 1930s and 1940s. They'll simply say that Pearl Harbor justified saving the Jews. You can show them how Pearl Harbor was intentionally provoked, how actions that might have saved the Jews were avoided, how the Jews became a justification for the war only long after it was over, and they'll just grunt at you. You can recount successful nonviolent resistance to the Nazis and the growth and development of nonviolent resistance in the decades since, and they'll drool, scratch their heads, or ask if you're going to vote for Hillary.

A few young people believe we simply must have wars, and every last one of them has the identical reason: ISIS. Because ISIS is something evil, there must be war. "Should we attack ISIS or do nothing?" they all ask. I imagine I'd laugh if I weren't trembling for our future. *Iraq III: The Return of the Decider* is becoming the worst parody of a humanitarian war in history. First George W. Obama gave himself[286] a waiver from his own dumb rules against killing unlimited civilians. Then he asked[287] for a special waiver in order to arm lots of really good people who happen to torture some folks and murder some folks and rape some folks and genocide some

---

286    http://www.commondreams.org/news/2014/10/01/us-relaxing-standards-killing-civilians-iraq-and-syria
287    http://bigstory.ap.org/article/03c6663be173479b9af8e9ae249af04a/obama-seeks-human-rights-waiver-war-funds

folks. This after he asked the CIA if arming rebels has ever worked out, and the CIA said "No, but we do it as a matter of principle," and he said "Let's roll!"

Just as nobody supposes World War II the Just and Noble could have arisen without World War I the Futile and Pointless, no serious analysis of ISIS can explain its birth without *Iraq II: The Liberation.* ISIS is made up of people tortured in U.S. prison camps and thrown out of the Iraqi Army by U.S. occupiers and driven into desperation by the hell the U.S. and its allies created. ISIS brutally murders just like, but on a smaller scale than, the U.S. and its new allies in fighting ISIS. The helpless-people-on-a-mountaintop story remains permanently present outside of time for Americans, even though the U.S. is now killing so many civilians that it needs laws changed (or simply ignored; anyone remember the UN Charter?), even though the story was a gross distortion at the time, and even though the bombing protected the oil contractors in Erbil, not the mountain.

People nod their heads and ask, "So, should we attack ISIS or do nothing?"

You can explain to them that ISIS explicitly said it wanted to be attacked. You can show them how ISIS is growing as a result. You can explain to them how hated the United States is now in that region. You can read them a RAND Corporation report showing that most terrorist organizations are ended through negotiations, virtually none through war. You can fill them in on how 80 percent of the weapons shipped into the Middle-East, not counting U.S.

weapons or weapons the U.S. gives to groups like ISIS and its allies, come from the United States. You can describe how the region could be demilitarized rather than further armed. You can discuss diplomatic possibilities, local cease-fires, aid and restitution. You can graphically make clear how a fraction of what's spent on bombing Iraq to fix the disaster created by bombing Iraq could pay for transforming the whole region into a healthier happier place to live with food, water, agriculture, clean energy, etc. You can detail emergency measures that are available, including peaceworkers, aid workers, doctors, journalists—measures that risk fewer lives than war.

And they'll blink their eyes and ask "So, should we attack ISIS or do nothing?"

Do you recall, you can say, that last year the White House wanted you to support attacking Syria, and wanted to attack the opposite side in that war? And people said no, remember? And now they want to attack the opposite side, while arming it, and this makes sense to you? They have no goal in mind, no plan, no estimated end-date or price-tag or body-count, and this makes sense to you?

Well, they'll say, it's that or do nothing.

But do you recall the year 2006 in which everybody said they'd elected Democrats in order to end the war, and the Democrats said they'd keep it going in order to run against it again in 2008? At that time, in 2006, as the big marches were just ending, having begun with the biggest marches ever on February 15, 2003, if you'd told anyone that in 2014 the war would be over and a new president would propose starting it up again, and nobody would protest, you'd have been laughed at. The America of 2006 would never have stood for this for a minute, at least not if the President were a Republican.

"Oh," they'll say, "I've heard of Republicans. They're the ones who like war, right? Do you think the military is letting women participate enough?"

It happened that while I was touring and talking, NATO claimed for something like the 89th time this year that Russia had invaded Ukraine. If it were ever true, I asked, would anyone believe it? The answer I got: Nobody cares.

Nobody with the easy ability to do something about it cares. The people under the bombs care. The world gets the wars Americans deserve.

## *Watchers of the Sky Falls in a Pit*

The United States is a society incapable of producing a major documentary film opposing the institution of war and explicitly advocating its abolition. If it did so, the major corporate media outlets would not sing such a film's praises.

Yet *Watchers of the Sky* is beloved by the U.S. corporate media because it opposes genocide, not war. I'm not aware of any opponents of war who don't also oppose genocide. In fact, many oppose the two as a single evil without the stark distinction between them. But the anti-genocide academic nonprofit industrial complex has become dominated by leading advocates for war.

As we watch people lament Bosnia, Rwanda, and Darfur while supporting mass killing in Palestine, Iraq, Afghanistan, and elsewhere, we seem to be witnessing a sort of extended victors' justice running 70 years from the hypocritical "justice" that followed World War II right through the establishment of the International Criminal Court (for Africans).

Right-wing war supporters oppose "terrorism" which means small-scale killing my government disapproves of. Liberal war supporters oppose "genocide" which means killing my government disapproves of and which is motivated by backward drives like race or religion rather than enlightened projects like control of fossil fuels, profiteering off weapons, or maintaining global hegemony.

Selective outrage over killing within a country has become a common justification for killing across borders (and oceans). Ben Ferencz, featured in *Watchers of the Sky*, was recently on my radio show[288] pushing his idea of criminalizing war while refusing to consider recent U.S. wars to fit the category of wars worth criminalizing. Samantha Power, star of *Watchers of the Sky*, supports mass killing[289]. I don't think she's pretending to be outraged by genocide any more than Madeline Albright who said killing a half million children had been a good policy is pretending

288 http://davidswanson.org/node/4477
289 http://www.alternet.org/world/samantha-power-obamas-atrocity-enabler

when she claims to be outraged by genocide. I think such people are outraged by evils they have permitted themselves to see as evil, while blinding themselves to horrors they prefer not to recognize.

I recently gave a talk at a college and happened to mention Hillary Clinton's comment about obliterating Iran. A professor interrupted me to state that such a thing never happened. A student pulled up the video of Clinton on several websites on a phone, but the professor still denied it stating that it made no sense. That is to say, it didn't fit into his worldview. I later happened to criticize Israel's treatment of Gaza, and the same professor got up and stormed out of the room. He could only deny what was done to Gaza by avoiding hearing it altogether. I have no doubt that he would have expressed sincere outrage over Rwanda if asked.

The problem with the focus on Yugoslavia and Rwanda is the pretense that there is something worse than, discrete from, and preventable by war. The myths about the origins and outcomes of those horrors play down the role that Western militarism had in creating them while playing up the role it had or could have had in preventing them. War is depicted as an under-utilized tool, while the effects of both war and genocide (such as refugee crises) are blamed entirely on genocide.

The odd thing is that people being slaughtered from the sky are almost always being slaughtered by the U.S. military and its allies. Those who can only see killing when it's done by people resisting U.S. domination can usually keep their eyes comfortably downward.

# *Watch Schooling the World, Stop Schooling the World*

It's becoming slightly more common in the Western industrialized world to propose radical cultural change away from consumerism and environmental destruction. It's not hard to find people making the case[290] that in fact nothing else can save us. But we should have one eye on what our governments and billionaires are doing to educate the rest of the world with the way of thinking that we are beginning to question.

What if the United States were to radically reform and abandon its role as leading destroyer of the environment and leading maker of war in the world, and we were to discover that U.S.- and Western-funded institutions had in the mean time created billions of teenagers around the globe intent on each becoming Bill Gates?

The remarkable film *Schooling the World*[291] brings this warning. It is not an overly simplistic or dreamy argument. It is not a rejection of the accomplishments of Western medicine or a pitch for adopting polytheistic beliefs. But the film documents that the same practice that "educated" thousands of young Native Americans into second-class U.S. citizens through forced boarding schools is running its course in India and around the world. Young people are being educated out of kindness and cooperation, and into greed and consumerism, out of connections to family and culture and history, and into a deep sense of inferiority of the sort created in the U.S.

290    http://truth-out.org/news/item/27392-abundant-clean-renewables-think-again
291 http://schoolingtheworld.org

by the separate-but-equal educational system of Jim Crow. People whose families lived happily and sustainably are being taken away from their villages to struggle in cities, the majority of them labeled as failures by the schools created to "help" them—many of them cruelly introduced to a modern invention called poverty.

Eliminated in the process are languages—referred to in the film as ecosystems of the mind—and all the wealth of knowledge they contain. Also eliminated: actual ecosystems, those that once included humans, and those simply damaged by heightened consumption rampaging around the globe. Young people are not taught to care for local resources as their parents and grandparents and great grandparents were.

And much of this is done with the best of intentions. Well-meaning Westerners, from philanthropic tourists to World Bank executives, believe that their culture—that of industrial extraction, competition, and consumption—is good and inevitable. Therefore they believe it helpful to impose an education in it on everyone on earth, most easily accomplished on young people.

But is a young person's removal from a sustainable healthy life rich in community and tradition, and their arrival in a sweatshop in a crowded slum, as good for them as it looks in the economic statistics that quantify it as an increase in wealth? And can we see our way out of this trap while screaming hysterically about the glories of "American exceptionalism"? Will we have to lose that stupid arrogance first? And by the time we've done that, will every African nation have its own Fox News?

# *What Is Imaginable*

## *Misplaced Lessons of Tahrir*

I still want *Dirty Wars* to win the Oscar, but *The Square* is a documentary worth serious discussion as we hit the three-year point since the famous occupation of Tahrir Square in Cairo that overthrew Mubarak—in particular because a lot of people seem to get a lot of the lessons wrong.

I suppose some people will leave *Dirty Wars* imagining that we need clean wars, whatever those would be. But too many people seem to be drawing from *The Square* lessons they brought with them to it, including these: Thou shalt have a leader; thou shalt work within a major political party; thou shalt have an identifiable group of individuals ready to take power. I don't think following these commandments would have easily changed the past three years in Egypt; I don't think they're where Egyptians should be heading; and I'm even more confident they're blind alleys in the United States—where they serve as supposed remedies for the supposed failings of Occupy.

Many lessons that might be drawn from *The Square* seem right to me. Did the people leave the square too early? Hell yes. Was the movement divided when the Muslim Brotherhood sought to claim victory exclusively for itself and not for all of the people of Egypt? Of course it was. Let that be a lesson to us indeed. We agree, virtually all of us in the U.S., on a lot of needed reforms.

We're all getting collectively screwed. But we divide ourselves over stupid petty stuff, irrelevant stuff, secondary stuff—cultural issues, ideologies, superficial identities, and—yes—big-name leaders (think how many opponents of militarism and Big Brother you could agree with if they weren't "Ron Paulers"). Preferring one tyrant to another because of their religion or race is not a flaw the Egyptians have a monopoly on (think of all the Christian support for Bush and African-American support for Obama).

Was trusting the military a horrible idea? No. It wasn't a horrible idea. It was the most catastrophically stupendously stupid notion ever to enter a human skull. Militaries don't support people. People support militaries through their useful and exploited labor. Costa Rica had to disband its military to stop having coups. When a military exists, appealing to the humanity of its individual members is wise indeed. But expecting the military as a whole to be democratic to the point of handing over power before it's compelled to do so is decidedly foolish. None of which is to say the Egyptians have had much choice or that their project is yet completed. Between them and us the question of which group is learning faster is no contest at all.

Do the people of Egypt need a Constitution rather than a pharaoh? Yes, absolutely. Does the Occupy movement need demands? Yes, of course it does. Must we all create an ongoing culture of nonviolent action? Yes, sir-ee. While *The Square* doesn't explicitly make the point, would better nonviolent discipline help? Undoubtedly. Is the key lesson to never give up? Indeed. All of these lessons should soak in deep.

But other points are less clear, in both *The Square* and common discussions of Egyptian revolution. Tahrir Square didn't begin in 2011, and neither did the Muslim Brotherhood. The foundations for the popular movement and for the religious party were laid over a period of years. Foundations are being laid for nonviolent revolution in other places now.

Did the Egyptians fail? And did they fail because they are great protesters but bad democrats who should be condescended to by enlightened Americans? No. First, it isn't over. Second, the United States has a failed system of government itself, as 80-90 percent of the people here have been telling pollsters for years. Third, although I caught only one very quick little hint at it in *The Square*, the major financial and military backer of the brutal, corrupt regimes in Egypt—before Tahrir and since—is the United States government. To the extent that Egyptians have failed they've failed with our help. And whether we're unaware of the billions of dollars of our grandchildren's unearned wages that we give to Egyptian thugs to assault the Egyptian people every year, or aware and unable to do anything about it—either way, our democracy hardly shines out as a model for the world.

A leader would have divided the Tahrir movement or the Occupy movement. That we don't think of ourselves as having leaders is a function of the corporate media giving no microphones to people who favor major improvements to the world. Ironically, just like coverage of New York Police Department brutality, this helps us to build a stronger movement. That is to say, it helps us in so far as it allows a movement not focused on a leader. Yes, we'd be much stronger with major media coverage, but the possible development of leaders recognized and named as such would be a downside. And a successful movement behind a leader would only be able to put that leader into power if it succeeded far beyond where Egypt arrived in 2011—and it would only be able to get that leader back out of power again if it succeeded even further.

Is the lesson of Tahrir that Occupiers should back candidates in the Democratic Party? Is an organized party that can challenge the Muslim Brotherhood or the Democrats the answer? Not within a corrupt system it isn't. When our goal is not a better regime but something approaching democracy, then what's needed is the nonviolent imposition of democracy on whatever individuals are in power, and the development of a culture of eternal vigilance to maintain it. You can't elect your way out of a system of corrupt elections. You can't impose a group of populist leaders on a government by coup d'etat and then write a democratic constitution afterwards.

No, that is not what happened in the United States, and not just because the old government got on ships and sailed away, but because the Constitution was fundamentally anti-democratic. The United States has gained democracy through nonviolent movements of public pressure, imposed reforms, amendments, court rulings, and the changing of the culture. Reforms are needed more badly than ever now, and whether they're imposed at the federal level or through the states or through secession, they must come through popular nonviolent pressure, as bullets and ballots are virtually helpless here.

The lesson I take away from *The Square* is that we must prevent the operation of business as usual until the institution itself, not its face, is fixed. We can put up giant posters of a black man followed by a white woman followed by some other demographic symbol, but the posters will still be on the walls of prisons, barracks, and homeless shelters, unless we fix the structure of things. That means:

Rights for people, and for the natural environment, not for corporations.

Spending money on elections is not a human right of free speech.

Elections entirely publicly financed.

The right to vote, to have time off work to vote, and to vote on a paper ballot publicly counted at the polling place.

Free air time, ballot access, and debate participation to all candidates who have collected sufficient signatures of potential constituents.

A citizens branch and public initiative power by signature collection.

The application of criminal laws to authorities who commit crimes or abuse their office.

Mandatory impeachment and recall votes for officials facing prosecution.

The right to a decent income, housing, healthcare, education, peace, a healthy environment, and freedom from debt.

The rights of the natural environment to continue and thrive.

The institution of minimum and maximum wages and a ban on extreme wealth.

Demilitarization.

Dismantling of the prison industry.

Give me all of that or give me death. Take your bullshit rhetoric about "liberty" and name a square after it.

# *One Nation the U.S. Actually Should Liberate*

*"Secretary Kerry? It's Ukraine on the phone asking about liberation again. Have you been able to get them a reference letter yet from Libya or Iraq or Afghanistan? How about Vietnam? Panama? Grenada? Kosovo maybe? Ukraine says Syria says you have a reference letter in the works from Kosovo. No? Huh. They said they'd accept one from Korea or the Dominican Republic or Iran. No? Guatemala? The Philippines? Cuba? Congo? How about Haiti? They say you promised them a glowing reference from Haiti. Oh. They did? No, I am not laughing, Sir. What about East Timor? Oh? Oh! Sir, you're going to liberate the what out of them? Yes sir, I think you'd better tell them yourself."*

Some nations the United States should probably not liberate— except perhaps the 175 nations which could be liberated from the presence of U.S. soldiers. But one nation I would make an exception for, and that is the nation of Hawai'i.

Jon Olsen's new book, *Liberate Hawai'i: Renouncing and Defying the Continuing Fraudulent U.S. Claim to the sovereignty of Hawai'i*, makes a compelling case—a legal case as well as a moral one. Olsen's case, in very condensed summary, looks like this: Hawai'i was an independent nation, recognized as such by the United

States and numerous other nations, with treaties in effect between Hawai'i and other nations, including the United States, that have never been terminated. In 1893 U.S. profiteers and U.S. Marines, in a criminal act, overthrew Hawai'i's government and queen, setting up a new government that lacked any legal standing. President Grover Cleveland investigated what had been done, admitted to the facts, and declared the new government illegitimate, insisting that the Queen retain the rule she had never abdicated. But the fraudulent foreign government remained, and in 1898 once William McKinley was U.S. president, handed over Hawaii (thought it had no legal power to do so) to the United States, as the United States also picked up the Philippines, Guam, Puerto Rico, and Cuba in a bit of a global shopping spree. By 1959, these events were growing lost in the mists of time, and the demographics of Hawai'i were radically altered, as Hawai'i was offered a vote between two bad choices: statehood or continued status as a colony or "territory" (liberation wasn't on the ballot). Thus did Hawai'i seem to become a state without legally becoming any such thing. In 1993, the U.S. Congress passed and President Clinton signed U.S. Public Law 103-150, admitted to and apologizing for this history, without of course doing the one thing legally and morally required—liberating Hawai'i.

The primary purpose of the U.S. grab for Hawai'i, even more than economic exploitation, was military expansion, as Olsen shows. The U.S. military wanted, and took, Pearl Harbor. Then it took a lot more land, occupied it, bombed it, poisoned it. Now the U.S. military holds 22% of O'ahu, 68% of Kaula, and chunks of all the major islands, with more planned, archaeological sites threatened, species threatened, air quality for telescopes threatened, and heightened tensions around the Pacific not just threatened but those heightened tensions being the actual purpose of this massive and disastrous investment by the foreign occupying nation claiming Hawai'i by force and fraud.

What can be done? And of, by, and for whom exactly? Who is a Hawaiian and who is not? Olsen does not advocate a Hawaii for the ethnically native Hawaiians alone. He recognizes that the term "Hawaiian" is used to refer to an ethnic group, and proposes the invention of the term "Hawaiian national" to refer to anyone who considers Hawaii home and supports its liberation. I think Olsen is on the right path but slipping slightly off it. Nationalism has not proved a wholly beneficial concept. Hawaii needs to be liberated from U.S. nationalism, but Hawaiians and the rest of us need to begin thinking of ourselves as citizens of the world, not of one nation over others. Nor do two wrongs, of whatever disparity, make a right (just ask Palestine). I'd like to see "Hawaiian" evolve to encompass all who consider Hawaii their home, without the addition of "national." Of course this unsolicited advice from me to Hawaiians may be unappreciated. But then, they are free to ignore it; I'm not using the Marine Corps as a delivery service, and my advice to the Marine Corps (unsolicited as well) is to disband and liberate the world from its existence.

There's an important point that I think Olsen's argument supports, although he does not develop it in his book, and it is this: If in 1941 Hawaii was not yet even purporting to be a U.S. state, but was rather an illegally and illegitimately seized territory, Pearl Harbor having been stolen from the Hawaiian people, then whatever else you might think of the *second* major crime committed at Pearl Harbor, the Japanese did not attack the United States. The Japanese attacked an imperial outpost in the middle of the Pacific that they viewed as a threat—and what else was it if not that?

Were Hawaii to liberate itself from the United States (for the United States is not actually going to liberate it voluntarily), would the point be moot as the practices of the United States and China and other nations drive the world's islands underwater? Actually, projections[292] show Hawaii surviving the flood. The question for Hawaiians may be this: Who do you want managing the influx of millions of Floridians looking for a new paradise to pave, your own manageable self-governed society or the tender mercies of the United States Congress?

## *When We're All Musteites*

We won't necessarily know what a Musteite is, but I'm inclined to think it would help if we did. I'm using the word to mean "having a certain affinity for the politics of A.J. Muste."

I had people tell me I was a Musteite when I had at best the vaguest notion of who A.J. Muste had been. I could tell it was a compliment, and from the context I took it to mean that I was someone who wanted to end war. I guess I sort of brushed that off as not much of a compliment. Why should it be considered

292 http://ngm.nationalgeographic.com/2013/09/rising-seas/if-ice-melted-map

either particularly praiseworthy or outlandishly radical to want to end war? When someone wants to utterly and completely end rape or child abuse or slavery or some other evil, we don't call them extremist radicals or praise them as saints. Why is war different?

The possibility that war might not be different, that it might be wholly abolished, could very well be a thought that I picked up third-hand from A.J. Muste, as so many of us have picked up so much from him, whether we know it or not. His influence is all over our notions of labor and organizing and civil rights and peace activism. His new biography, *American Gandhi: A.J. Muste and the History of Radicalism in the Twentieth Century* by Leilah Danielson is well worth reading, and has given me a new affection for Muste despite the book's own rather affection-free approach.

Martin Luther King Jr. told an earlier Muste biographer, Nat Hentoff, "The current emphasis on nonviolent direct action in the race relations field is due more to A.J. than to anyone else in the country." It is also widely acknowledged that without Muste there would not have been formed such a broad coalition against the war on Vietnam. Activists in India have called him "the American Gandhi."

The American Gandhi was born in 1885 and immigrated with his family at age 6 from Holland to Michigan. He studied in Holland, Michigan, the same town that we read about in the first few pages of *Blackwater: The Rise of the World's Most Powerful Mercenary Army*, and at a college later heavily funded by the Prince Family, from which Blackwater sprang. The stories of both Muste and

Prince begin with Dutch Calvinism and end up as wildly apart as imaginable. At the risk of offending Christian admirers of either man, I think neither story—and neither life—would have suffered had the religion been left out.

Muste would have disagreed with me, of course, as some form of religion was central to his thinking during much of his life. By the time of World War I he was a preacher and a member of the Fellowship of Reconciliation (FOR). He opposed war in 1916 when opposing war was acceptable. And when most of the rest of the country fell in line behind Woodrow Wilson and obediently loved war in 1917, Muste didn't change. He opposed war and conscription. He supported the struggle for civil liberties, always under attack during wars. The American Civil Liberties Union (ACLU) was formed by Muste's FOR colleagues in 1917 to treat symptoms of war, just as it does today. Muste refused to preach in support of war and was obliged to resigned from his church, stating in his resignation letter that the church should be focused on creating "the spiritual conditions that should stop the war and render all wars unthinkable." Muste became a volunteer with the ACLU advocating for conscientious objectors and others persecuted for war opposition in New England. He also became a Quaker.

In 1919 Muste found himself the leader of a strike of 30,000 textile workers in Lawrence, Massachusetts, learning on the job—and on the picket line, where he was arrested and assaulted by police, but returned immediately to the line. By the time the struggle was won, Muste was general secretary of the newly formed Amalgamated Textile Workers of America. Two years later, he was directing

Brookwood Labor College outside of Katonah, New York. By the mid-1920s, as Brookwood succeeded, Muste had become a leader of the progressive labor movement nationwide. At the same time, he served on the executive committee of the national FOR from 1926-1929 as well as on the national committee of the ACLU. Brookwood struggled to bridge many divides until the American Federation of Labor destroyed it with attacks from the right, aided a bit with attacks from the left by the Communists. Muste labored on for labor, forming the Conference for Progressive Labor Action, and organizing in the South, but "if we are to have morale in the labor movement," he said, "we must have a degree of unity, and, if we are to have that, it follows, for one thing, that we cannot spend all our time in controversy and fighting with each other—maybe 99 per cent of the time, but not quite 100 per cent."

Muste's biographer follows that same 99 percent formula for a number of chapters, covering the infighting of the activists, the organizing of the unemployed, the forming of the American Workers Party in 1933, and in 1934 the Auto-Lite strike in Toledo, Ohio, that led to the formation of the United Auto Workers. The unemployed, joining in the strike on behalf of the workers, were critical to success, and their commitment to do so may have helped the workers decide to strike in the first place. Muste was central to all of this and to progressive opposition to fascism during these years. The sit-down strike at Goodyear in Akron was led by former students of Muste.

Muste sought to prioritize the struggle for racial justice and to apply Gandhian techniques, insisting on changes in culture, not just government. "If we are to have a new world," he said, "we must have new men; if you want a revolution, you must be revolutionized." In 1940, Muste became national secretary of FOR and launched a Gandhian campaign against segregation, bringing on new staff including James Farmer and Bayard Rustin, and helping to found the Congress of Racial Equality (CORE). The nonviolent actions that many associate with the 1950s and 1960s began in the 1940s. A Journey of Reconciliation predated the Freedom Rides by 14 years.

Muste predicted the rise of the Military Industrial Complex and the militarized adventurism of the post-World War II United States in 1941. Somewhere beyond the comprehension of most Americans, and even his biographer, Muste found the wisdom to continue opposing war during a second world war, advocating instead for nonviolent defense and a peaceful, cooperative, and generous foreign policy, defending the rights of Japanese Americans, and once again opposing a widespread assault on civil liberties. "If I can't love Hitler, I can't love at all," said Muste, articulating the widespread commonsense that one should love one's enemies, but doing so in the primary case in which virtually everyone else, to this day, advocates for the goodness of all-out vicious violence and hatred.

Of course, those who had opposed World War I and the horrible settlement that concluded it, and the fueling of fascism for years— and who could see what the end of World War II would bring, and who saw the potential in Gandhian techniques—must have had a harder time than most in accepting that war was inevitable and World War II justified.

Muste, I am sure, took no satisfaction in watching the U.S. government create a cold war and a global empire in line with his own prediction. Muste continued to push back against the entire institution of war, remarking that, "the very means nations use to provide themselves with apparent or temporary 'defense' and 'security' constitute the greatest obstacle to the attainment of genuine or permanent collective security. They want international machinery so that the atomic armaments race may cease; but the atomic armaments race has to stop or the goal of the world order recedes beyond human reach."

It was in this period, 1948-1951 that MLK Jr. was attending Crozer Theological Seminary, attending speeches by, and reading books by, Muste, who would later advise him in his own work, and who would play a key role in urging civil rights leaders to oppose the war on Vietnam. Muste worked with the American Friends Service Committee, and many other organizations, including the Committee to Stop the H-Bomb Tests, which would become the National Committee for a Sane Nuclear Policy (SANE); and the World Peace Brigade.

Muste warned against a U.S. war on Vietnam in 1954. He led opposition to it in 1964. He struggled with great success to broaden the anti-war coalition in 1965. At the same time, he struggled against the strategy of watering down war opposition in an attempt to find broader appeal. He believed that "polarization" brought "contradictions and differences" to the surface and allowed for the possibility of greater success. Muste chaired the November 8 Mobilization Committee (MOBE) in 1966, planning a massive action in April 1967. But upon returning from a trip to Vietnam in February, giving talks about the trip, and staying up all night drafting the announcement of the April demonstration, he began to complain of back pain and did not live much longer.

He did not see King's speech at Riverside Church on April 4. He did not see the mass mobilization or the numerous funerals and memorials to himself. He did not see the war ended. He did not see the war machine and war planning continue as if little had been learned. He did not see the retreat from economic fairness and progressive activism during the decades to come. But A.J. Muste had been there before. He'd seen the upsurges of the 1920s and 1930s and lived to help bring about the peace movement of the 1960s. When, in 2013, public pressure helped stop a missile attack on Syria, but nothing positive took its place, and a missile attack was launched a year later against the opposite side in the Syrian war, Muste would not have been shocked. His cause was not the prevention of a particular war but the elimination of the institution of war, the cause also of the new campaign in 2014 World Beyond War[293].

What can we learn from someone like Muste who persevered long enough to see some, but not all, of his radical ideas go mainstream? He didn't bother with elections or even voting. He prioritized nonviolent direct action. He sought to form the broadest possible coalition, including with people who disagreed with him and with each other on fundamental questions but who agreed on the important matter at hand. Yet he sought to keep those

---

293 http://worldbeyondwar.org

coalitions uncompromising on matters of the greatest importance. He sought to advance their goals as a moral cause and to win over opponents by intellect and emotion, not force. He worked to change world views. He worked to build global movements, not just local or national. And, of course, he sought to end war, not just to replace one war with a different one. That meant struggling against a particular war, but doing so in the manner best aimed at reducing or abolishing the machinery behind it.

I'm not, after all, a very good Musteite. I agree with much, but not all. I reject his religious motivations. And of course I'm not much like A.J. Muste, lacking his skills, interests, abilities, and accomplishments. But I do feel close to him and appreciate more than ever being called a Musteite. And I appreciate that A.J. Muste and millions of people who appreciated his work in one way or another passed it on to me. Muste's influence on people everyone knows, like Martin Luther King, Jr., and people who influenced people everyone knows, like Bayard Rustin, was significant. He worked with people still active in the peace movement like David McReynolds and Tom Hayden. He worked with James Rorty, father of one of my college professors, Richard Rorty. He spent time at Union Theological Seminary, where my parents studied. He lived on the same block, if not building, where I lived for a while at 103rd Street and West End Avenue in New York, and Muste was apparently married to a wonderful woman named Anne who went by Anna, as am I. So, I like the guy. But what gives me hope is the extent to which Musteism exists in our culture as a whole, and the possibility that someday we will all be Musteites.

# *Imagine There're No Countries*

A serious case has been made repeatedly by unknown scholars and globally celebrated geniuses for well over a century that a likely step toward abolishing war would be instituting some form of global government. Yet the peace movement barely mentions the idea, and its advocates as often as not appear rather naive about Western imperialism; certainly they are not central to or well integrated into the peace movement or even, as far as I can tell, into peace studies academia. (Here's a link[294] to one of the main advocacy groups for world government promoting a U.S. war on ISIS.)

All too often the case for world government is even made in this way: Global government would guarantee peace, while its absence guarantees war. The silliness of such assertions, I suspect, damages what may be an absolutely critical cause. Nobody knows what global government guarantees, because it's never been tried. And if national and local governments and every other large human institution are any guide, global government could bring a million different things depending on how it's done. The serious question should be whether there's a way to do it that would make peace more likely, without serious risk of backfiring, and whether pursuing such a course is a more likely path to peace than others.

Does the absence of world government guarantee war? I haven't seen any proof. Of 200 nations, 199 invest far less in war than the United States. Some have eliminated their militaries entirely.

---

Costa Rica is not attacked because it lacks a military. The United States is attacked because of what its military does. Some nations go centuries without war, while others seemingly can't go more than half an election cycle. In their book *One World Democracy*, Jerry Tetalman and Byron Belitsos write that nations do not go to war because they are armed or inclined toward violence but because "they are hopelessly frustrated by the fact that they have no legislative or judicial forum in which their grievances can be heard and adjudicated."

Can you, dear reader, recall a time when the U.S. public had a grievance with a foreign country, lamented the absence of a global court to adjudicate it, and demanded that Congress declare and the Pentagon wage a war? How many pro-war marches have you been on, you lover of justice? When the Taliban offered to let a third country put Bin Laden on trial, was it the U.S. public that replied, "No way, we want a war," or was it the President? When the U.S. Vice President met with oil company executives to plan the occupation of Iraq, do you think any of them mentioned their frustration at the weakness of international law and arbitration? When the U.S. President in 2013 could not get Congress or the public to accept a new war on Syria and finally agreed to negotiate the removal of chemical weapons without war, why was war the first choice rather than the second? When advocates of world government claim that democracies don't wage war, or heavily armed nations are not more likely to wage war, or nations with cultures that celebrate war are not more likely to wage war, I think they hurt their cause.

When you start up a campaign[295] to abolish the institution of war, you hear from all kinds of people who have the solution for you. And almost all of them have great ideas, but almost all of them think every other idea but their own is useless. So the solution is world government and nothing else, or a culture of peace and nothing else, or disarmament and nothing else, or ending racism and nothing else, or destroying capitalism and nothing else, or counter-recruitment and nothing else, or media reform and nothing else, or election campaign funding reform and nothing else, or creating peace in our hearts and radiating it outward and nothing else, etc. So those of us who find value in all of the above, have to encourage people to pick their favorite and get busy on it. But we also have to try to prioritize. So, again, the serious question is whether world government should be pursued and whether it should be a top priority or something that waits at the bottom of the list.

There are, of course, serious arguments that world government would make everything worse, that large government is inevitably dysfunctional and an absolutely large government would be dysfunctional absolutely. Serious, if vague, arguments have been made in favor of making our goal "anarcracy" rather than world democracy. These arguments are overwhelmed in volume by paranoid pronouncements like the ones in this typical email I received:

> "War is a crime, yes agreed totally, but Man-made Global Warming is a complete scam. I know this to be a fact. Aurelio Peccei, co-founder of the Club of Rome, offered me a job as

---

295 http://worldbeyondwar.org

> *one of his PAs (my uncle, Sir Harry, later Lord Pilkington*
> *went to the first ever Bilderberg Conference in 1954, a year*
> *before he came a Director of the Bank of England and was*
> *a loyal member of the global corporate elite) and he told me*
> *that this was all a scheme to help frighten the world into*
> *accepting global governance on their terms. Be very careful,*
> *you are unwittingly playing their game.*
> *Best wishes*
> *Justin"*

One of the huge advantages of global government would seem to be that it might globally address global warming. Yet the horror of global government is so great that people believe the droughts and tornados destroying the earth all around them are somehow a secret plot to trick us into setting up a world government.

A half-century ago the idea of world government was acceptable and popular. Now, when we hear about those days it's often in sinister tones[296] focused on the worst motivations of the worst players at the time. Less common are accounts[297] reminding us of a hopeful, well-meant, but unfinished project.

I think advocates for a world federation and global rule of law are onto an important idea that ought to be pursued immediately. Global warming leaves us little time for taking on other projects, but this is a project critical to addressing that crisis. And it's a project that I think can coexist with moving more power to provinces, localities, and individuals.

296    http://www.salon.com/2013/09/20/elites_strange_plot_to_take_over_the_world
297 http://www.laprogressive.com/whos-afraid-of-world-government

The bigger the Leviathan, claims Ian Morris, the less war there will be, as long as the Leviathan is the United States and it never stops waging wars. Advocates of world government tend to agree with the first part of that, and I think they're partially right. The rule of law helps to regulate behavior. But so do other factors. I think Scotland could leave the UK or Catalonia leave Spain, Quebec leave Canada, Vermont leave the United States without the chance of war increasing. On the contrary, I think some of these new countries would be advocates for peace. Were Texas to secede, that might be a different story. That is to say, habits of peace and cultures of peace necessary to allow a world federation might render such a federation less necessary—still perhaps necessary, but less so. If the U.S. public demanded peace and cooperation and participation in the International Criminal Court, it would be ready to demand participation in a world federation, but peace might already have—at least in great measure—arrived.

Extreme national exceptionalism, which is not required by nationalism, is clearly a driver of war, hostility, and exploitation. President Obama recently said that he only wakes up in the morning because the United States is the one indispensible nation (don't ask what that makes the others). The theme of his speech was the need to start another war. Republican presidential candidate Ron Paul was once booed at a primary debate, not for opposing war, but for suggesting that the golden rule be applied to relations with foreign countries. Clearly we need to become world citizens in our minds as well as in written law.

Rudolf Gelsey recently sent me his book, *Mending Our Broken World: A Path to Perpetual Peace*, which led me on to Tetalman and

Belitsos's book. I think these authors would benefit from the wisdom of the 1920s Outlawry[298] movement, but I think they do an excellent job of recognizing the successes and failures of the United Nations, and proposing reforms or replacement. Should we be scared of an international rule of law? Tetalman and Belitsos reply:

"In truth, living under a system of war and anarchy with WMDs readily available for use on the field of battle—*that* is the really frightening choice when it is compared with tyranny."

This is the key, I think. Continuing with the war system and with environmental destruction threaten the world. Far better to try a world with a government than to lose the world. Far better a system that tries to punish individual war makers than one that bombs entire nations.

How do we get there? Tetalman and Belitsos recommend abolishing the veto at the United Nations, expanding Security Council membership, creating a tax base for a U.N. that currently receives about 0.5 percent what the world invests in war, and giving up war powers in favor of U.N. policing. They also propose kicking out of the United Nations any nations not holding free elections, or violating international laws. Clearly that would have to be a requirement going forward and not enforced retroactively or you'd lose too many big members and spoil the whole plan.

The authors envision some transition period in which the U.N. uses war to prevent war, before arriving at the golden age of using

---

298 http://davidswanson.org/outlawry

only police. I'm inclined to believe that imagined step would have to be leapt over for this to work. The U.S./NATO/U.N. have been using war to rid the world of war for three-quarters of a century with a dismal record of failure. I suspect the authors are also wrong to propose expansion of the European Union as one way to get to a global federation. The European Union is the second greatest purveyor of violence on earth right now. Perhaps the BRICS or other non-aligned nations could begin this process better, which after all is going to require the United States either rising or sinking to humility unimaginable today.

Perhaps a federation can be established only on the question of war, or only on the question of nuclear disarmament, or climate preservation. The trouble, of course, is that the willingness of the dominant bullies to engage in one is as unlikely as, and intimately connected to, each of the others. What would make all of this more likely would be if we began talking about it, thinking about it, planning for it, dreaming it, or even just hearing the words when we sing John Lennon songs. The U.S. peace movement is currently drenched in nationalism, uses "we" to mean the U.S. military, and thinks of "global citizen" as a bit of silly childishness. That needs to change. And fast.

## Which Is Worse, a Libertarian or a Humanitarian-Warrior?

Is it worse to put into Congress or the White House someone who wants to end wars and dismantle much of the military but also wants to abolish Social Security and Medicare and the Department of Education and several other departments they have trouble remembering the names of, OR someone who just wants to slightly trim all of those departments around the edges while waging countless wars all over the world in the name of every heretofore imagined human right other than the right not to get blown up with a missile?

Can dismantling the military without investing in diplomacy and aid and cooperative conflict resolution actually avoid wars? Can a country that continues waging wars at every opportunity actually avoid abolishing domestic services? I would hope that everyone would be willing to reject both libertarians and humanitarian-warriors even when it means rejecting both the Republican and the Democratic Parties. I would also hope that each of those parties would begin to recognize the danger they are in and change their ways.

Democrats should consider this: States within the United States are developing better and worse wages, labor standards, environmental standards, healthcare systems, schools, and civil liberties. The *Washington Post* is advising[299] people on which foreign nations to go to college in for free—nations that both tax wealth and invest between 0 and 4 percent of the U.S. level in militarism. A federal government that stopped putting a trillion dollars a year into wars and war preparations, with all the accompanying death, trauma, destruction, environmental damage,

---

299        http://www.washingtonpost.com/blogs/worldviews/wp/2014/10/29/7-countries-where-americans-can-study-at-universities-in-english-for-free-or-almost-free/

and loss of liberties, begins to look like a decent tradeoff for a federal government ending lots of other things it does, from its very minimal security net to massive investment in fossil fuels and highways. Of course it's still a horrible tradeoff, especially if you live in one of the more backward states, as I do. But it begins to look like less of a horrible tradeoff, I think, as we come to realize that representative democracy can work at the state and local levels, and the major crises of climate and war can only be solved at the global level, while the national government we have is too big to handle our local needs and is itself the leading opponent of peace and sustainability on earth.

With that in mind, consider a leading face of the Democratic Party: Hillary Clinton. She's openly corrupted[300] by war profiteers. She was too corrupt[301] to investigate Watergate. Wall Street[302] Republicans back her, and she believes in "representing banks[303]." She'd be willing to "obliterate[304]" Iran. She laughed[305] gleefully about killing Gadaffi and bringing Libya into the liberated state of hell it's now in, with violence having spilled into neighboring nations since.

She threw[306] her support and her vote behind attacking Iraq

300     http://www.washingtonpost.com/politics/for-hillary-clinton-and-boeing-a-beneficial-relationship/2014/04/13/21fe84ec-bc09-11e3-96ae-f2c36d2b1245_story.html?hpid=z1

301          http://www.truthorfiction.com/rumors/c/clinton-watergate.htm#.VFeh6IeJmfl

302     http://www.politico.com/story/2014/04/wall-street-republicans-hillary-clinton-2016-106070.html#ixzz30nimFjqt

303    http://www.commondreams.org/views/2014/07/14/hillarys-candid-motto-democratic-party-represent-banks

304 https://www.youtube.com/watch?v=857guwaNbRc

305 https://www.youtube.com/watch?v=Fgcd1ghag5Y

306 https://www.youtube.com/watch?v=DkS9y5t0tR0

in 2003. She is[307] a leading militarist[308] and authoritarian[309] who turned the State Department into a war-making[310] machine pushing weapons and fracking[311] on the world, and she supports the surveillance[312] state. There's a strong feminist argument[313] against her. The pull of superior domestic rhetoric is strong, but not everyone will see a candidate who backed a war that killed a million dark-skinned Iraqis as the anti-racist candidate.

Republicans should consider this: Your star senator, Rand Paul, can be relied on to talk complete sense about the madness of war, right up until people get scared by beheading videos, and then he's in favor[314] of the madness of war[315], if still so far short of all-out backing of war-on-the-world as to horrify the *Washington Post*[316]. He has backed cancelling all foreign aid, except[317] for military foreign "aid" up to $5 billion, mostly in free weapons for Israel. He

307      http://www.wideasleepinamerica.com/2014/09/hillary-clinton-friends-kissinger.html

308      http://www.thenation.com/blog/180020/left-ought-worry-about-hillary-clinton-hawk-and-militarist-2016?utm_source=Sailthru&utm_medium=email&utm_term=email_nation&utm_campaign=Email      Nation %28NEW%29 20140527&newsletter=email_nation_tuesday

309      http://www.alternet.org/civil-liberties/ex-cia-analyst-ray-mcgovern-sues-state-dept-putting-him-watch-list-after-hillary

310      http://www.commondreams.org/views/2014/06/06/hillary-clinton-and-weaponization-state-department

311      http://www.huffingtonpost.com/2014/09/10/hillary-clinton-fracking_n_5796786.html?utm_hp_ref=tw

312      http://www.thenation.com/article/180564/nsa-hillary-clinton-either-fool-or-liar?utm_source=Sailthru&utm_medium=email&utm_term=email_nation&utm_campaign=Email Nation %28NEW%29 - Headline Nation Feed 20140708&newsletter=email_nation

313      http://www.thenation.com/article/174442/feminist-case-against-woman-president-response-jessica-valenti

314 http://www.newyorker.com/magazine/2014/10/06/revenge-rand-paul

315 ttp://www.kentucky.com/2014/11/02/3514678/paul-distances-himself-from-himself.html

316      http://www.washingtonpost.com/blogs/right-turn/wp/2014/10/29/rand-paul-cant-hide-his-isolationist-views/

317 http://www.newyorker.com/magazine/2014/10/06/revenge-rand-paul

used to favor serious cuts to military spending, but hasn't acted on that and now has[318] John McCain's support as a good "centrist." He supports[319] racist policies while hoping not to be seen doing so, and was against[320] the Civil Rights Act before he was for it. He thinks[321] kids should drive 10 miles to find a good school or get educated online.

Everyone should consider this: Candidates like the above two are so horrible, and end up moving ever closer to each other's positions, that the real choice is between them and someone decent. If the choice ever really arises between a libertarian who opposes war (many self-identified libertarians love war and are only against peaceful spending) and a humanitarian warrior with something to offer domestically (many humanitarian warriors don't have much of an upside elsewhere) it could shake up some people's blind partisanship. By why wait? Why not shake it up now? Why not start now investing energy in activism rather than elections, including activism to reform elections and how they are funded? Why not start now voting for candidates we don't have to hold our noses for? Six years into the Obama presidency, we have peace groups—not all of them, thank goodness—but we have peace groups putting everything into electing Democrats, after which they plan to oppose advocating for peace, instead backing limited war. It isn't the lesser-evil voting that kills us; it's the lesser-evil thinking that somehow never gets left behind in the voting booth.

318 http://www.newyorker.com/magazine/2014/10/06/revenge-rand-paul

319 http://thinkprogress.org/election/2014/11/02/3587580/rand-paul-supports-voter-id-laws-but-says-republicans-shouldnt-campaign-on-it/

320 http://www.kentucky.com/2014/11/02/3514678/paul-distances-himself-from-himself.html

321 http://thehill.com/homenews/senate/222533-rand-paul-courts-the-black-vote

## *Mark Udall and the Unspeakable*

President Obama, who is just now un-ending again the ending of the endless war on Afghanistan, has never made a secret of taking direction from the military, CIA, and NSA. He's escalated wars that generals had publicly insisted he escalate. He's committed to not prosecuting torturers after seven former heads of the CIA publicly told him not to. He's gone after whistleblowers with a vengeance and is struggling to keep this Bush-era torture report, or parts of it, secret in a manner that should confuse his partisan supporters.

But the depth of elected officials' obedience to a permanent war machine is usually a topic avoided in polite company -- usually, not always. Back in 2011, the dean of the law school at UC Berkeley, a member of Obama's transition team in 2009, said[322] publicly that Obama had decided in 2009 to block prosecutions of Bush-era criminals in part because the CIA, NSA, and military would revolt. Ray McGovern says he has a trustworthy witness to Obama saying he would leave the crimes unpunished because, in Obama's words, "Don't you remember what happened to Martin Luther King?" Neither of those incidents has interested major media outlets in the slightest.

As we pass the 51st anniversary of the murder of President John F. Kennedy, many of us are urging[323] Senator Mark Udall to make the torture report public by placing it into the Congressional Record, as Senator Mike Gravel did with the Pentagon Papers in 1971. Gravel is alive and well, and there's every reason to believe

322        http://davidswanson.org/node/3390
323        http://releasethetorturereport.com/?code=RootsAction

that Udall would go on to live many years deeply appreciated for his action. But there is -- let us be honest for a moment -- a reason Udall might hesitate that we don't want to speak about.

The general thinking is that because Udall's term ends this month, he doesn't have to please those who fund his election campaigns through the U.S. system of legalized bribery, and he doesn't have to please his fellow corrupt senators because he won't be working with them any longer. Both of those points may be false. Udall may intend to run for the Senate again, or -- like most senators, I suspect -- he may secretly plan on running for president some day. And the big payoffs for elected officials who work to please plutocracy always come after they leave office. But there is another consideration. The need to please the permanent war machine ends only when one is willing to die for something -- what Dr. King said one must be willing to do to have a life worth living -- not when one leaves office.

Presidents and Congress members send large numbers of people to risk their lives murdering much larger numbers of people in wars all the time. They have taken on jobs -- particularly the presidency -- in which they know they will be in danger no matter what they do. And yet everyone in Washington knows (and no one says) that making an enemy of the CIA is just not done and has not been done since the last man to do it died in a convertible in Dallas. We've seen progressive members of Congress like Dennis Kucinich leave without putting crucial documents that they thought should be public into the Congressional Record. Any member of Congress, newly reelected or not, could give the public the torture report. A group of 10 of them could do it collectively for the good of humanity. But nobody thinks they will. Challenging a president who does not challenge the CIA is just not something that's done.

To understand why, I recommend reading Jim Douglass' book JFK and the Unspeakable. Douglass is currently writing about three other murders, those of Malcolm X, Martin Luther King Jr., and Robert Kennedy. Distant history? Something that doesn't happen anymore? Perhaps, but is that because we've run out of lone nuts with guns? Clearly not. Is it because the permanent war machine has stopped killing its enemies? Or is it, rather, because no one has presented the same challenge to the permanent war machine that those people did? Peace voices are no longer allowed in the U.S. media. Both political parties favor widespread war. War has become a matter of routine. Enforcement has become unnecessary, because the threat, or other influences that align with it, has been so successful.

I recommend checking out ProjectUnspeakable.com, the website of a play by Court Dorsey that recounts the killing of JFK, Malcolm, Martin, and RFK. (Or check out a performance[324] in Harlem planned for February 21.) The play consists almost entirely of actual quotes by public figures. While no attempt is made, of course, at including a comprehensive collection of information, enough evidence is included in the play to completely erase belief in the official stories of how those four men died. And evidence is included showing who actually killed them, how, and why.

---

324 http://projectunspeakable.com/events/upcoming-events/

As if that weren't enough to persuade the viewer that our society is mentally blocking out something uncomfortable, the glaring obviousness of what happened in those years of assassinations is highlighted. President Kennedy was publicly asked if he might be murdered exactly as he was, and he publicly replied that it could certainly happen. His brother discussed the likelihood of it with Khrushchev for godsake. The killing of Malcolm X was not the war machine's first attempt on his life. He and King both saw what was coming quite clearly and said so. Bobby Kennedy knew too, did not believe the official account of his brother's murder. King's family rejects the claim that James Earl Ray killed MLK, pointing instead to the CIA killer shown in the photographs of the assassination but never questioned as a witness. A jury has unanimously agreed with King's family against the government and the history books.

The attention to President Kennedy has always been so intense that fear and suppression have been required. The doctors said he was shot from the front. Everyone agreed there were more bullets shot than left the gun of the official suspect, who was positioned behind the target. But investigators and witnesses have died in very suspect circumstances. The other deaths have not been in exactly the same glaring spotlight. New evidence in the killing of Robert Kennedy emerges every few years and is chatted about as a curiosity for a moment before simply being ignored. After all, the man is dead.

Let's try an analogy. I live in Charlottesville, Va., where the University of Virginia is. This week, Rolling Stone[325] published an article about violent gang rapes of female students in a fraternity

325 http://www.rollingstone.com/culture/features/a-rape-on-campus-20141119

house. I had known that rape victims are often reluctant to come forward. I had known that rape can be a hard charge to prove. But I had also known that young women sometimes regret sex and falsely accuse nonviolent well-meaning young men of rape, and that UVA held rallies against date rape, and that opposition to sexual assault and harassment was all over the news and widely accepted as the proper progressive position. With California passing a law to clarify what consent is, I had assumed everyone knew violent assault had nothing to do with consent. I had assumed brutal gang attacks by students who are expelled if they cheat on a test or write a bad check could not go unknown. And now it seems there's something of a widely known unspoken epidemic. In the analysis of the Rolling Stone article, women deny rape goes on to shield themselves from the fear, while men deny it in order to shield themselves from any discomfort about their party-going fun-loving carelessness. And yet some significant number of students knew and stayed silent until one brave victim spoke, just as every whistleblower in Washington exists alongside thousands of people who keep their mouths shut.

What if someone in Washington were to speak? What if the unspeakable were made speakable?

## 57 Candidates and Nothing On

I was lucky to attend a debate among the candidates for Congress from Virginia's Fifth District just before game 7 of the world series. This was the kind of event you can write about while drinking beer and yelling at a television with your family. In fact, I'm not sure there's any other way you could write about it. Here are our choices for the House of Misrepresentatives:

The incumbent Robert Hurt, a fairly typically horrendous Republican, if a bit less of a warmonger than his Democratic predecessor, didn't make a fool of himself *at all* on Wednesday evening. On the contrary, he disgraced himself by not showing up. Of course, the debate was in the left-leaning corner of a district gerrymandered to keep him in Washington for life, barring a mass movement of a few thousand people for one of his opponents. He would have answered most of the evening's questions as badly or worse than anyone else there, and that's saying something. One of the questions, submitted by me on a 3x5 card, was this:

> *Roughly 53% of federal discretionary spending goes to militarism. How much should?*

I doubt very much that Hurt would have answered the question clearly and directly had he been there.

Ken Hildebrandt, an Independent Green who spoke often if vaguely about cutting the military, answered my question by offering arguments that UFOs had visited Roswell. Asked about climate change, he argued that chem-trails from airplanes are manipulating our weather. Pretty much all the other questions he answered: "Hemp." Hildebrandt is a bit of a mixed bag. He wants progressive taxation but no gun laws. He wants single-payer health coverage but calls it "public option" and claims that life expectancy in the United States is in the 40s. (During the whole debate, neither the moderator nor any candidate ever corrected another's factual errors, and the opportunities were plentiful.) Hildebrandt wants to stop subsidizing Lockheed and Boeing, but has nothing to say on a lot of topics, seems to think the two men sitting next to him would be about as good in office as he would, runs for office every two years as a routine, has a wife running in the next district, and—less peacefully than one might wish—calls the incumbent a "monster."

Behind Curtain 2 is Paul Jones, a Libertarian. He said he'd cut military spending in half immediately, that it's not defensive. "Who's going to attack us?" he asks. "It's ludicrous! The reason they would attack us is that we're over there all the time. . . . Nobody ever wins a war." Not bad, huh? He wants to end the surveillance state too. Of course, you had to be there to hear him mumble it all. But here's the downside. He wants that $500,000,000,000 to all go into tax cuts. He also objects to the term "discretionary spending." It's all discretionary, he says, no matter what some politician says (such as in a *law* putting Social Security out of his government-shrinking reach). Also he'd like to cut most of the rest of the government too, including eliminating a bunch of departments—although, unlike Rick Perry, he didn't attempt to name any of them. He also wants to pay off the debt, use the free market for healthcare (while assisting the poor) and get immigrants to start paying taxes (huh?). He claims no laws can keep guns from criminals or the mentally ill. He claims that India produces more greenhouse gases than the United States.

Last up is Democrat Lawrence Gaughan. He was the most professional, articulate presence. He said he agreed with the other two gentlemen a lot, but it wasn't clear what he meant. He said he agreed "100%" with Jones on military spending. So, does he want to cut it by 50% right away? Will he introduce a bill to do that? He criticized Hurt for supporting the new war in Iraq. He called the Pentagon a "Department of Offense." But he said repeatedly that he would cut $1 trillion in military spending, which obviously meant $1 trillion over some number of years, probably at best 10 years, which would mean $100 billion a year. He claimed that the Democratic Party opposes war. And he claimed that his pro-war predecessor Tom Perriello is working with President Obama to reduce overseas bases. (All of this with a very straight face.)

That combination of comments makes Gaughan by far the best Democratic or Republican candidate in this district in living memory, but a bit of a question mark in terms of follow through. Hildebrandt said he wouldn't have compromised on "public option." Gaughan said that he both favored "public option" (clearly meaning to say "single payer") and would have sought a "more bi-partisan solution." Wow. Gaughan is not even in DC yet and he's talking as if we're bothered by "gridlock" more than bad healthcare. He wants to tax corporations and billionaires. He mentions "the 1%" a lot. But he favors a "leaner, more efficient government." Hildebrandt mentioned publicly financed elections. Gaughan said he wanted to "get the money out of elections" without saying how. He wants immigrants to have a path to citizenship, and he wants to "tighten borders." He sees the top problem as the concentration of wealth and power, but he sees the root cause of that as low voter turnout (what?). He's for background checks on guns and recognizing the reality of climate change, but one doesn't sense a major push for radical transformation. He talks about saving the climate by creating a better America, not a better planet.

Gaughan said he wasn't taking money from the Democratic Party in Washington. That makes him different from Perriello, who proved very obedient to his "leaders." No doubt the DCCC isn't offering money because they don't think any Democrat has a chance in VA-05. If we were to elect Gaughan, he might not lead Congress toward peace and justice, but he'd come a lot closer to actually meriting the praise that liberal groups gave Perriello, and he just might be answerable to the people who elected him rather than the party that didn't buy his ticket to Washington. A liberal Democratic Party elections group, the Progressive Change Campaign Committee, is basing its national elect-Democrats work out of Charlottesville, but none of the candidates[326] they're backing are from Virginia.

## *Things, Not People, You Can Vote For*

"Vote. It's the American thing to do!" read an email I received yesterday. Actually it's the just-about-anywhere-else thing to do. U.S. voters lead[327] the world in staying home and not bothering. There are three schools of thought as to why, all of which I think are largely correct.

1. They don't make it easy. Americans, in many cases, have to work long hours in unlivable cities, go through a hassle to register to vote, wait in long lines, produce photo IDs, and get past

326 http://boldprogressives.org/candidates
327 http://en.wikipedia.org/wiki/Voter_turnout

intimidation, scams, and fraudulent removal from voter rolls.

2. Americans are idiots. This explanation is not always thought through, but the U.S. public is constantly indoctrinated with a belief in its own powerlessness, informed that action will make no difference, and distracted from civic engagement by bread and circuses.

3. There's nobody on the ballot worth voting for. The districts have been gerrymandered. The media, the debates, and the ballot-access rules all favor the incumbent or, at best, the two corporate political parties. The candidates flooding the airwaves with often quite accurate negative advertisements about how awful their opponents are have been bribed to hold similarly awful positions by the extremely wealthy interests paying for the show. And your vote for the greater or lesser evil of the two similar candidates is often counted on a completely unverifiable machine. Why bother?

Well, one trick that candidates and parties have come up with to get more people into voting booths is the public initiative or referendum. If people can vote to make a direct decision on something they're passionate about, many of them will also go ahead and vote for the candidates whose platforms are infinitesimally closer to their own positions. Thus you have Democrats and Republicans supporting placing measures on the ballot that they believe will attract either more Democrats or more Republicans.

In 2004, Floridians put a minimum wage vote on the ballot, meant both to raise the minimum wage and to elect Democrats. But John Kerry opposed Florida's minimum wage initiative.

Floridians (assuming, based totally on faith, that the count was accurate) rejected Kerry while, of course, passing the minimum wage. So, as a trick to win votes for candidates, this tool requires candidates who aren't bigger idiots than voters are. But as a positive development on its own, the referenda and initiatives on ballots around the country today offer good reason to vote in some places.

Alaska, Arkansas, Nebraska, and South Dakota, San Francisco, and Oakland will almost certainly raise (that is restore lost value to) the minimum wage.

Alaska, Florida, Oregon, Washington, D.C.; Guam; South Portland, Maine; Lewiston, Maine; and lots of localities in California, Colorado, Massachusetts, Michigan, and New Mexico will vote on various forms of marijuana legalization.

In 50 localities in Wisconsin and in countless others across the country, people will vote for funding for schools.

In Illinois, voters can vote to tax all income over $1 million an additional 3 percent to fund schools. Localities in California, Ohio, and Texas will have the opportunity to ban fracking by popular vote. In Washington state and elsewhere, voters can vote to impose background checks on gun purchases. Betting on passage, the gun companies are urging people (criminals in particular, I guess) to buy now before it's too late.

So, my recommendation is to check out what things, if any, rather than people, you have a chance to vote for. By all means, stop being an idiot who imagines activism is pointless. But don't jump to the conclusion that voting is one of the top priorities. Check whether there isn't perhaps something actually worth voting for, or a way to make there be such a thing next time.

# Who Says Ferguson Can't End Well

Just as a police officer in a heightened state of panic surrounded by the comfort of impunity will shoot an innocent person, the Governor of Missouri has declared a state of emergency preemptively, thus justifying violence in response to something that hasn't happened. Bombing Iraq in response to nonexistent weapons and Libya in response to nonexistent threats worked out so well, we may as well try it domestically, the Governor is perhaps thinking. "There Is No Way That This Ends Well" is a headline I actually just read about Ferguson.

Well, why not? Who says it can't end well? The police may want continued impunity. The justice system may be rigged against any sort of reconciliation. The government may want—or believe it rationally expects—violence. But all of those parties are capable of changing their behavior, and the people of Ferguson are capable of determining their own actions rather than following a script placed before them.

We should understand that the violence in Ferguson is not new and is not limited to Ferguson. It did not begin with a particular shooting. It did not begin with any shooting. It began with a system of oppression that keeps people in misery amidst great wealth. Just as that injustice is inexcusable, so is any violence in response to it. But the outrage at an angry man knocking over a trashcan conspicuously exhibited by people who cheer for mass-murder in Iraq isn't well thought-through or helpful. And the disproportionate focus on such small-scale violence misses more than the larger picture. It also misses the courageous, disciplined, principled, and truly loving actions of those resisting injustice creatively and constructively. Such actions are not always successful and not always well-planned to the satisfaction of scholars. But they have long been far more common than is acknowledged on the television or in the history books.

Back in 1919 in Lawrence, Massachusetts, some 30,000 textile workers went on strike for decent pay. The mill owners and the police sought to provoke them, infiltrate them, intimidate them, and brutalize them. The workers held strong. The police set up machine guns along the streets, toying with the model of domestic war now exhibited in Ferguson. Organizer A.J. Muste spoke to the workers on the morning that the machine guns appeared:

> "When I began my talk by saying that the machine guns were an insult and a provocation and that we could not take this attack lying down, the cheers shook the frame building. Then I told them, in line with the strike committee's decision, that to permit ourselves to be provoked into violence would mean defeating ourselves; that our real power was in our solidarity and in our capacity to endure suffering rather than give up the fight for the right to organize; that no one could 'weave wool with machine guns'; that cheerfulness was better for morale than bitterness and that therefore we would smile as we passed the machine guns and the police

*on the way from the hall to the picket lines around the mills. I told the spies, who were sure to be in the audience, to go and tell the police and the mill management that this was our policy. At this point the cheers broke out again, louder and longer, and the crowds left, laughing and singing."*

And, they won. The powers that owned the mill and put the weapons of war on the streets of that town conceded defeat, and conceded it without the bitterness that would have come had the workers and their supporters somehow been able to defeat the machine guns with violence.

That type of incident is as common as water, but little recounted. It's what organizers in Ferguson are calling for right now, and they are being preemptively ignored by the media. But it doesn't come easy. And it doesn't come without solidarity. If the people of the United States and the world chip in to support the people of Ferguson in their struggle for full justice, if we nonviolently and smilingly take on the forces of militarism and racism everywhere at once, and in Missouri in particular, we need not defeat the police or the Governor. We need only defeat cruelty, bigotry, and brutality. And that we can do. And that would be ending well.

## One Day We Will All Strike for More Than One Day

An international one-day strike by fast-food workers is something new, and also something old. People without a union are organizing and acting in solidarity. Others are joining in support of their moral demand for a living wage. They're holding rallies. They're shutting down restaurants. They're using Occupy's people's microphone. They're targeting the one-percenter CEO of McDonald's who apparently is paid $9,002 per hour for the public service of ruining our health with horrible tasting processed imitation food.

Jeremy Brecher has released a revised, expanded, and updated edition of his 40-year-old book, Strike, that includes the origins of these fast-food worker strikes and puts them in the context of a history of the strike in the United States dating back to 1877. This opening passage of Chapter 1 sets the context beautifully:

> "In the centers of many American cities are positioned huge armories, grim nineteenth-century edifices of brick or stone. They are fortresses complete with massive walls and loopholes for guns. You may have wondered why they are there, but it has probably never occurred to you that they were built to protect America not against invasion from abroad but against popular revolt at home."

And what revolts there have been! Brecher's book should be read for inspiration. The most marginalized of workers have repeatedly taken matters into their own hands and won radical changes for the better. Success has followed selfless acts of solidarity. Failure has followed strategic calculation and compromise. The potential for greater victories has been frustrated time and again by the decision not to press working people's advantage forward—a decision generally made by labor unions.

The vision of replacing capitalism has driven the efforts that have reformed it. A century ago, World War I provided the excuse to beat back workers. But their demands exploded upon the war's conclusion. Workers took over Seattle and ran the city, effectively replacing the government. In the 1930s, coal miners opened their own coal mines. Unemployed workers during the great depression joined picket lines in support of striking workers rather than competing with them. Workers at a rubber factory in Akron developed the sit-down strike, which spread like wildfire and might work well in McDonald's restaurants all over the world today. Customers could join workers by sitting in at tables and not eating. We could bring our own food; McDonald's has internet.

Brecher's book brings the story of strikes, including general strikes, up to the present. The lessons it teaches open up possibilities not usually considered. Brecher sums up what we're up against:

> "The ideology of the existing society exercises a powerful hold on workers' minds. The longing to escape from subordination to the boss is often expressed in the dream of going into business for yourself, even though the odds against success are overwhelming. The civics book cliché that the American government represents the will of the people and is therefore legitimate survives even in those who find the government directly opposing their own needs in the interests of their employers. The desire to own a house, a car, or perhaps an independent business supports a belief in private property that makes expropriation of the great corporations seem to many a personal threat. The idea that everybody is really out for themselves, that it can be no other way, and that

*therefore the solution to one's problems must come from beating other people rather than cooperating with them is inculcated over and over by the very structure of life in a competitive society."*

One day we will all strike, and we will strike for more than a day. We will strike until we replace the "very structure of life" with different ones. We'll strike forever, occupy everything, and never give it back.

CPSIA information can be obtained
at www.ICGtesting.com
Printed in the USA
FFOW01n1608071214
9235FF